PROLOGUE TO WAR

By Elizabeth Wiskemann

COMPLETED just before the outbreak of the war, this book gives a penetrating account of the impact of the Nazi totalitarian machine upon the countries lying both to the east and to the west of the Rome-Berlin Axis, and thus provides the indispensable background for any clear understanding of the forces that led inevitably to the outbreak of hostilities. Germany has developed an elaborate technique (a combination of political propaganda, economic pressure, and unrelenting agitation of German minorities) by which to gain domination over smaller states. It is this technique, in all its various aspects, which Miss Wiskemann, with her customary clarity and brilliance, sets out to examine. Her book falls naturally into two parts: In the first she deals with German policies to the east of the Axis; in the second with those policies as they affect the smaller countries to the west of the Axis. Examining in turn each country that has fallen prey to Pan-German aspirations, she first describes its general historical structure, and then proceeds to analyze Nazi methods of penetration in both the racial and economic spheres from the Baltic to the Balkans on the east and from Denmark to Switzerland in the west.

In examining German success in what Miss Wiskemann calls the Undeclared War, she compares and contrasts the effect of Nazi pressure

(Continued on back flap)

PROLOGUE TO WAR

in eastern and western Europe. After reviewing
developments in the socially backward states
east of Germany, she finds in Switzerland the
most representative community in the west, and
describes the powers of resistance manifested
by this really democratic, highly industrialized
and multi-racial State. She shows, too, how well
anti-Semitism served the purposes of the Nazi
penetration by its disintegrating effects of one
kind or another, varying as they did between
the east and west of Europe.

Also by Elizabeth Wiskemann

CZECHS AND GERMANS
A study of the Struggle in the
Historic Provinces of Bohemia
and Moravia

Prologue to WAR

ELIZABETH WISKEMANN

OXFORD UNIVERSITY PRESS

NEW YORK   TORONTO

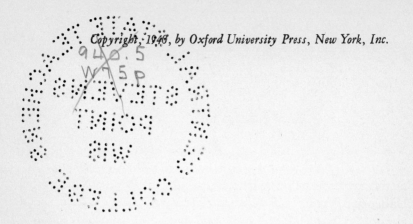

Copyright, 1946, by Oxford University Press, New York, Inc.

Printed in the United States of America

PREFACE

I WAS originally asked to write something about Europe after the Munich Agreement; to do so automatically resolved itself into an account of Germany's Undeclared War. If this overlaps with other contemporary books I can only say that it was written independently of anything other than the publications to which I have referred in the text, and presents my own particular approach as historian, traveller, or whatever I may be. The contrast between the effect of the German campaign East of the Axis Powers and its effect to their West is striking, and, I believe, deserves emphasis. If the greater space I have devoted to Eastern Europe is an insult to symmetry I can only excuse this by saying that I prefer to write at length only about the countries and problems I know at first hand, and it seemed more satisfactory to examine certain areas with care rather than to glance hastily at the whole map of Europe; I was also anxious to avoid repetition. Although the situation in Alsace is exceedingly relevant to the theme of this book, I have deliberately avoided the subject of France because it was impossible to deal with it adequately in the available space and time. Further, I have not concerned myself directly with the peoples—not even the Slovaks—who are already admitted to be Germany's subjects. The permanent international crisis, that very state of undeclared war in which we live, itself

v

constantly adds to the difficulty of describing it accurately. I can, therefore, only beg for indulgence. And whether I receive it or not, the least I can do is to express my gratitude to all kinds of long-suffering friends at home and abroad, and, of course, to the staff of Chatham House. Finally, I am anxious to thank the Editors of *Foreign Affairs*, *The Fortnightly Review*, *The Nation*, *The New Statesman and Nation*, *The Scotsman* and *The Spectator* for permission to incorporate small portions of my articles published by them.

ELIZABETH WISKEMANN.

LONDON,
    August 1939.

POSTSCRIPT

I FINISHED writing this book towards the end of July, and added the foregoing preface in the second week of August; Poland's currency difficulties and a further German encroachment in Slovakia had occurred in the interval, but I felt that my text had provided for these. A new situation has now been created by the Anglo-French war against Hitlerism which followed the Russo-German Pact and Germany's assault upon Poland, events which did not, I believe, take me entirely by surprise. If Stalin had annihilated his political enemies on the plea that they had conspired with Germany, Hitler had destroyed the Czecho-slovak Republic ostensibly on account of its treaty with the U.S.S.R., and the Soviet-Nazi Agreement was a fittingly cynical conclusion to the six months which had covered the occupation of Prague and the plan for the expulsion of the South Tyrolese. The Ukrainian question remains, "Promethean" ambitions live on, and Herr von Ribbentrop's sympathy with the ideas of Paul Rohrbach and Alfred Rosenberg with regard to the partition of Russia may well have outlived his journey to Moscow.

The most satisfactory outcome of the Russo-German *rapprochement* was the immediate reconciliation of the Croats with the Belgrade Government, after protracted negotiations which had reduced many Yugoslavs to something like despair. A fortnight after the Serbo-Croat Agreement, an amnesty released men like Professor Dragoljub Jovanović, who was well known for his hostility to the totalitarian Powers.

Since *Prologue to War* was an attempt to provide an accurate review of some of Germany's pre-war preparations, its validity remains as an account of the state of affairs leading up to the war in which we are now engaged. I have therefore decided not to attempt to bring it strictly up to date, but to publish it as it was written for what it may be worth.

E. W.

September 1939.

CONTENTS

PART ONE

EAST OF THE AXIS POWERS

		PAGE
INTRODUCTORY - - - - - -		3
I. HUNGARY - - - - - - -		7
II. ROUMANIA - - - - - - -		47
III. THE SOUTHERN SLAVS OF YUGOSLAVIA AND BULGARIA; THE EASTERN MEDITERRANEAN -		102
IV. POLES, UKRAINIANS AND BALTS - - -		177

PART TWO

WEST OF THE AXIS POWERS

V. WEST OF THE AXIS POWERS - - - -		253
VI. CONCLUSION - - - - - - -		310
INDEX - - - - - - - -		325

ix

PART ONE
EAST OF THE AXIS POWERS

INTRODUCTORY

THE Peace Settlement of 1919 was based upon the principle of self-determination, a principle which was inapplicable to Eastern Europe where centuries of savage conflicts had prevented the evolution both of mature national consciousness and of some machinery by which it could be in the least accurately expressed. Instead the natural greed of victors in a decimating struggle attempted to exploit quasi-tribal passion in the place of national feeling and hoped to justify its claims by holding semi-terroristic plebiscites in the name of natural choice. The men who really made the peace modified these evils as best they could and very conscientiously considered factors of every kind, and there can be little doubt that according to the Peace Settlement far fewer people were subjected to alien rule against their will than according to the frontiers existing before 1914. The great difficulty was that the nationalistic idea, which had never lost a fundamental relationship to political principle in the French Revolution, had, thanks to German influences, degenerated during the nineteenth century into the more primitive physical conception of racialism. In Eastern Europe, certainly, there was no satisfactory way of reconciling racial homogeneity with the territorial assumptions implied in the drawing of frontiers. For "blood and soil" involved a hopeless contradiction in terms. The peacemakers fell back upon strategic and economic considerations, and upon the hope that time and tranquillity would cause the

3

principles of political freedom to weld together the
different racial elements within the frontiers they drew.

In the East of Europe the Russian, the German, the
Austro-Hungarian and the Turkish Empires had
broken down by the end of 1918, and of these, as
Albert Sorel had foreseen, the Habsburg Empire left
behind it the most overwhelming series of problems,
whose complexity malicious forces eagerly exploit
to-day. Two satisfactory things are possible where
men of different language and tradition live together
in territorial confusion. Either they assimilate and
amalgamate, finding common ideas to bind them
together and dropping their flagrant differences—in
this way Angevins, Normans, Gascons and the rest
developed into the nation of the French. Or again, as
in Switzerland, the differences are deliberately retained
and a political union based upon their existence is
worked out. In Austria-Hungary as a whole, while
the Germans and the Magyars regarded political and
social privilege as their right, Slav races were actually
in the majority; in spite, and indeed because, of this
fact, a strong tendency was at work to keep them in
an inferior social condition. In Transleithania [1] or
Hungary the Magyars aimed at a process of assimilation, which either began too late in relation to the
development of national and racial ideas, or was too
constantly undermined by rigid social distinctions:
the Slovak or Roumanian or Serb in old Hungary was
no sooner attracted by the pleasures and benefits of
Magyar civilization than he felt repelled, perhaps, by
the disturbing assumption that his mother-tongue

[1] The River Leitha formed part of the frontier between Austria and
Hungary and accounts for the appellations, Transleithania and Cisleithania.

doomed him to social inferiority unless some merciful dispensation should reverse Fate's decrees. In Cisleithania or Austria the more cosmopolitan attitude of the regime gradually provided more scope for Czechs or Slovenes to advance without becoming Germanized, and towards 1914 there was more and more talk of a Swiss system for Austria. But again some of the Germans in Austria, unlike the Germans in Switzerland, felt too certain of their social and general superiority to allow such a thing to develop, though the *Reichsrat*, the Austrian Parliament, between the introduction of universal suffrage in 1907 and the outbreak of war, had something of the face of a multi-national federal assembly.

Thus in the years preceding 1914, and especially after 1908, the Slav and Roumanian majority in Austria-Hungary was bitterly discontented, and the Habsburg Empire had collapsed before the Armistice without any help from the Peace Conference, which is unjustly blamed for breaking it up. Though prosperity was great and increasing in pre-war days, social inequality was great too, and the conditions in which the working-classes lived in centres of luxury like Vienna or Carlsbad was appalling. This was not, however, so deeply resented as the poverty of to-day, which, following the social upheavals all over Europe between 1917 and 1920 and a far wider acceptance of the ideal of social justice, is robbed of pre-war excuses; pre-war poverty, therefore, has now been forgotten. In fact, in setting up the new Successor States, which were directed by the enemies of the old feudal classes, the peacemakers positively facilitated a certain degree of salutary reform.

Developments in the last twenty years have thus provided magnificent material for the nihilism [1] of the Nazis in the Successor States. Wilsonianism could not make sense in Eastern Europe. Czech or Serb or Polish Chauvinists, on account of some mediaeval victory which should have made some stretch of soil forever theirs, wanted more than they got, while many Germans, Hungarians and Bulgars were obviously not treated to very much self-determination. To offer to apply that inapplicable principle really this time gave the Nazis a wonderful battle-cry fifteen and twenty years later, though any well-informed person knew that no satisfactory racial frontier could be drawn in Bohemia or Transylvania or Bosnia. And plebiscites which had been a rough business round about 1920 could still be claimed as sounding just, though the whole perfection of Nazi technique had gone into the paralysis of the independent judgment of the individual in elections or plebiscites. Since the great depression the sting of poverty has been added to the disappointment of those who had either lost through the Peace Settlement or found their gains illusory; nearly everyone who was impoverished could be persuaded to blame the *status quo* and to glorify forgotten pre-war circumstances, while those who had gained economically from the post-war state of affairs had the lukewarm attitude of those on the defensive in any war of words.

The Munich Agreement, taking a long step as it did back to a big German Central European Empire, caused the propagandistic material of the Nazis in

[1] See H. Rauschning, *Die Revolution des Nihilismus.* Europa-Verlag. Zürich, 1938.

Danubian Europe to double and treble in value. Since Austria and the major part of Czechoslovakia have now been absorbed into the Reich, it is perhaps in the three remaining Successor States, in Hungary, Roumania and Yugoslavia, that the undeclared war waged by Nazi Germany can most profitably be studied in the East of Europe. Poland and Italy, also Successor States in a sense, though they are not usually classified as belonging to the group, provide more particular cases and will be dealt with more or less briefly below. There is, of course, a sharp demarcation to be drawn between Hungary on the one hand and Roumania and Yugoslavia on the other, since Trianon-Hungary was the poor rump of the Hungary of pre-war times while the other two were greatly extended by the Peace Settlement. Nor am I here concerned with pre-Munich conditions except in so far as familiarity with them provides an indispensable explanation of the post-Munich situation and the undeclared war of to-day, that brilliant totalitarian German campaign in which propaganda is intertwined with politico-military threats—war is only the continuation of policy—with economic pressure, and the fullest exploitation of the presence of a German minority.

CHAPTER I

HUNGARY

(a) *Political Development*

In spite of a long tradition of resisting encroachments by the Habsburgs, always hated in Hungary as more German than they in fact were, the Hungarians had found themselves, ever since 1867, drawn towards the Germans in mutual defence against the growing strength of their Slav subjects. Defeat and a passionate determination to undo the Peace Settlement then drew German and Magyar perhaps closer still. But a passive Weimar Germany, where the Trades Unions played so important a rôle, was an uncongenial partner in Hungarian eyes, which looked more eagerly towards Italy from the time of the Italo-Hungarian Treaty of 1927. In 1933 the situation, from Hungary's point of view, was most agreeably transformed. Both the regime and public opinion as a whole were delighted with Hitler's anti-Communist talk, since they could never forget their resentment over the short-lived Communist experiment in Hungary under Bela Kun. They, too, detested internationalism and were all for manly talk, and Brown Shirt activities were merely reminiscent of what their own Condottiere had done to Communists and Jews in the White Terror which brought back the magnates and the gentry to power after 1919. As for Hitler's racialism, the Hungarians were singularly undisturbed by the sanctification of the Nordic Man, derogatory to the blood in their own veins though it was; they merely welcomed the aspersions cast upon both the Slavs and the Jews.

To the Westerner both Magyar and Jew may seem to be at least semi-oriental, and yet no two traditions are more diametrically opposed than those of Hungary and Jewry. With the mysticism and laziness of the one, the rationalism and the industry of the other sharply contrast. The Magyar acquires with difficulty any sense of money values, with him the feudal tradition, which conceives of value in terms of land, dies astonishingly hard, and he feels morally elevated above the "materialism" of those whose criteria are necessarily different. In old pre-war Hungary there were innumerable administrative jobs for members of the ruling Magyar race. They lived in their country mansions and regarded with benevolent contempt the groups of Jewish intellectuals who gathered in those, in Hungary, rare, and, in Hungarian eyes, deplorable phenomena, towns. In the early twentieth century, when a movement in favour of industrialization in Hungary, with a view to depending less upon Austria, developed, the value of the odd, industrious, urban Jew, with his strange comprehension for the mysteries of banking and organization, became rather more evident; he was not therefore any better liked.

But it was only after the war that the Jews became bitterly and generally hated in Hungary. Their numbers were increased by immigration from the areas of the Eastern War Front, and they were very far from skilful—except in growing rich—in their behaviour in the subsequent period of inflation. Meanwhile Hungarian civil servants from the lost territories crowded into Hungary and clamoured for employment, while that widespread post-war malady, the over-crowding of the universities together with the over-production of the *Herr Doktor*, developed apace. Certain anti-Semitic regulations were already enforced, notably a *numerus clausus* which restricted the admission of Jewish students by the universities to a mere 8 or 9 per cent.[1] In the later 'twenties, however, a bubble prosperity smoothed over the difficulties.

[1] After 1926. From 1921 to 1926 it was even more restricted.

Hungarian corn and wine sold at good prices and the Jews could send their sons to universities abroad. The great depression then abruptly swept away all alleviations. Foreign outlets were blocked because foreign exchange could no longer be obtained. And at home the Hungarian magnate or squire, who was rescued by loans from Jewish bankers, repaid these loans with hatred, not gratitude. The growing middle class, dispossessed officials or the next generation of university graduates, searching desperately for employment, found that the new system of high tariff barriers, which had so greatly injured Hungary's traditional agricultural exportation, had been utilized by Jewish *entrepreneurs* to establish new industries. They thereupon resented, not their own incapacity to have done the same thing, but the initiative taken by the Jews. Meanwhile the slump caused the Jewish industrialists severe losses, since, though they were fairly well protected against foreign competition, the collapse of agricultural prices left both big and medium landowners, as well as the peasantry, with next to no purchasing capacity.

It is certainly not difficult to account, then, for the popularity in Hungary of the anti-Semitic doctrines which overflowed from Germany in ever-growing volume from the time of the German elections in 1930, and which received the blessing of authority with Hitler's appointment as Chancellor of the Reich. The Jews of Hungary, like the Jews of Germany, were prominent in literature, journalism, the theatre and the cinema, for much the same reasons, since the Hungarians, like the Germans, slightly despising the effeminacy of the professional *littérateur*, had monopol-

ized the posts supplied by the administration, by the
Army and Diplomacy. Indeed the Hungarians had
had a far smaller middle class from which the professions could possibly be recruited and habitually fell
back upon Jews,[1] unless, curiously enough, they had
already made use of the fairly steady German immigration; this professional competition between Jews and
German immigrants in Hungary is not without
interest. From 1933 the idea of a literary purification
grew increasingly popular in Hungary, and the burning
of books in the Reich was fairly generally applauded,
or at least not condemned, among considerable sections of the population. The whole pattern of Nazi
ideology was difficult to resist, even for Hungarians
who realized the dangers it presented. The idea that
Jewish journalists, many of them as full of Magyar
enthusiasm as any Magyar, if they spoke of the practical need for co-operation between the Danubian
states, were in league with the mainly Slavonic Little
Entente to maintain the peace settlement, was seductive.
For the Peace Treaties were regarded as a subjection
of races born to rule, like the Magyars and if you will
the Germans (the Magyar accepted the German thesis
provided he heard no whisper of Germans ruling
Magyars, to avoid which he frequently had to turn a
very deaf ear), to the ignorant misrule of the Slavs,
who in many Magyar eyes were nothing but their
liberated serfs. The Hitlerist assumption that inferior
persons like the Jews naturally intrigued with inferior

---

[1] On the eve of M. Imrédy's anti-Semitic legislation

50 per cent of the lawyers
35 ,, ,, journalists
33 ,, ,, medical men
28 ,, ,, engineers
} in Hungary were Jews.

peoples like the Slavs to prolong an unnatural state of affairs provided an easy explanation of what most Hungarians disliked, and effectively stimulated their revisionist ardour.

In spite of the fact that only about half the population of pre-war Hungary had been Magyar, even according to the Hungarian official census,[1] all Hungarian schools after the war directly or by implication brought up the younger generation to believe that they must never rest until the old frontiers were restored. Their national symbol, St. Stephen's crown with its crooked cross, stood for the integrity of the lands united by the great king round about the year 1000, and there were few moderates who aimed only at minor rectification of frontiers except when discussing the question with visitors from the west. This flagrant Magyar divergence from the racial principle upheld by Herr Hitler until the occupation of Prague led to intermittent friction between Budapest and Berlin, especially in the autumn of 1938.[2] But in effect it created feelings so much more bitter against the Little Entente that the difficulties between the Hungarians and the Germans counted for less and less as Hitler's policy of breaking up the Little Entente in order to destroy Czechoslovakia was revealed.

---

[1] According to the official census figures the Magyars comprised

| 46·65 per cent of Hungary's population in 1880. |
| 48·61 ,,   ,,   ,,   ,,   1890. |
| 51·4 ,,   ,,   ,,   ,,   1900. |
| 54·5 ,,   ,,   ,,   ,,   1910. |

As heavy pressure was put upon people to declare themselves Magyar, and as there are many authentic stories of, say, Slovaks who could not speak Magyar who were nevertheless registered as Magyar, these percentages may be regarded as exceedingly generous. Since the birth-rate of the Slavs and Roumanians was probably higher than that of the Magyars the effects of Magyarization are evident.

[2] See below, p. 21.

The Little Entente, an alliance between Czecho-slovakia, Roumania and Yugoslavia, aimed frankly at the maintenance of the Treaty of Trianon according to which Hungary's frontiers had been drawn in 1919. It was an alliance between the Slav and Daco-Roman subject races of pre-war Hungary, and an alliance between three new regimes which each introduced agrarian reform; this in its turn was bound to result in dispossessing the big landed class which had enjoyed estates all over old Hungary and which still expected to rule new Hungary. The leading partner in the Little Entente was Czechoslovakia, a state in every way repugnant to the majority of Magyars. They had regarded the Czechs as their hereditary enemies at least since 1848, and the Slovaks as their hereditary serfs. The Czechoslovak Republic, a democracy organized by professors, was almost a monstrosity to them, an incredible state without an upper class, provided quite superfluously for the former cab-drivers, cobblers and tailors of Habsburg Vienna. It was also widely agreed that the southern frontier of Slovakia, comprising the *Grosse Schütt* island in the Danube, was unduly unfavourable to Hungary, though there was next to no case for the Hungarian claim to Bratislava where the Hungarian population was far behind the Slovaks and even the Germans as well. Since Czech officials were notoriously tactless and not very easy to buy, the Hungarian public was fed upon a diet of tales against the Czechs. From the time of the Franco-Russian pact of May 1935, to which the Czechs adhered, Czechoslovakia became the focus of hostile German propaganda; from this moment traditional indictments of Panslavism and new reproaches of Bolshevism were incessantly hurled at the all too western-in-outlook Government of Prague from all the wireless stations of the Reich. Most Hungarians were infinitely susceptible to both the Pan-Slav and the Communist cry, and although the Translyvanian question had hitherto mostly made Roumania into Hungary's "Enemy No. 1," Czecho-slovakia now succeeded to the title; if Germany could break the Czechoslovak Republic, let Hungary be on the alert for gain.

The tremendously uneven distribution of land in Hungary had been little ameliorated by the insignifi-cant changes brought about by Count Bethlen in the 'twenties, and in the following decade, although new industries had drawn the population away from the land, about three million people, out of the nine millions inhabitating Trianon Hungary, were depend-ent upon the land, yet practically landless. The magnates and gentry who ruled the country, perhaps deliberately turned the attention of the public away from their own overgrown estates in order that public enthusiasm should be concentrated upon the lost territories beyond the new frontiers; some of these territories comprised their own lost estates. Here and there the question of large-scale land-reform was raised, but more than once men who studied the question in earnest, in order to make practical pro-posals for reform, were imprisoned for their pains, more particularly if they spoke in democratic language. In 1932, just before Hitler came to power, General Gömbös became Prime Minister of Hungary. This man, like a considerable number of Hungarians, was half German by descent and almost Nazi in outlook, and from 1933 Nazi propaganda from Germany, countenanced by him and his protégés, playing upon so many Magyar prejudices, made great strides. While from the time of the expulsion of Bela Kun in 1919 no opposition from the Left was able to make itself seriously felt, a conflict between conservatives and Nazis now became acute because the latter seized upon the peasants' land-hunger and their post-depression misery to raise the issue of agrarian reform from the Right. Hungarian Nazis of various kinds combined revisionist fervour with desire for land-reform (thus spoiling the magnates' game), and in this they were vigorously seconded by their German friends, and Hungary was quickly invaded by pamphlets in Magyar printed in Germany. Though the Nazis in Germany had come into power as something like the saviours of the East Elbian Junkers, and although their land policy in Germany has been less radical than their other activities, they showed instinctive feeling for this Achilles' heel of Hungary's social system.

At first Hungarian National Socialism did not seem formidable since it was represented by small warring groups led by rival *Führer* of an unimpressive kind. The largest of these groups was that of the *Pfeil-kreuzler* or "Arrow-Cross" people, who indulged in green shirts; there was also a Scythe-Cross party (*Sensenkreuzler*) directed by M. Böszörményi, who led his peasant forces upon an expedition to Budapest in 1936 only to meet with ignominious disarming and plentiful arrests. After a time one heard more and more of Major Ferenc Szálasi, and one heard—what many simple people had said of Adolf Hitler—that he compelled allegiance because he seemed so tremendously sincere. Szálasi had been with Admiral Horthy at the counter-revolutionary headquarters at Szeged in 1919 when he was only twenty-two. He was promoted Captain in 1924, but was reproved in 1927 for propagandistic activities; he already had many supporters at Debrecen. Having served as a staff officer for some years, he was retired on a pension in 1935 on account of his subversive tendencies, and he was able to pursue his political aims with less interruption for the next two or three years. At one time or another Szálasi published various pamphlets advocating intransigent revisionism, extreme anti-Semitism and uncompromising dictatorship. The chief of these publications was his "Plan for the construction of the Hungarian State" which came out in 1933; whoever hesitated to accept his notions, he wrote, "must be taught them with the knout." At one time he had also shown enthusiasm for Magyar racial purity, but this was impaired by the discovery of his own mixed Armenian-Slovak-German descent. He called his party the "Party of the National Will," and his prestige was enhanced by the support of the historian, Edmund Málnási; he also came into association with Dr. Rainis' "National Front" and the Catholic Nazis whose badge was the blue cross. Fascist movements in Hungary, incidentally, have never yet displayed the anti-Christian character of the German National Socialists, indeed this is the only visible distinction between them. Although the *Putsch* he attempted in spring 1937 proved abortive, Szálasi continued to gain a good deal of support, especially among students and unemployed workmen, many of whom were ex-Communists. In spite of recurring difficulties with the authorities,

Germany's seizure of Austria strengthened Szálasi
further, and in August 1938 his party was fused with
the "Arrow-Cross" party led by the big landowner,
Count Alexander Festetics, but nevertheless supported
by many land-hungry peasants ; [1] the united followers
of Szálasi now called themselves Hungarists. Actually
Szálasi had prophesied his own certain triumph for 1938,
but the end of it was that he was put into prison for
three years; by this time, however, his ally, M. Hubay,
had been elected to the Hungarian Chamber, and the
Hungarist movement had become a serious affair.

The year 1938 must have been one of the most
confused in all Hungarian history; the country as a
whole became aware that Nazi Germany was dangerous, yet the Hitlerist *élan* was able to carry Hungary
along with it. In February the *Gleichschaltung* of
Austria was tumultuously welcomed by the Szálasists
even in Budapest cafés; they seemed quite unable to
realize the implications. Some of them indeed spoke
secretly of amalgamation, or at least a Customs Union,
with this new and glorious Germany with its full
understanding for the freedom of neighbouring races.
The disappearance of Austria further weakened the
Hungarian conservatives by putting the Legitimist
party in an impossible position. But yet one received
the impression that, although most Hungarians had
long spoken of the *Anschluss* as inevitable, when it
came as it did it shocked them considerably. Old
memories of the historic struggles against the Habsburgs revived, and slowly, still surprisingly slowly,
realization seemed to come that the new Germany

---

[1] It was, incidentally, the peasants who had a little land, rather than the
agricultural workers with none, who betrayed the greater appetite for land.

now in pre-war Hungarian territory in Burgenland
was a grimmer neighbour than the old Austria had
ever been. And it was clear that the pre-war Leitha
frontier was gone for good, dream what the revisionists might. That the followers of Szálasi demonstrated
in Budapest might be dismissed as unimportant ex-
uberance, but German demonstrations at the Hungarian town of Sopron near the Austrian frontier were
disagreeable—there was a German minority of half a
million[1] in the country, and where would the influence
of German propaganda now end? Though those
who have studied Hungarian folklore and know the
peasants from long years of village life will tell one
that the traditional peasant songs are anti-German and
never anti-Slav, one heard in the summer of 1938 of
Hungarian villages where the peasants were so mystic-
ally impregnated with the swastika gospel that they
were praying that Hitler would come because their
own masters were incapable. The educated classes
had long felt irritation at the impudence of German
visitors who often explained to them that the rôle of
Hungary in future would be that of a *gleichgestellte
Hilfsmacht*, an obedient auxiliary for Germany.
Another annoying German habit was to refer to the
Tolna district of Hungary as *die Schwäbische Türkei*,
an old German phrase dating from the settlement of
the Swabian Colonists around the Danube in Hungary
after the Turks had been gradually evicted by a series
of Austrian generals ending with Prince Eugene. It
was not a very pleasant recollection that so recently as
1848 Budapest itself had been three-quarters German,
though by 1890 it had become 68 per cent. Magyar.

[1] See below, p. 28.

Very nationalist talk now aroused a certain Magyar feeling against, not only the Magyarized Jews, but also the Magyarized Germans, in their midst. This was not a question of the minority which had kept to speaking German, but of the relatively large number of people who had become completely Magyarized superficially, though their parents or grandparents had been German. Many people of this kind held high administrative posts; they had included General Gömbös among their number; purer Magyars suspected that their blood would out and that it was dangerous to have so many Ministers and Civil Servants of this kind, they would certainly be more susceptible to pressure from Berlin.

As a matter of fact, from the time of Austria's fall, if not even earlier, bureaucrats and important police officials and even one or two highly placed members of the judiciary seemed to be preparing, like many Austrian officials before them, to stand on the right side of Hitler; they intended to be safe from dismissals or reprisals should any kind of Nazi regime— German or dependent upon Germany—be installed at Budapest. As for the Army, it was said to be strongly infected with Szálasi doctrines, the younger officers, of course, in particular.

For a time the attitude of the Regent, Admiral Horthy, was uncertain; he had been brought into power years before as the head of a group of reactionary officers, some of whom were now undoubtedly attracted by Hitlerism and the "Party of the National Will." But in April 1938 the Regent broadcast his "Hands off the Army" speech in which he made it exceedingly clear that he at any rate meant to

resist the new German offensive, the steady pressure
of propaganda, together with economic threats and
bribes, political and military *faits accomplis* and the
Trojan Horse trick of over-stimulating the local
German minority. In the middle of May he appointed
the Imrédy Cabinet to put down Hungarian National
Socialism, overt Szálasi sympathizers were turned out
of the officers' corps, and Count Paul Teleki, as
Minister of Education, took steps to abolish Szálasi
influence from the schools. Yet German influence
upon the Hungarian press had now become paramount,
and there remained something alarmingly anomalous
about this regime; it seemed to combine the complexion of the strong-minded "baronial" Cabinet of
Herr von Papen in Germany in 1932 with that of the
Schuschnigg regime in Austria, for several of its
members, men like M. Bornemisza and M. Sztrányávszky, were known to be more than half Nazi, while
the same thing was true of many members of the
Government Party in the Lower House. M. Imrédy's
policy, moreover, consisted of nothing but to take
the wind out of the Nazis' sails, and he began with a
mild anti-Jewish law and more vigorous rearmament;
to finance the latter he launched his Milliard-pengö
Plan, which included arrangements for raising 600
million pengö by a capital levy assessed at a higher
rate upon industry than upon land.

   In September the partition of Czechoslovakia
absorbed Hungary's attention. At first she was with
Germany with all her heart against Beneš, but it was
extremely disagreeable for the Magyars to observe
that, whatever was to happen to Bratislava (which
they always claimed as an old Hungarian capital), it

would be dominated by the German troops who
occupied the bridgehead of Engerau, Hungarian
though this territory had been before Trianon. The
Munich Agreement indeed left the fate of Hungary's
pre-war provinces of Slovakia and Ruthenia un-
decided. Intriguers of all kinds were despatched
across the frontiers to strengthen all pro-Magyar
elements, and Hungarian soldiers were smuggled into
both areas to make trouble and to help create "spontaneous" demands for a return to Hungary. The end
of it was the Belvedere Award of November 2nd by
which Germany still insisted upon the maintenance of
the much trumpeted racial principle, though Italy
persuaded her to allow it to be interpreted about as
generously in Hungary's favour as the new German-
Czech frontiers had been drawn to Germany's advantage. The settlement was nevertheless regarded
by the Hungarians both as an insult and an injury, and
indeed the new frontiers were farcical from every
point of view, whether racial, economic or strategic.
Lively polemics were exchanged between German and
Hungarian newspapers, the Germans furiously attack-
ing the archaic imperialism of the Magyar belief in
the integrity of the lands of St. Stephen, and on
November 21st Hungary was reproved by the German
and Italian Governments for her disobedient de-
meanour. Meanwhile Germany had become the
champion of the Slovaks and almost of the Czechs
against the Hungarians, and she proceeded to turn
Chust (Huszt), the new capital of Ruthenia, into a
centre of Great-Ukrainian propaganda,[1] an enterprise
big with consequences for all Eastern Europe.

[1] See below, p. 225.

At this stage Hungarian opinion seemed alive at last to the danger presented to the country by Germany; the Prime Minister, however, pursued his efforts to forestall the Nazis so vigorously as to render him indistinguishable from them. He allowed it to emerge that he aimed at getting rid of Parliament and establishing a dictatorship, and he announced his intention of introducing new very severe anti-Semitic legislation—it was not clear how far Berlin was insisting upon this at the time. The position was complicated by whispers that M. Imrédy was not innocent of Jewish blood himself, a suggestion which he emphatically rejected in a speech at Baja [1] on January 15th, 1939. The Regent had become more and more restive, and he now received unimpeachable evidence that the Prime Minister's statement was inaccurate; he thereupon placed this evidence before M. Imrédy, who sensationally collapsed and was ill for three days. Admiral Horthy accepted his resignation on February 14th, and then with relief appointed Count Paul Teleki in his place. It is not without interest that, after his recovery, M. Imrédy was known to be collaborating with the notoriously pro-Nazi deputy M. Mécser, who had, it is true, always contrived to remain within the Government Party.

In the next six weeks Hungary's relations with Germany were almost indescribably intricate. Towards the end of February Count Teleki dissolved the Hungarists and sent Count Louis Széchenyi and other of their leaders to join Major Szálasi in prison. On March 15th, as the Germans occupied Prague, the Hungarians quite frankly crossed the Belvedere frontiers to invade

[1] On this occasion he admitted not only to German, but to Czech descent.

the remains of Ruthenia; from the tone of certain German newspapers [1] it appeared that the Germans had not been consulted. To this second act of defiance the Budapest Government added yet something more; on March 23rd, the day on which Germany signed a treaty undertaking "to protect the independence of Slovakia and the integrity of her territory," the Hungarians advanced into south-eastern Slovakia and took possession of the Ung Valley railway line, a gain to which the Slovaks were subsequently forced to agree in spite of the presence of German troops in Prešov and elsewhere in Slovakia. It appeared that the Hungarian Government had triumphed all along the line and had spoilt an elaborate German game in the Carpatho-Ukraine, where in fact a number of officers of the Sič or Ukrainian National Guard were shot by the Hungarians and thereupon discovered to be Germans.[2] Small power triumphs over Hitler have, however, mostly turned out to have boomerang qualities. Already before M. Imrédy's fall Hungary had been forced to join the Anti-Comintern Pact, and for the moment it was worth Hitler's while to drop Ruthenia in order to be able to play off Hungary against Roumania, as Hitler virtually announced to the Reichstag on April 28th.[3] On March 23rd also the German-Roumanian Commercial Treaty was signed, containing, as it did, the implication that Germany guaranteed the existing frontiers of Roumania. The Hungarians' appetite for revision had only been whetted and an implied threat to their Transylvanian hopes was enough, in the general cir-

---

[1] e.g. *Der Grenzbote* of Bratislava.
[2] See below, p. 226.   [3] See below, p. 236.

cumstances of 1939, to bring them to heel. As in most other countries, there was also in Hungary a much greater scepticism towards Hitler after March 15th, especially, it was thought, in Hungarian military circles. The Germans since that day had admitted, even to the outside world, an imperialistic claim to *Lebensraum* and to the heritage of the mediaeval Reich, so that even they could no longer use racial arguments against the revisionist programme of the Magyars with full effect. But this fact, like many, cut in two directions and seemed to facilitate a frankly imperialistic Hungaro-German alliance. In Hungary itself the situation remained as ambiguous as ever. There were still Cabinet Ministers like M. Homan or M. Jaros whose sympathies were strongly pro-Nazi with whose services Count Teleki seemed unable to dispense. The Hungarists were dissolved but the Hungarist deputy, M. Hubay, had been allowed to form a new Arrow Cross or Hungarian National Socialist Party on March 12th. The position was summed up perhaps by a remarkable incident which took place in Budapest on March 15th, 1939. The day upon which the Germans chose to enter Prague is celebrated in Hungary as the day of the liberal anti-Austrian revolution in 1848. At a public function attended by the Regent that day several youths made a demonstration crying out in chorus, "Justice for Szálasi." The elderly Admiral Horthy, before he could be missed, dashed up two flights of stairs and made as if he would strike them, exclaiming, "You wretched traitors, do you wish to ruin your country?" This was the talk of Budapest for a week or so, but the fact remains that the Regent is seventy and the young men are young.

Matters were put to the test some two months later, when on May 28th (Whitsunday) elections were held, the first to take place according to the electoral reform law of early 1938. In order to weaken the influence of the young and the destitute, who had naturally shown themselves most susceptible to German Nazi propaganda, the age at which voters became eligible had been raised, while educational and long residence qualifications were extended or maintained. At the same time growing protests against open voting—it had, since Count Bethlen reorganized the administration, only been secret in the towns—had been accepted, and a secret ballot generally introduced; conservatives hoped that this would restrict Nazi pressure from the Reich, while the Hungarists claimed that the peasants would now dare to vote against the big estate owners and in favour of the Radicals of the Right. During the election campaign the Hubay party evidently had large supplies of money at its disposal which could only have come from Germany in the main, for there was no one in Hungary who would or could have provided them. There also suddenly appeared in Hungary at this time a Green Book [1] or pamphlet which had certainly not been printed in Hungary, but on the contrary usually arrived there by post from Munich. It was dedicated to Szálasi and other imprisoned Hungarian Nazi personalities, attacked the Teleki Government for its "reactionary regime detrimental to the interests of the Hungarian people," and urged the latter to elect a Nazi Parliament. Among its assertions it stated that one-third of Hungary's national wealth belonged to a handful of Jewish capitalists and

[1] See *Times*, May 24th, 1939.

another third to a handful of feudalistic landowning aristocrats, so that equitable redistribution must be brought about without delay.

There was a good deal of Magyar indignation against Germany's interference in the Hungarian elections in spite of all the concessions in foreign and minority policy which had been made to Berlin; M. Hubay and his friends, indeed, publicly disavowed the "Green Book." The indignation, however, was felt by the more cultivated and articulate members of Hungarian society, already full of resentment as they were with regard to the severely anti-Semitic legislation which had just, not without much hesitation and amendment, gone through the Hungarian Parliament on May 5th. The new laws, it was true, were not so cruel as those prevailing in Germany, for one could only be branded as Jewish by two Jewish grandparents instead of one, small quotas [1] of Jews were to be allowed in cultural and economic life, and, even with four Jewish grandparents, one was saved by baptism before 1919 if one's ancestors had consistently lived in Hungary since before 1867. Few people supposed, however, that the Hungarian Nazis could have pushed through laws of this kind without vigorous "diplomatic" insistence from Germany, and members of the gentry, who had been bitterly anti-Semitic in their talk hitherto, were now suddenly attacked by Nazis as the friends and protectors of the Jews.

Meanwhile the lower strata of society were caught in the toils of propaganda. Though contemporary press comments abroad exaggerated the Nazi land-

---

[1] Something slightly over 6 per cent. in cultural organizations and something over 12 per cent. in economic life according to all kinds of complicated regulations.

slide, the results of the elections undoubtedly indicated
the success of the unceasing pressure from Germany.
Hitherto there had only been in the Lower Chamber
M. Hubay himself and two other Arrow Cross men,
and besides these, two or three independents with
strong Nazi sympathies. On May 28th, however,
twenty-eight Szálasi people were elected, together
with another fifteen pro-Nazis, bringing the group
up to 43; it was exceedingly significant that Budapest
with its big working-class vote had become a Szálasi
stronghold, for the voting had been secret in the towns
before, so that the change could not be attributed to
electoral reform. The Government retained a big
majority—180 seats out of 260—but this in Hungarian
terms was not as impressive as an Englishman might
think. Though the elections were said to have been
held correctly, the administration in Hungary has
great opportunities for bringing its influence to bear,
and the peasants naturally disbelieved in the secrecy
of the ballot. Moreover, perhaps half the Government Party itself sympathized actively with the Nazis,
for it included, not only the pro-Nazi ministers, but
also old quasi-Nazi supporters of General Gömbös,
men like M. Mécser or again men like M. Mécser's
new friend, M. Imrédy, elected to represent Pécs;
it also included two representatives of the Nazi wing
of the German minority.[1] On the other hand, those
parties which stood for liberal democracy in a western
sense and were regarded as the country's anti-Nazi defences lost considerably, especially M. Eckhardt's Small
Farmers' Party which was associated with the non-
Nazi members of the German minority [2] in Hungary.

[1] See below, p. 37.   [2] See below, p. 38.

The small Liberal group led by Dr. Rassay held its ground, but the Social Democrats, whose very survival so near the German frontier was a remarkable anomaly, were reduced from 11 deputies to 5.

Thus Germany, against whom Hungary has no defensive frontier, can now play more mischievously than ever with the better emotions of the younger generation and the natural desires of the peasantry by keeping the question of agrarian injustice in evidence. For both good and evil motives the old aristocracy,[1] which most fully appreciates the German menace to Hungary, is most hostile to any really fundamental change in the distribution of land, and it is not unjust to attribute the fall of M. Imrédy from office to his enthusiasm for land-reform as well as to his Nazistic proclivities. A small degree of land redistribution is now necessarily under way, since everyone has to-day been brought to admit the importance of the question. While men like the Regent and Counts Bethlen and Paul Teleki are strongly opposed to the harsh anti-Semitic laws which Berlin has undoubtedly thrust upon them, they are perhaps glad enough to see the few big Jewish landed estates divided up among peasants, though this process can only stimulate a cry for more and postpone the evil day.

(b) *The Minority Aspect*

The events of autumn 1938 and spring 1939 have brought to Hungary a minority of some half million Ruthenes or Ukrainians newly over-stimulated by

---

[1] There are a certain number of Nazi Hungarian aristocrats like Count A. Festetics and Count L. Széchenyi, but they are few enough to be regarded as exceptional.

Great Ukrainian propaganda; the Slovak minority in Hungary has also been greatly increased up to nearly half a million, while Hungary's German minority has received a number of over-excited recruits in the Slovak and Ruthene towns. The extended Hungary of to-day is certainly more formidable in appearance, and the Budapest wireless has been eloquent about the return of the Ruthene brothers and the autonomy they will receive. Ruthenian autonomy, however, has shown no signs of materializing for the present,[1] and it would be contrary to the whole Magyar tradition that it should do so. Germany has had triumphant experience in using the self-determination cry as a disintegrating instrument; it may be only too satisfactory to let Hungary conquer various territories and load herself up with minorities, and then to bring about her disintegration and swallow her piece by piece.

There was a good deal to be said for the old cultural imperialism of the Magyars. They regarded themselves as a race born to rule and to civilize, and they therefore expected to assimilate their non-Magyar subjects; as Mr. Macartney has made clear,[2] they successfully attracted many converts, and once a German or Slovak or Roumanian had accepted Magyarization there was little discrimination against him. Unfortunately for Hungary these conceptions conflicted increasingly with the nationalistic ideas of the nineteenth century, as these ideas gradually,

[1] At the time of the Hungarian elections the Government nominated deputies to represent the Slovak and Ruthene territories acquired by Hungary in 1938 and 1939.

[2] See C. A. Macartney, *Hungary and Her Successors*. Oxford University Press, 1937.

and mainly thanks to German influences, became
more racial and even more tribal. As the Turks
were driven back across Hungary Swabian immigrants had been settled around Budapest from the
seventeenth century onwards; they soon appeared
in Transdanubia around Pécs, and later still in
the Banat territory which now belongs to Roumania
and Yugoslavia.[1] Even after the eighteenth century
there was a thin stream of arrivals from Germany and
Austria; together with the Germans of the Burgenland
the Germans in all pre-war Hungary numbered about
two million. They had kept their language and
customs, but as a whole the Hungarian authorities
presumed that the Germans should enjoy a purely
Hungarian education except for a few denominational
schools mostly in the territory taken from Hungary
in 1919. The Germans in pre-war Hungary did retain
a certain prestige—though this again was true rather
of the Transylvanian Saxons or even the Swabians of
the Banat—because the Magyars after all had accepted
a German dynasty and an at least superficially German
sister-state.

The Treaty of Trianon left Hungary with a German
minority of about half a million, which until 1936 was
mainly educated in schools without any teaching in
German; the majority of German children in Hungary
until then went to Hungarian schools, where they were
only considered to the extent of ensuring them a certain
number of German lessons. In 1928 the Germans in
Hungary were in fact educated in 316 of these Hungarian schools, with 98 schools where the teaching was
about half-and-half in Magyar and German and only 49

[1] See below, pp. 75, 145.

where the teaching was altogether in German; in
1933 the latter type of school had fallen to 40 in
number, but the mixed type had increased up to 191
schools, while the schools with purely Hungarian
teaching for Germans had diminished from 316 to 265.
Nor was there any secondary or higher education to
be had in German; religious instruction and most
religious services were conducted in Hungarian in
most German districts. Further, the German minority
in Hungary was not represented in Parliament and it
enjoyed an extremely limited right of non-political
association. In 1924 it was allowed to found a cultural
organization known as the *Ungarländisch-Deutscher
Volksbildungsverein* (or U.D.V.), which was able to
publish a weekly newspaper, the *Sonntagsblatt*, but
which encountered a good deal of obstruction from
the Hungarian authorities. In the early 'thirties the
position was made particularly unfortunate by a
Magyar chauvinist campaign in favour of the Magyarization of the names of Hungarians of foreign origin;
only people who had freely accepted assimilation were
supposed to be concerned, but inevitably ill-feeling
was engendered between the Hungarians and the
members of the actual German minority. German
resentment was also aroused by the publication of the
preliminary figures of the 1930 census in Hungary,
which showed a drop in the various minorities, a drop
which represented a natural tendency of minorities
but against which the new spirit of the Reich was
beginning to raise wild cries of protest—inferior
peoples, ran the legend, were deliberately accelerating
the dying out of German groups abroad.[1] In 1933

---

[1] This indictment was much to be heard among the Sudeten Germans.

the leader of the German minority in Hungary, Professor Bleyer, protested in the Budget debate against German disabilities, and especially against the lack of mixed schools (which were all he himself advocated) and the way in which various legal rights were in practice ignored, for instance the right of a 20 per cent. (or bigger) minority in any commune to deal with the authorities in its own language. Bleyer's protest was indignantly received by most Hungarians; indeed the National Socialist Revolution in Germany synchronized with an embittered situation between Hungary and its German minority.

After Hitler came to power, the German Legation in Budapest pressed more and more insistently for some noticeable change. After all, the Reich was now ruled by the Nazi party, the first point on whose programme was "*Wir fordern den Zusammenschluss aller Deutschen auf Grund des Selbstbestimmungsrechtes der Völker zu einem Gross-Deutschland.*" The Pan-German organizations like the *Verein*, which soon became the *Volksbund, für das Deutschtum im Auslande*, now busily imbued all Germans outside Germany [1] with the idea that they owed allegiance primarily to Hitler, the leader of their race, and that this race was inherently superior to others with a mission to rule over them. German minorities in other countries thus became the outpost of a future world empire; in accordance with such a conception they were to acquire a privileged position as of a superior caste among natives. The essential claim they must make, though this was not published to the world for some time, not really clearly,

[1] At first these activities were indignantly denied, but as time went on there was less and less reason not to admit to them.

indeed, until Herr Henlein's speech at Carlsbad in April 1938,[1] was to a corporate personality, making them into something like a state within each state. This demand served a number of purposes. It was consistent with the anti-individualism of National Socialism, it denied the right of an individual to be guided by his judgment as against his descent, and it ensured the triumph of one-party and leadership notions in each minority group. Any German who chose, as an independent individual to do homage to the state in which he lived, or who resisted the authority of the local Nazi leader, more and more ran the risk, as a *Volksverräter*,[2] of ostracism and other more unpleasant experiences. In this way the German minorities became much more clearly marked off, much more difficult for the local administration to control, and much easier for the Reich authorities to manipulate.

Magyar tradition had immensely retarded such developments in Hungary, and in 1933, it has been seen, the infinitely more palatable requests of Professor Bleyer had been rejected. This had the effect of immediately transferring the allegiance of some of the younger Germans in Hungary to the Reich, which now fed them with a stronger diet than they can ever have dreamt of. The pressure from Germany steadily increased, and at Christmas 1935 the Hungarian Government consequently decreed that the German minority schools should all be gradually transformed into the type in which about half the teaching took

---

[1] Actually this claim was first publicly raised in Henlein's speech at Eger in June 1936. It was a claim for minority rights such as none of the Minority Treaties of 1919 had ever envisaged.

[2] Traitor to his *Volk*, a conception half-way between nation and race.

place in German and the other half in Magyar. Hungarian official promises were well known to get easily shelved, but by the spring of 1938 most of the German minority schools had been transformed into the half-and-half type. Otherwise little had been changed, and there had now arisen the ludicrous situation that Germany more and more openly demanded the dismemberment of Czechoslovakia as the oppressor of Germans, though the Sudeten Germans had enjoyed many rights (if no privileges) and would have felt indescribably outraged at the offer of schools with only half the teaching in German. Yet Germany remained in an anti-Czech alliance with Hungary, where the Swabians had far fewer rights either as Magyar citizens in general or as German-speaking ones in particular. With M. Imrédy's appointment as Prime Minister in May 1938 German pressure was accepted to the extent of at length agreeing to transform the bilingual schools into purely German ones. After the Munich Agreement Germany's tone everywhere became much more brusque, especially in minority affairs, and German-Magyar friction in November and December only stimulated German complaint.

M. Imrédy was in any case not disinclined to offer concessions, and in a Christmas supplement to the semi-official *Pester Lloyd* he announced that there would in future be a German daily newspaper in Hungary, that German would be used in churches with German congregations, that there would now be training colleges for German teachers and German teaching in clerical seminaries, and that the newly started German *Volksbildungsvereine* should be allowed to indulge in propaganda freely. It was also conceded, at about the same time, that in any commune where the Germans were in the majority and expressly asked for it, purely German schools should be opened. In spite of his Nazi sympathies and perhaps because of his German descent, M. Imrédy had still offered less than the Sudeten Germans ever had, and there was a certain amount of irony in the ecclesiastical nature of some of the concessions to the co-racialists of the Pope's enemy, Herr Hitler.

In spite of the successes of National Socialism and the activities of the V.D.A., the majority of the Germans in Hungary had not yet been disturbed by the National Socialist spirit. Many of them are small farmers in the Tolna district and have habitually voted for M. Eckhardt's Small Farmer Party. The Nazi attitude, was, however, maintained and inflamed by a local *Führer*, Dr. Franz Basch, who in December 1938 was elected President of a new and Nazi *Volksbund der Deutschen in Ungarn* with no use for the *Ungarländisch-deutsche* idea. Dr. Basch now organized German requests for German schools, sending round forms for the Germans to sign; it is not without interest that a number of the Swabian peasants resisted the pressure from the *Volksbund* in this matter, because they had always taken the extraordinarily sensible view that it was preferable for their children, who would have to live in Hungary and who could speak German at home, to have a Hungarian education. On the other hand, since the beginning of 1939 new "*Völkisch*" feeling has been aroused among the Swabians, and there are fears [1] that a growing number of apparently

---

[1] See above, p. 19.

assimilated Hungarians of German descent may wish
to revert to the Germanism which nowadays involves
the possibilities of privilege. Dr. Basch himself was
once a Hungarian chauvinist. He has now made use
of the ever-growing pressure from Berlin upon Budapest to work up the tone of his new paper, *Deutscher
Volksbote*. To anyone aware of the character of the
leading Henleinist daily, *Die Zeit*, in pre-Munich
Czechoslovakia, the contents of Dr. Basch's paper
seem all too familiar; one finds complaints about the
schools, of course, and just the same accusations about
brutal gendarmes, just the same glorification of the
Reich and its foreign policy. On the occasion of his
election as President of the *Volksbund* in December
1938, Dr. Basch also raised the crucial Henleinist
demand for the legal recognition of the corporate
personality of the German *Volksgruppe* in Hungary.
Now anything of this kind is unprecedented in Hungary, and a good Hungarian chauvinist, who is all for
an alliance with Germany for what Hungary can get
out of it, is infuriated when he discovers this sort of
thing going on within his own country. Several
unpleasant incidents were the result. There was, for
instance, an occasion in February 1939 when some
Hungarians attended a German meeting at Pécs rather
with the idea of keeping an eye on the proceedings;
soon cries of "Out with the Hungarian dogs!" arose,
and the visitors were compelled, to their great indignation, to leave. With the annexation of Bohemia
and Moravia and the anomalous treatment of Slovakia,
which really made the German-Hungarian frontier
continuous (if ambiguous) from somewhere near
St. Gotthard to somewhere near Prešov, the Reich

began to press harder for greater liberty—or should one say licence?—for all German so-called cultural organizations abroad; these, since the books they have circulated have expressed nothing but the Nazi *Weltanschauung*, have become attractive and attracting political propaganda bureaux. In spite of the mounting resentment in Hungary, the authorities were forced to allow a new German performance on April 30th, when Dr. Basch's *Volksbund* paraded out-of-doors at Ciko. Thanks to Nazi influence, both German and Hungarian, upon the Cabinet, the Government Party proceeded to take up Dr. Basch's following and to offer them three seats in the new chamber to be elected on May 28th, while the anti-German, M. Eckhardt, whom Count Teleki would perhaps privately have welcomed as a colleague, was decried in Germany as the ally of the un-German Germans led by M. Eckhardt's supporter, Herr Anton Klein. In the election campaign a tremendous pressure was exerted upon the Swabian minority in Hungary through German bribery and intimidation of one kind and another. Bribery took the form of attractive promises of employment in Germany offered by the *Volksbund* candidate to the inhabitants of a hotly contested place like Bonyhad, while intimidation was most strongly exercised in the mixed town of Sopron on the frontier where Nazi threats of direct annexation were loud. As many indignant Hungarians pointed out, the *Volksbund* leaders dropped the old claims to be loyal and frankly abused the Hungarian state; later, on June 22nd, Herr Klein attacked them in Parliament for this and they did not deny it. The voting, like that in Czechoslovakia in 1935, showed that about two-thirds of the

German minority had been won to Dr. Basch, who
again, like Konrad Henlein in 1935, did not himself
stand for parliament, but left Dr. Mühl, a medical man
from Bonyhad itself, to take his place there. Herr
Klein was elected to represent the non-Nazi Swabians,
and, incidentally, the old pro-Magyar Swabian leader,
Dr. Gustav Gratz, was returned to Parliament as a
member of the Rassay Liberal group. In Sopron
Count Csáky successfully defeated the Nazis, but there
were many who regarded him as no very real enemy
of theirs. Although hitherto the pro-Nazi Germans
had not, as in other countries, ostensibly had much
to do with the totalitarians in Hungary itself in this
election campaign, though they were officially attached
to Count Teleki and the Government Party, they made
no secret of their sympathy for the Hungarist opposition. Even in Hungary the German Minority is thus
being used to bring the Hungarian Government Party
closer to the Axis and to weaken resistance, like that
of M. Eckhardt, to the Nazi drive to the south-east.

(c) *Economic Pressure*

The term *Gleichgestellte Hilfsmacht* very accurately
indicates the rôle Germany wishes Hungary to play,
especially from an economic point of view. The
Hungarian plain is naturally a great corn-producing
area, and, since the industrialization of her Austrian
and Bohemian neighbours, it has been natural that
Hungarian wheat should be sent mainly to them, and
beyond them, to Germany. Already before 1914 the
Hungarian Government, regretting its dependence
upon imported manufactures, even those coming from

Austria, made determined attempts at industrialization, efforts which were not, however, in time to bear very much fruit before the Great War. It was natural, therefore, that Hungary should export large quantities of grain to the industrial cities of Germany after the war; after her commercial relations with Czechoslovakia were broken off in 1930 it became still more imperative that she should do so. The great depression brought a collapse in agricultural prices, and it was obvious that, when Nazi Germany showed a revived appetite for foodstuffs and was willing to offer unusually good prices though in fact she was unable or unwilling to provide normal payment, Hungary would willingly fall in with her plans. It was only later observed that Germany was deliberately creating a situation in which the Hungarians had to accept what German goods were sent to them as the only payment for which they could hope. In this way Hungarian wheat, and to a much less extent maize, production became partly dependent upon the German market, though the Rome protocols of 1934 gave her convenient trade relations with Italy and Austria which were also willing to take some of her grain until Austria disappeared and Italy [1] became impoverished. It should be observed that the export of wheat was chiefly interesting to the big landowners of Hungary, and that their growing hostility towards Hitler's Reich has been restrained by the advantages Dr. Schacht and his successors offered them. And while her agents whip up the land-hunger of the Hungarian peasants Ger-

---

[1] During the first four months of 1938 Hungary's exports to Italy were only worth 11·1 million pengö, though in the same period in 1937 they had been worth 33·9 million pengö.

many has an interest in preventing the break-up of the big Hungarian estates, not only because of transitional disorganization but also because large areas are much more satisfactory as units for the production of corn.

Post-war tariffs and post-slump autarchy have brought about a marked industrialization in Hungary, though agriculture still employs substantially more people than industry. The development of the textile industry has been most extensive, while the production of machinery has considerably increased. This has led to competition with Germany for Balkan markets.

The disappearance of Austria and Czechoslovakia as independent states has radically changed the economic situation as between Germany and Hungary. Budapest, having itself been the centre of an Empire, had no tradition of economic dependence upon Vienna to preserve, such as characterized the relations of Yugoslavia and, to some extent, Roumania with post-war Austria, still less had Hungary depended upon the Czechs. But since Mussolini had for a time particularly fostered the economic relations of Hungary with Austria, the Magyars found themselves in a very much more dependent position when their trade with Austria came under German control—Hungary lost a more or less free currency market, and Germany could bargain in bigger and therefore more forcible terms. It also became clear that Germany would become more competitive with regard to raw materials required for industry, and that she would gradually cut off the supplies of Austrian timber upon which Hungary had relied. Indeed Germany became altogether more disagreeable to deal with, and in particular, more impatient of any industrial competition. The

events of autumn 1938 and the spring of 1939 greatly
accentuated the new German scowl, for the Reich had
mostly acquired industrial areas which increased her
shortage of food and raw materials, while, on the
other hand, by becoming so large an economic unit
her economic threats or blandishments enormously
increased in significance—they were, of course, always
manipulated in skilful relationship to political and
directly strategical pressure, either positive or negative.
The demands which Germany now formulated with
more and more insistence in the countries to her
south-east amounted to something not far from
economic annexation to the Reich—long-term trade
agreements involving the monopoly of the small
countries' foreign trade together with the virtual
linking of their currencies with that of Germany.
This new German economic programme was associated with Dr. Schacht's successor, Dr. Funk.

Now Hungary had gained a certain amount of iron
ore in Southern Slovakia in November 1938, and in
March 1939 Ruthenia brought her a valuable salt-mine
at ·Akna Szlatina and about enough timber to compensate her for her disappearing Austrian supplies.
She therefore appeared to be in a stronger position,
and her increasingly valuable production of bauxite
and the sinking of several new oil-wells opened out a
promising prospect. With the virtual absorption of
Czechoslovakia, Germany, however, was taking about
50 per cent. of her total exports,[1] and nearly as high
a proportion of her imports now came from the new

---

[1] The habit has been adopted of assessing trade with the Greater Reich
of to-day in terms of the trade formerly done with Germany, Austria and
Czechoslovakia added together. Apart from the questions of Slovakia and
Ruthenia, this leaves room for inaccuracy, but it is not really misleading.

big Reich with its Slovak dependency. Far more than half of Hungary's agricultural produce now goes to Great Germany, indeed in January and February 1939 about 90 per cent. of this was taken by Germany with Austria, Bohemia, Moravia and Slovakia, and Hungary is constantly faced with a far too "active" balance in her trade with Germany which then necessitates more purchases from the Reich. All this comes dangerously near to a German monopoly in itself and cuts Hungary off from the free currency countries. Meanwhile Germany has been pressing more and more insistently for a long-term commercial treaty to run for three to five years, which would in itself restrict Hungary's freedom of action and ability to adapt herself to new circumstances. Germany has also, in return for the preferential wheat prices she has offered, insisted upon an artificially high rate of exchange for the mark,[1] a demand she has been pressing wherever she could, and with particularly unfortunate consequences in Yugoslavia.[2] The practical effects of this currency dictation on the part of Germany have been to make the high prices she has offered partially and increasingly fictitious, while prices have been driven up in the selling country so that the latter has found it difficult to compete in the open world market; in this way, too, Hungary has found herself harnessed to the economic system of the Reich. It is said that on the occasion of the Hungarian official visit to Germany in August 1938 the German Government pressed for a direct Hungarian-German Customs

---

[1] Cf. *South-Eastern Europe*. Royal Institute of International Affairs, 1939. P. 122.

[2] See below, p. 163.

Union, but was stoutly resisted by the then Hungarian Foreign Minister, M. de Kánya.[1] More recently Germany is known to have been urging a plan for a Customs Union between Hungary and Slovakia which, since March 1939, would also in effect bring Hungary into the German customs area; in return it was suggested that Slovakia, at least as far as the River Vág, should be handed over politically to Budapest.

For Germany has made no secret of the fact that she wishes to destroy Hungarian industry so that Hungary shall cease to compete with her in any way, but shall, on the contrary, concentrate upon producing food and aluminium for the Reich. The anti-Semitic legislation, but especially the much severer project initiated by M. Imrédy at Christmas time 1938 and only finally legislated some four months later, has undoubtedly been insisted upon by the Germans with a view to the paralysing effects upon Hungarian industry to which it was bound to conduce. Until 1938 about three-quarters of the personnel of Hungary's commercial organization was Jewish, if banking and industry, very closely linked as they were, be considered together. Out of a total of, roughly, 3000 factories, about 1500 were in Jewish hands, and this 1500 included all the major concerns. According to the earlier law only 20 per cent., according to the later one only about 12 per cent., of the posts and salaries in any business may be Jewish; hitherto, in spite of a slow squeeze-out which has long been in progress, the percentage was on the average perhaps 40 to 50 per cent. There are simply not enough Magyars qualified to take their place, and while many concerns are preparing to close

---

[1] See Graham Hutton, *Danubian Destiny*, p. 195.

down it seems also to have been the case that Reich Germans have to a slight extent replaced Jews. While roundly objecting to competition from the Hungarian machine and textile industries, the Germans are said also to have protested against the erection, recently, of plants to smelt bauxite in Hungary—the growing importance of aluminium makes Hungary's bauxite production increasingly valuable to her. The German-Roumanian commercial treaty of March 23rd, 1939,[1] seems likely to have unfortunate results for Hungarian industry, to which it, too, suggests Germany to be hostile; a customs connection with the Reich direct or via Slovakia would also be hard upon Hungarian manufacturers. On the other hand, if Germany felt able to supply sufficient new personnel in Hungary's industrial concerns this might constitute in her view a satisfactory penetration, and Hungary's industry in direct German control could be moulded to Germany's pleasure. Nor will the oil-well at Lispe in Trans-danubia have escaped Germany's notice; it is not fantastic to suppose that if the oil flows at all freely the German Minority's claim to the sacred soil around there will be still more loudly heard. Many Hungarians bitterly resent the various forms of German economic pressure, and regard as particularly insolent the demand that their country should abandon its industrial life. M. Kunder, the not very strong Minister of Trade and Industry, who is thought to be rather pro-German than not, in a speech held on March 31st, 1939, was forced to voice the determination which is felt that Hungary's economy shall not "degenerate into one-sidedness." He pointed out that

[1] See below, p. 92.

Hungary's population had increased in November 1938 and March 1939 by 17½ per cent., while her industrial production had only been increased by 6 per cent., a salutary piece of de-industrialization, probably, in the German view; M. Kunder, on the other hand, chose to regard the change as calling for industrial expansion.[1] It has been interesting, in recent times, to hear people in Hungary, who formerly could not find enough epithets with which to abuse the Jews, complain that they would as soon keep their Jews as give their Jews' jobs to Germans. Unfortunately it may take a long time before such feelings penetrate into Hungarist circles. It is characteristic of Germany's undeclared war that she whips up revolutionary agrarian emotions on the one hand, and on the other presses Hungary to de-industrialize, a process which, in depriving thousands of workmen of their livelihood, would send them "back to the land," and in fact into the ranks of the landless masses who are already so numerous that their desires cannot possibly be fulfilled. It is particularly ironical that the industrial working-class of Budapest appears to have been largely decoyed into the Nazi camp where its very existence is endangered. Even the Hungarist leaders, in so far as they accept Germany's de-industrializing and Customs Union plans, are deluded into doing so by their quite exaggerated belief in the blessings quickly to be realized through the redistribution of the land. The uncertain situation in Hungary is agreeable to Germany, who, not wishing to find her Hungarian grain supplies diminished by

---

[1] Pester Lloyd, March 31st, 1939. Count Paul Teleki said very much the same thing in an election speech in May.

temporary disorganization, has no desire to see an idealistic agrarian reform really carried out. But it is thoroughly convenient for the Germans to be able to refer, in the words of the *Völkischer Beobachter*,[1] to the "urgent need for the establishment of political harmony between the people and its ruler" in Hungary; how easily in these circumstances could Germany's interference be made to seem necessary, how easily, as people already whisper among themselves, could M. Imrédy become the Seyss-Inquart, scarcely the Hácha, of Hungary. Meanwhile the Lajos affair, the prosecution suddenly announced in July 1939 of the author of an extremely popular book, which had implied that Germany might not win the next war, shows the extent to which Hitler has already reduced Hungarian independence.

[1] March 25th, 1939 (Vienna edition).

CHAPTER II

ROUMANIA

(a) *Political Development*

THE Roumanian is perhaps the most difficult continental mentality for an Englishman to comprehend, and he usually dismisses the Roumanians from his mind as corrupt scoundrels, brigands and savages. He is able to do this mostly because he is ignorant; he does not know that the history of "less happier lands" has prevented the development of "clean" administration which requires undisturbed prosperity to afford ample salaries for administrators. Still less does he realize that the Roumanians have been subjected to series after series of destructive invasions interspersed with corrupt and brutally oppressive government—if indeed one should honour it with the name of government—by Turks, Phanariot Greeks and the rest. It is not worth working if invaders are about to wipe out the traces of your work; it is not worth being honest if alien tax-collectors take everything you confess to having from you—it is only worth taking everything you can find and enjoying it quickly. Indeed to study the history of Roumania [1] is to marvel at how often virtue can still raise her head in the ancient Principalities of Moldavia and Wallachia. The Roumanians have another perplexing quality, a blend of an immensely ancient, civilized inheritance—which makes

---

[1] See *A History of the Roumanians*, by R. W. Seton-Watson. Cambridge, 1934.

the very children seem tired, sophisticated but essentially intelligent—with the rawness and anxiety of a nation that is new. Though their enemies sneer at their claim to be the direct descendants of the Daco-Romans and declare that only their Parisian studies have supplied their Latinized veneer, and though it is true that they disappeared from historical record from the end of the third century to the beginning of the thirteenth, it is wholly impossible to dismiss the story of their Latin descent so frivolously. No doubt their racial impurity is as great as anyone's, no doubt Roumanian contains a great deal of Slav blood, but quite apart from historical monuments it is almost impossible to imagine that a wholly un-Latin people like the Bulgars or the Serbs could have had so Latin a language imposed upon it by a few intellectuals. Nor will Sofia or Belgrade ever make upon one the impression one receives in Bucharest of being in a Naples stripped of baroque.

Napoleon III, in his strange interested quixotism, was the first European notable to concern himself seriously with the aspirations of the Danubian Principalities, but it is characteristic that Bismarck then exploited the question which Napoleon had raised, and despatched the thinly disguised Charles of Hohenzollern down the Danube to become the first Prince of united Roumania just before the outbreak of the Austro-Prussian war in 1866. To Roumanian patriots, however, the process of emancipation had only begun, for across the Transylvanian Alps there were thousands of peasants in Transylvania who spoke much the same language as their own, but who were treated by the dominant Magyar and German groups there as an

inferior caste which must be kept in its place. The
Great Prince of Transylvania was still at this time the
Habsburg Emperor of Austria, who, distant though
he was, was regarded by the Transylvanian Roumanians as their only protector. The arrival of the
Hohenzollern Prince to rule the Principalities naturally
caused these other Roumanians to look to Bucharest,
indeed Bismarck may not altogether have regretted a
little extra pinpricking of the Habsburgs in 1866. In
the following year, however, Francis Joseph abandoned his Roumanian subjects (except those of the
Bukovina), and allowed Transylvania to be incorporated with the new, all but independent, Hungary, to
whose authority he agreed by the compromise of
1867. From this time on systematic Magyarization
set in throughout Transleithania, and the Transylvanian Roumanians looked more and more to the
south-east; it was only the alliance of Roumania with
the Central Powers until she joined the Allies during
the Great War which prevented the Roumanians of
the Regat, the Kingdom whose independence was
recognized in 1878, from more active co-operation
with their brothers in Hungary. The bitterness felt
by the German Austrians against the Czechs for their
active sympathy with the Allies during the war was
equalled by that which the Hungarians felt against the
Transylvanian Roumanians for exactly similar reasons;
it combined with the social contempt which they
entertained for them.

Since the Roumanians were the largest ethnical
group in Transylvania, the Peace Treaties handed
Transylvania, together with much of the Hungarian
Banat and an extra strip of territory to include the

valuable Oradea-Arad railway, over to Roumania. She also received the Bukovina from Austria, Bessarabia and Southern Dobrogea. Her problems thus became exactly the opposite from the problems of post-war Hungary—they arose out of the need for a greatly expanded administrative machine to be applied to an approximately doubled territory. The existing mechanism had not had time to become efficient. It now had to deal with many different racial groups and to reconcile four or five conflicting traditions, and it was called upon to handle the problem of Transylvania, perhaps the most intricate problem in Europe.

The history of the 'twenties is not in itself particularly instructive with regard to the circumstances which have subsequently facilitated the waging of the Germans' undeclared war in Roumania; these circumstances, as elsewhere, were largely created by the World Slump. Certain characteristics of Roumanian life at the time need, however, to be mentioned. The Roumanians, mostly easy-going as they are, are yet subject to fierce chauvinistic explosions, and anti-Semitism among them had long been easy to arouse. One of history's prettiest ironies is the story of how Germany in Bismarck's day harried the Roumanians because they hesitated to implement the rights ensured to their Jews under the Treaty of Berlin. The humiliation of the Magyars and the disruption of their kingdom did nothing to make the Roumanians love them more, and very bitter hatred continued. In Roumanian schools the children learnt, as they learn to-day, that the Magyars were a set of brutal savages from Asia before whom the poor Roumanians had all but gone under. Statues of Romulus and Remus suckled by the she-wolf were set up in the centre of old Hungarian towns like Cluj (Kolozsvár), as an indication of restored Latin culture. In the Transylvanian or Banat towns many of the Jews were enthusiastically Magyarphil, and in consequence the Jews were often abused as Magyars and the Magyars as Jews. The new administrative problems presented great difficulties; the system of communications was quite inadequate, and kept the Old Kingdom and the new lands apart rather than holding them together, and the whole economic life of the country inevitably lacked co-ordination. Officials from the Regat claimed to reap the fruits of victory and crowded into Transylvania, the Banat, Bukovina, Bessarabia and Southern Dobrogea. Their behaviour contrasted as Balkan with that of, for instance, their Hungarian predecessors, who, if not fundamentally industrious, had not been fundamentally corrupt. The Transylvanian Roumanians felt that they, who had perhaps risked most, were slighted in spite of their—as they felt—more European education,[1] and the friction between them and the Regat Roumanians was reflected in political party life. The democratic National Peasant Party which was born in 1926 of a marriage between the Transylvanian M. Maniu's pre-war Roumanian National Party and M. Mihalache's pre-war Regat Peasant Party was frowned upon by its Liberal opponents as Transylvanian; M. Maniu, who had spent the flower of his youth fighting against the Hungarian Government on behalf of its Roumanian

---

[1] The intellectual difference between Transylvanian and Regat Roumanians may be summed up by saying that the former had mostly gone to Vienna University and the latter to the Sorbonne.

subjects, was and is still sometimes spoken of in angry
tones as "that old Hungarian." When at last in 1929
he became Prime Minister until 1931 it seemed as if
this gulf were bridged.

The National Peasant or Tsaranist Party owed its
strength to the Agrarian Reform Law of 1921,
according to which King Ferdinand's promise in
April 1917 that the land should be given to the
people was gradually and imperfectly but yet essentially
carried through, and large estates were diminished
or broken up for the purpose. Though a landed
aristocracy survived more noticeably than in Yugoslavia, Roumania, unlike Hungary, became a country
of small peasant farmers. By emasculating the pre-war
Conservative Party land reform also played into the
hands of the Liberals, who governed the country up
to M. Maniu's Premiership, and then again most of
the time between 1931 and 1937. Already in the
'twenties corruption and intrigue in Roumania, as
elsewhere, disillusioned many people, and especially
the young, with regard to the joys of parliamentary
democracy and the freedom which peace was to have
brought. Foreign policy was unswervingly pro-
French, and though the Liberal Party, which represented industrial and banking circles, was opposed to
the introduction of foreign capital, it was inevitable
that large French, British and American investments
should be made. The oil industry had begun to arouse
interest during the last years of the nineteenth century,
and in the early twentieth century German *entrepreneurs* had been prominent and had, for example,
owned the oil company now known as the *Steaua
Romana*. But like bauxite in Hungary, it was only after

the war that there was reason for oil production to go up by leaps and bounds,[1] and by this time all German investments had been liquidated and the oil fields lay open, as it were, for exploitation by the French, the British, the Americans and the Dutch. The general prosperity of the later 'twenties helped temporarily to smooth over the difficulties, administrative and other, to which reference has been made.

One other characteristic of Roumanian life cannot be ignored. Unlike the small Slav nations, the Roumanians have long felt the deepest distrust of Russia. This is not ideological in origin, but the result of Russian invasions at different times in modern history; it is particularly to be attributed to the Russo-Turkish war of 1877-78, when the Roumanians fought with Tsarist Russia against Turkey only to lose Southern Bessarabia by the Treaty of Berlin. The Soviet Government refused to recognize the return of all Bessarabia between Dniester and Pruth to Roumania in 1919, and until 1934, therefore, there were no diplomatic relations between Bucharest and Moscow.

The World Depression brought about a crystallization of the disappointments and prejudices which have been recorded above. The Balkan *nouveau riche*, whether Roumanian, Serb or Greek or Eastern Jew, has an unblushing complexion which may be due as much to inexperience as to original sin. His lack of shame could be stomached while the peasants were reasonably well off, but when the fall in world grain prices ruined them, the glaring inequalities displayed by life in the night clubs of Bucharest, as compared

[1] See below, p. 88.

with the poverty of the peasants who in Balkan countries are in and out of the towns and do not think to spare one's feelings by avoiding the luxurious quarters, became infinitely provocative. The Liberals were assailed as a set of profiteer bankers fattening upon the spoils of office and as altogether too tolerant towards their collaborators in industry and finance, the Jews. The National Peasant Party was discredited by being in office when the slump became apparent and by an unfortunate scandal in which a relative of M. Maniu's was involved with a representative of Škoda's, the Czech armament firm. The plethora of university graduates had not made itself felt so quickly in Roumania as in Hungary because an enlarged state had more jobs available for some time, but now these people, looking around for a creed, took refuge in that of the Iron Guard.

It has been seen that anti-Semitism was a very old story in Roumania, and anti-Jewish organizations like Professor Cuza's Christian Defence League dated from before the war, while a man like the Transylvanian, Dr. Vaida Voevod, long prominent in the National Peasant Party, professed a strongly anti-Semitic racial ideology for which he claimed scientific evidence. The Jews, if often very primitive in type, were more hard-working, more frugal and less easily demoralized by urban life—all qualities which those without them resent. But the Iron Guard Movement which arose was not one of mere jealousy: it was, like National Socialism in Germany, based upon disillusionment with all aspects of post-war society. It cried out, therefore, for regeneration based upon a stern dictatorship in the place of parliamentary intrigue, for a narrow nationalism in the place of internationalist aspiration and the recognized equality of the nationless Jew. Above all, it revolted against rationalism. It was a mystical reaction even more than in Germany; it was eager, indeed, to identify itself with the *mystique* of the national, the Orthodox Church, and was supported by many young priests. Its adherents nevertheless, like the Nihilists, Anarchists, Macedonian Revolutionaries, the Black Hand of Serbia or the Fascists or the Nazis, adopted a technique of terrorism. The leader of this movement, which first became notorious through an attempted outrage in 1927, was Zelea Codreanu, a young man of romantic appearance who maintained to his death at least a reputation for sincerity and courage; like Major Szálasi in Hungary, however, his theories were somewhat disproved by his foreign descent, for his name had been Zilinsky and he was of Ukrainian, and, some said, of German or even Hungarian descent.

Codreanu's movement was naturally stimulated by the National Socialist revolution in Germany, and contact between the Iron Guard and the Nazis was fairly soon established. In addition to demanding that the Jews, the capitalists, the Liberals should be simply "thrown out," Codreanu soon attacked Roumania's alliances with democratic France and the Little Entente. With the pact in 1935 between France and Czechoslovakia on the one hand and Soviet Russia on the other, Iron Guard complaints against Liberal Foreign Policy swelled up into a roar. Their hatred of Russia and their hatred of Communism were well fed by their German friends, who taught them all the phrases about the Czechs being Reds and under the control of Free-

masons and Jews; when M. Blum became Prime
Minister of France in 1936 the roar became a yell; the
fact that the French Minister in Bucharest, M. Thierry,
was married to a Rothschild provided an additional
incitement. It was perfectly clear at this time that the
Iron Guard was drawing an income from Germany
and that its whole revolutionary *élan* was stimulated
by German whispers and intrigue. Many Iron
Guardists were genuinely poor or genuinely eager to
help the poor and, for instance, to get more land for
the peasants, but the idea that got abroad among many
of the peasants and the poverty-stricken in general was
that somehow France was their enemy and Germany
their friend; they often knew a little German and
would tell one about it with enthusiasm, adding rather
pointedly that French was what the fine people spoke.
Meanwhile students and all sorts of other Roumanians
were invited as guests to the Olympic Games in 1936,
or whatever it might be; they had never seen anything
so impressive before; far more Roumanians or Yugoslavs than Hungarians were quite untravelled and easy
to influence in this way. The amount of German
publications on a Bucharest news-stand soon became
remarkable and could only be explained in one way.
It should be observed, incidentally, that the Iron
Guard was harshly opposed to the minorities in
Roumania and demanded their merciless assimilation.
The Nazis remained their close collaborators, though
in 1936 the German campaign against "oppressive"
Czechoslovakia was getting well under way—Czechoslovakia, where the minorities were immensely better
off and the Government anxious to safeguard their
rights.

The attitude of the Liberal Government, which ruled Roumania from December 1933 to November 1937, towards the Iron Guard movement was exceedingly obscure. They had suppressed it on the eve of the election in December 1933, but it at once reappeared as the "All for the Fatherland" movement under General Cantacuzino; everyone, however, continued to refer to the Iron Guard, for no one had taken the suppression seriously. The Liberals were frightened of the unrest which the slump had necessarily provoked, and the state of nerves induced by German propaganda among the ruling classes everywhere had the excuse in Roumania that, if there were few Roumanian Communists, Russia was next door; it was possible, too, if one insisted upon doing so, to decry certain Jewish intellectuals and the Left Wing of the Tsaranists led by Dr. Lupu as "bolshevik." In fact the Peasant Party as a whole remained the most formidable political opponent of the Liberals, for it was believed to retain the support of a clear majority of the people, all the Nazi propaganda and Codreanu hero-worship notwithstanding. The Roumanian Ministers, therefore, reacted like many other authorities in the face of a totalitarian offensive; they secretly helped it a little and at the same time they took certain dictatorial steps themselves, such as the introduction and maintenance of martial law, which might be regarded as impeding Iron Guard activities but which in fact proved more irksome to the National Peasant Party. Indeed at this time anti-Semitic demonstrations were much more leniently treated than democratic demonstrations, which were actually in more exact accord with the spirit of the constitution. The ambiguity of the

Liberals' policy towards Codreanu and his followers
was further complicated by the fear of assassination
and by the attitude of the Court. The Minister of the
Interior, M. Inculeţ, who was said to stand close to the
King, is believed to have paid the Guardists consistently, whether mainly as an answer to blackmail
threats of murder is not clear. Further complications
were introduced by the position of Madame Lupescu,
furiously condemned by Codreanu as partly Jewish
and as the temptress of the King, who should, the
Guardists held, be setting the example of a blameless
life to his subjects. It seems certain that Madame
Lupescu herself protected members of the Iron Guard
for a time in the hope of averting their attacks upon
her. Hostile whisperers could easily make copy out of
this kind of reaction from the people they wished to
discredit. Perhaps the most hated enemy of the Iron
Guard was M. Titulescu, the brilliant Foreign Minister
who stood very definitely for co-operation with the
Western Powers and the Little Entente, and for two
even worse things in Iron Guard or Nazi eyes—
reconciliation with Russia, and warm collaboration
with the League of Nations, especially at the time of
the Abyssinian war. In June 1934 M. Titulescu had
indeed succeeded in establishing diplomatic relations
with the Government of the U.S.S.R. in spite of
Bessarabia, but he was tremendously attacked from
the Right for his pro-Czech policy, which implied
Roumanian permission for the passage of Russian
troops across the Bukovina if Germany should follow
up her press and wireless attacks upon Czechoslovakia
more drastically. M. Titulescu's policy did in fact
succeed in arousing the naturally anti-Russian feeling

of the Roumanians, while he irritated King Carol by his extraordinarily high-handed behaviour. When the King dismissed him in August 1936 it was inevitably gratifying for Germany abroad and the Iron Guard at home.

In November 1937 parliamentary elections fell due in Roumania. At this point the National Peasant Party, the only body in the country potentially capable of resisting totalitarian pressure in a straightforward way, fell into the kind of *gaucherie* which has so constantly characterized democratic opposition to the "Fascintern" drive; one wonders whether the Nazis and their allies do not deserve congratulation for an almost mysterious ability of depriving their enemies of political common sense and reducing them to the "hypnotized rabbit" condition. M. Maniu, who had been responsible for bringing King Carol back to the throne in 1930, had subsequently fallen out with him, and M. Mihalache had become the National Peasant Party leader. Before the dissolution, King Carol had offered the Premiership to M. Mihalache, stipulating, it is true, that the renegade Tsaranist, Dr. Vaida Voevod, the head of the pro-German "Roumanian Front," should be included in the new Cabinet. The royal excuse for this condition was the argument that it alone would prevent the Reich from feeling affronted, and the royal intention, possibly, to ensure M. Mihalache's refusal. Now in Eastern Europe it is of vital importance to control the executive during an election if only to be able to forestall the tricks of one's opponents, and it is difficult not to feel that the National Peasants, with their less easily mobilized electorate, should have taken office at all costs, making

sure of the man to whom they gave the Ministry of the
Interior; after the elections they could probably have
spoken to the King and Dr. Vaida Voevod with
greater authority. Having thrown away this opportunity, however, they proceeded to make an election
pact with—of all people—the Iron Guard, the sworn
enemies of nearly every principle for which the National
Peasants stood. Long afterwards National Peasant
leaders eagerly explained to one that they had made
no concessions whatever by making this pact, but it
was obvious to everyone that it was based upon one
thing, hatred of the King, and the conclusion of it
inevitably suggested to the public that the National
Peasant Party was guided by petty factiousness above
everything else. Even M. Maniu's high reputation
was injured by the natural assumption that he had
helped to bring about the short-sighted action of his
party. For what could suit Nazi intrigue better, nor
confuse the Roumanian peasant more, than the easily
circulated news that the Peasant Party had joined with
the Iron Guard?

In the end the election, then, was held under Liberal
auspices again, the Liberals nevertheless obtaining
only 38 per cent. of the votes, to 22 per cent. for the
National Peasants and 17·2 per cent.—a remarkable
increase—for the "All for the Fatherland" Party: this,
translated into the percentages probable in the western
circumstances of the Government exerting no per-
ceptible influence, might be estimated to imply that
about 25 per cent. of the electors were Liberal, at least
30 per cent. National Peasant, about 25 per cent. Iron
Guard, and the rest supporters of the National Christians and dissident Liberals. This state of opinion

created an unfortunate *impasse* to which the King replied by appointing as Premier the leader of the smaller violently anti-Semitic National Christian group which had officially received 8·7 per cent. of the votes. The National Christians had appeared in 1935 as the result of a fusion between the followers of old Professor Cuza and those of the Transylvanian poet, M. Octavian Goga; it was M. Goga, with nothing but anti-Semitism for a programme, who now came into office for forty-five days.

M. Goga's term of office is generally dismissed as a brief fiasco, but it had important results. It was very satisfactory from the Nazi point of view that M. Goga, who was strongly anti-French and pro-German, should conduce to the paralysis of the Little Entente until the eve of the German march into Vienna. Since he had next to no public support M. Goga established a more rigid form of martial law and wiped out the mildly Liberal newspapers, which were all in Jewish hands; since then a much stricter press censorship has prevailed. Further anti-Semitic measures appeared to · be about to ruin Roumania's economic life,[1] and having allowed M. Goga to discredit extreme anti-Semitism and to destroy the last safeguards of political liberty, King Carol took advantage of the situation to dismiss the elderly poet (who expired abroad not long afterwards) and perfect a royal dictatorship. The democratic constitution of 1923 was superseded by a new constitution, according to which ministers would be responsible only to the Crown, though two Chambers elected on a corporative basis by voters over 30 were later to be called into existence.

[1] See below, p. 90.

This raising of the voters' age from 21 to 30 was aimed, of course, at the disfranchisement of most of the followers of M. Codreanu, who dissolved his party as helpless forthwith. In April all other parties were abolished by the King, who had in the meantime formed a Cabinet of notables; presumably with a view to identifying the national Church with himself as opposed to M. Codreanu, he chose to be Premier the Orthodox Patriarch, a man no more popular than King Carol himself, and whose age, like M. Goga's, aroused the contempt of many young people. In February 1938 the King had resorted to the dictatorial device of a yes-vote on the constitution, and in the following December he completed the royal totalitarianism by making Roumania, too, a One-Party State with a Front of National Rebirth as the only legitimate political organization in the country.

King Carol, during 1938, was undoubtedly in a very difficult position, both geographically and otherwise. When in November Codreanu and a number of his associates were shot "while attempting to escape," many foreign observers applauded, insisting that terroristic methods were the only ones which terrorists would understand. The German press was full of violent protestation, but because Herr Hitler was annoyed Roumania had not therefore escaped the German menace; on the contrary, the Codreanu incident, like the Czech mobilization on May 21st, 1938, may only have hardened the determination in Berlin or Berchtesgaden to break Roumanian resistance. Within the country German intrigue has as much material as ever, and the democratic opinion which was opposed to it was gagged by the royal system, according to which National Peasant leaders might not even be mentioned in the press; only the King's old tutor, Professor Jorga, who was something of a Grand Old Man of Roumania, was allowed to publish his paper, the *Neamul Romanesc*, without submitting it to censorship. Roumanians are probably the most sceptical people in Europe, and not a child seemed willing to accept the King's explanation, everyone believed that he had ordered Codreanu's death; and in any case people were inclined to think if these were King Carol's methods, what was wrong with Herr Hitler's? The Iron Guard was left leaderless, but M. Calinescu, the Minister of the Interior, who became Prime Minister on the Patriarch's death in March 1939, is said to have little expectation of escaping assassination by Guardists sooner or later. The young people were not even attracted by the dazzlingly blue uniforms supplied to members of the Front of National Rebirth nor by its adoption of their own salutation and that of all fascists, the raising of the right arm to which the Roumanian word for *Heil*, *Sanatate*, is spoken. In fact a number of serious and competent people, many ex-Tsaranists and admirable people like M. Gafencu, were with the King, and signs of salutary administrative reform emerged, but at first the new administrators were scornfully received and their "non-party" efforts, it was said, were directed towards settling old party scores.

In foreign affairs the King behaved very correctly towards his Czechoslovak ally in September 1938, resisting the territorial bribes pressed upon him by the enemies of Prague. The attitude of Hungary helped him to maintain his course, but there was only

anti-Magyar feeling in Roumania, no Slavonic pro-
Czech feeling such as that in Yugoslavia where King
Carol's policy might have brought him real popularity.
In Roumania, in fact, once the public realized what had
happened at Munich the pro-Germans were exultant,
and the whole post-war policy of friendship with
France and Great Britain was so horribly discredited
that the National Peasants and all Liberal and pro-
western opinion lost immensely in influence. The
Little Entente was smashed and there was nothing left
of Roumania's alliance system but the Polish Alliance
and the Balkan Entente. Post-war Roumania, like
Czechoslovakia, was the child of the Paris Peace
Conference, and now only German protection, some
whispered, could save her from a similar fate. Of
course, the Roumanians—like all other nations—
flattered themselves that they would not allow themselves to be tricked like the Czechs; many of them
nevertheless regretted that the King saw fit to fly in
the face of Berlin with the Codreanu business in
November. German and pro-German gossip complained that King Carol was no good Roumanian,
nothing but a foreigner—a member of the German
family of Hohenzollern, in fact. German publications,
incidentally, were being delivered gratis in greater
quantities than before; it is interesting that they came
through the letter-boxes, now, of people who were
well known to be anti-Nazi in sympathy.

The crisis created in March 1939 affected Roumania
more directly than the excitements of the previous
September. That Hungary should seize an adjacent
province and extend her frontier with Roumania was
disturbing in itself, but in addition the Ruthenian

authorities positively appealed to Roumania, which already had some half-million Ruthene or Ukrainian subjects, to annex their territory. Actually Bucharest fought shy of prickly Ukrainian entanglements and ignored the appeal, but on the other hand there were a few Roumanian villages around the Szlatina salt-mine [1] in the south of Ruthenia, and the Roumanians were not at all eager to see the railway line running up to Poland in the east in Hungarian hands. It was suggested from Bucharest to Budapest, accordingly, that the Hungarians should keep out of a south-eastern section of Ruthenia. The Hungarians, to whom the salt-mine was important, rejected the suggestion and indeed chose to feel provoked by it into suspicions of Roumania's aims; Hungarian troops were, therefore, massed along a good deal of the Roumanian frontier. The Roumanian military authorities, who, like most authorities of the kind, had known what to expect, had also begun to mobilize on the day before the Germans actually occupied Prague—no one after all knew where Germany would stop, and the Hungarians, what with their volunteers in Slovakia and Ruthenia, had been militarily restive for some time and were known to be bent, now, upon a serious move. After Ruthenia, Transylvania, was the thought in many Roumanian minds, and was Berlin backing Budapest? Mobilization revealed the shortcomings of Roumanian rearmament, and the Škoda, Vitkovice and Brno factories, upon which Roumania depended for weapons, ammunition and the rest, had suddenly come into direct German control; indeed the Germans threatened to hold up the most necessary supplies. Since the middle of February

[1] See above, p. 41.

the German negotiator, Dr. Wohltat, had been in Bucharest virtually demanding a German monopoly of Roumania's foreign trade, and after March 15th he could bang on the table. It was an extremely unpleasant situation, and the Roumanian Government was glad to escape from it with nothing worse than the commercial treaty of March 23rd,[1] which was announced to the public as a very favourable affair; most Roumanians took it to imply a German guarantee of their frontiers since it specifically referred to the exploitation of the natural resources of Transylvania and the Dobrogea. Roumania's mobilization, like Hungary's, continued and increased; to watch, as the present writer did, a continuous stream of Roumanian troop trains, complete with Red Cross trains, etc., proceeding day after day from Cluj towards the Hungarian frontier was to fill one's mind with very disagreeable conjecture. Both sides glowered at each other and refused to take the first peaceful step. All this aroused a certain amount of Roumanian national feeling, but one heard almost as much cynicism as enthusiasm, especially with regard to hypothetical resistance to Germany. After all, the Government was afraid to allow anything derogatory to the Germans to appear in the press, which was often less cautious in critizing the Western Powers. The prestige of France and Britain had sunk so low in the autumn that protests in Paris or London against German action in Bohemia or Memel-land or against the Italian seizure of Albania were not seriously regarded, and the British guarantees to Roumania and Poland were at first received with incredulity. German propagandists

[1] See below, p. 92.

used every opportunity to the full, and their expatia-
tions on Western degeneracy and unwillingness really
to fight underlined the conclusions already drawn
from Munich. The Germans' ingenuity was inexhaust-
ible. If the British Council, by chance, sent out a
lecturer with a title, the talk would be of England's
feudal decadence. In May they discovered that the
British commercial negotiators were all Jews and had
only come to Bucharest to do a deal with the Jews in
Roumania at the expense of the Roumanian nation.
All the hitches, of course, in the Anglo-Russian
negotiations could be exploited to the full. The
Roumanians knew perfectly well that against a serious
German onslaught they would have no hope of
successful resistance unless they called in the Russians,
but they still feared a Russian at least as much as a
German occupation; the difference to them, they
would say, between the German and the Russian
armies was the difference for a condemned man
between being shot or being hanged. The less heroic
Roumanians might be heard to say that if they went
to bed any night saluting with the word *Sanatate* and
woke up the next morning making the same gesture
to *Heil Hitler*, it would not make so very much difference anyway. A typical instance of the popular confusion of mind at the time was that of a Roumanian
peasant girl in Transylvania, who was perfectly reconciled to the Hungarian speech of her employers, but
when they perforce spoke German with their visitors
she was incensed that they all should be speaking what
she could only suppose to be the language of the Jews.
There were no Jews present, but she had heard
stories of their iniquities in the neighbouring town,

while she made no distinction between German and Yiddish.

Soon after the international disturbances of March and April and a day or so after the Hungarian elections, a new Chamber and Senate were elected in Roumania. Large numbers of people who had hitherto been electors were disfranchised, not only by the raising of the voters' age, but also by literacy qualifications. Eleven large electoral districts were created, of which newly expanded Bucharest with its environs constituted one. In these districts, long lists of candidates belonging to the Front of National Rebirth, and grouped in three professional categories, were presented, from which the electors were asked to choose about half by secret ballot. The elections were indeed so arranged as to tell one comparatively little about public opinion. Supporters of the Government pointed out that over 80 per cent. of the eligible voted, but those who did not were subject to considerable fines. Only about 2 per cent. of the voting papers were said to have been spoiled in accordance with the instructions the Iron Guard was alleged to have given out, but then most of the Guardists had been disfranchised. The Ministers were most of them returned with large majorities. A few representatives of the minorities were elected, though except for the Germans, they were very few in proportion to the minority populations. The minorities were also represented in the Senate, a body chosen partly by royal nomination, partly by certain selected groups; there were also *ex-officio* Senators, for instance men who had been elected to be deputies a certain number of times under the superseded constitution. A number of oppositional leaders such as MM. Maniu, Mihalache and Lupu, were brought into the Senate in this way, and this led to further friction with them because they objected to certain forms with which they were expected to comply. The two Houses, however, were given no political power, so that it was only a right to criticize which was at stake. By the time the elections of June 1st and 2nd were over, Great Britain had made her alliance with Turkey, introduced a restricted conscription, and provided credits and extended markets for Roumanian produce. On the other hand, friction with the revisionist powers, Germany, Hungary and Bulgaria, had remained or revived, stimulated as it easily could be by Roumania's minority questions.

(b) *The Minority Aspect*

The Kingdom of Roumania, as delimited in 1919, contained a population of which something not far short of 30 per cent. was non-Roumanian. The aggravation of minority disputes in Czechoslovakia during 1937 and 1938 had not been without its repercussions in Roumania, and the excitements of spring 1939 made the question of Roumania's biggest minority, $1\frac{1}{2}$ million Magyars, necessarily acute. It need scarcely be emphasized that this was all in the German plan for the undeclared war, since no weapon is more deadly, in this campaign, than that of disruption on the self-determination plea.

According to the last Roumanian census held

in 1930 Roumania was racially composed as follows:—

Roumanians	12,980,000 or	71·9 per cent.	
Hungarians	1,426,000 or	7·9 per cent.	
Germans	740,000 or	4·1 per cent.	(Figures
Jews	722,000 or	4·0 per cent.	to nearest
Ukrainians	578,000 or	3·2 per cent.	thousand)
Russians	415,000 or	2·3 per cent.	
Bulgars	361,000 or	2·0 per cent.	

Since then it is likely that the Roumanian percentage has increased, because, on the one hand, for those who may have shown hesitation it has become more convenient to call themselves Roumanians, and, on the other, the Roumanians are more prolific than the two biggest minorities, the Magyars and the Germans. Against this it should be noted that the census-taking officials will have made the minority figures as small as they could, especially among the more illiterate minorities, the Ukrainians, Russians and Bulgars, who are less able to exercise any control.

The Ukrainian or Ruthene population in and around Cernauți (Czernowitz) in the Bukovina, and sprinkled over Northern Bessarabia as well, was certainly disturbed by the Great Ukrainian commotion stirred up from Chust by German agents during the winter of 1938-9.[1] The Roumanians found this an extraordinarily tiresome addition to the minority difficulties, and it has been seen that they in no way responded to the subsequent Ruthenian appeal.[2] They regard Ukrainians as particularly troublesome "toughs"; it is not altogether without significance that Codreanu

---

[1] See below, p. 225.   [2] See above, p. 65.

was of Ukrainian descent, for a strikingly high pro-
portion of his followers who were rounded up before
Christmas 1938 had Ukrainian names, and the Iron
Guard might have been directly useful to Germany in
the prosecution of the Great Ukrainian programme.
It is known that Ukrainians, for instance the Russian
Ukrainians in Tsarist days, easily became enthusiastic
Jew-baiters, and Roumanian officials sometimes complain that the really brutal anti-Jewish outrages in
Roumania are usually perpetrated by Ukrainians or
Germans. Since, however, Chust has been ignomini-
ously sacrificed to the Hungarians, Ukrainian feeling
in Roumania has subsided again; in so far as it counts
it seems to have reacted bitterly against Germany and
to be looking to Russia instead. As for the Russians
in Bessarabia, theirs is perhaps the hardest lot of all the
non-Roumanian-speaking inhabitants of Roumania.
They look back to pre-war days when they were part
of an enormous country which offered an unlimited
market for their fruit and other produce, while as a
neglected portion of Roumania they languish in hopeless poverty. It is, moreover, absolutely forbidden
to speak Russian, and all signs of Russian civilization
have been obliterated as completely as possible. The
upper social class thinks longingly of Tsarist Russian
days, while the peasants are perhaps more inclined to
imagine wonderful conditions across the frontier
to-day. And the Roumanian authorities' behaviour
is marred by suspicion, for they are well aware that,
in spite of M. Titulescu's conciliation of Russia,
diplomatic relations between Moscow and Bucharest
do not signify that the U.S.S.R. has lost all interest
in Bessarabia.

The whole problem of Bulgaria's frontiers has been made to become very prominent in 1939, raising with it the issue of the Southern Dobrogea (Dobruja), which means the two closely related questions— should the Roumano-Bulgar frontier be corrected, and what of the Bulgars under Roumanian rule? The frontier question, complicated as it is by Black Sea rivalry and the proximity of Bucharest, is being hotly disputed, but if opinions differ as to whether revision here is a good or a bad answer to the threats of to-day, it is fairly generally agreed that Bulgaria came off a little shabbily by the Treaty of Neuilly in 1919; it is interesting that Turkey, the good friend of Roumania, is said to have proposed that Roumania should lease the Southern Dobrogea to Bulgaria for a hundred years. The position was unfortunately complicated by the Belița incident on May 10th when a clash between Roumanian gendarmerie and Dobrogea Bulgars took place. Accounts of the incident are so conflicting that it is impossible to describe it with any accuracy whatever [1]—the Roumanians said Bulgar brigands were wholly to blame, while the Bulgars believe that the Roumanian gendarmes perpetrated something like a massacre of Bulgarian deserters from the Roumanian army. While the Bulgarian Government at first forbade press references to the matter, the Hungarian and Axis newspapers eagerly took it up as a Roumanian outrage. Germany and Italy, especially since the seizure of Albania, have every reason to be the fervent champions of Bulgaria,[2] but in itself the question of the Bulgarian minority, a smaller group than either the Russians or Ukrainians in

[1] See *Times*, May 15th, 1929.   [2] See below, pp. 137-138.

Roumania, is not necessarily of first-rate importance; it is complicated by the facts that a good many Turks live in the Southern Dobrogea, while a number of Bulgars live north of the Danube Delta actually in Bessarabia.

It is, then, the Germans and Hungarians in Roumania who constitute the more serious part of her minority question. Some 70,000 to 80,000 Germans live in Bukovina and a very slightly larger number in Bessarabia, but the fundamental problem consists of the racial confusion and the historic difficulties existing in Transylvania and the territories of Crișana-Maramureș and the Banat, which were cut away from Hungary by the Treaty of Trianon. Transylvania deserves its exquisite name. To the loveliness of its woods and its valleys and its hills must be added its marvellous remoteness, both in detail and as a whole. This has brought the most different groups of settlers to live there close together yet in isolation and completeness through the centuries, as their ancient towns and castles still bear witness. This has sheltered Transylvania from some of the major European catastrophes, such as the Thirty Years' War, during which Count Bethlen's ancestor ruled Transylvania in prosperous tranquillity. This has allowed as much diversity of religion as of race. In no area in the world could self-determination slogans be more disastrously inapt and therefore more thoroughly destructive.

In mediaeval times Transylvania had been dominated by the three so-called ruling nations, the Székelys, the Magyars and the Saxons. The Székelys spoke Magyar and were traditionally said to have been the oldest Magyar settlement in Europe, though it is

probable that they were sent from Hungary in the
twelfth century; their home is in South-eastern
Transylvania, right away from Hungary, and they
have been the despair of those who think in terms of
tidy homogeneous nations neatly arranged within
straightforward frontiers. The Székelys have never
succumbed to the feudalism which has characterized
Hungary proper, but have continued community
tenure of land to this day; even the Transylvanian
Hungarians nearer to Hungary seem less bowed down
in homage to a feudal lord. Before the great Turkish invasions these two groups held rights from the kings of
Hungary in common with the " Saxons," who were in
fact settlers from West Germany in the twelfth century
too, the builders of old towns like Sibiu (Hermannstadt) and Braşov (Kronstadt). Although the Habsburgs succeeded the native Bethlens and Rákóczys, as
the Great Princes of Transylvania, the Reformation
had here been too uncurbed for the Austrians to undo
it. The Magyars had mostly become Calvinist, or, in
the Székely counties, Unitarian; the Saxons were
Lutheran; in the eighteenth century, however, the
Habsburgs sent the Catholic Swabians to settle in the
Banat. To add to the diversities of Transylvania there
were not only these two distinct Magyar groups, but
also Magyarized German villages with a character of
their own, Jewish groupings, Armenian towns, and
last, but by no means least, the Roumanians. For,
centuries before, Roumanian shepherds and herdsmen,
some of them from across the mountains which
divided Transylvania from the Principalities, had
appeared; when trouble overtook the Principalities
they were found in greater numbers in Transylvania.

But they were despised as Wallachians or Vlachs and they were subject to religious persecution. Their national religion was that of the Orthodox Church— it should not be forgotten that a man's creed in south-eastern Europe is as good as a national badge—and, by way of not completely denationalizing them, Transylvania's rulers allowed the Roumanians to belong to the Uniate Church, that strange refuge of the Ruthenians where the Papacy is acknowledged but Byzantine ritual preserved. It has already been seen that, since the despised Roumanians had long before become the largest group and in fact formed an absolute majority of the whole population of Transylvania,[1] the territory was, after incorporation with Hungary in 1867, attached to the Old Kingdom of Roumania in 1919.

Roumania was thus established with a German minority of about three-quarters of a million in which the two most important elements were some 225,000 Transylvanian Lutheran Saxons, and some 350,000 Catholic Swabians in the Banat with Timişoara (Temeschburg) as one of their chief centres. Under Magyar rule these Germans, like those in Transdanubia, had accepted a certain Magyarization;[2] indeed a good many jokes have been cracked over the sudden discoveries of German consciousness which have been overtaking hitherto ostensibly good Magyars in Roumania ever since, and particularly in the last five or six years. Roumanian policy, based on a short view, favoured the German minority with rights, for instance with regard to schools and economic life, which were, in practice if never in theory,

---

[1] See Professor Seton-Watson, *op. cit.*   [2] See above, p. 30.

withheld from the Magyars. The Germans, nevertheless, continued to regard the Roumanians as an inferior species, and when from 1933 the *Kleindeutsch* policy was reversed in Berlin and Pan-German agitation developed, the Swabians, and especially the Saxons, were only too ready to accept the theory of their own inherent superiority and of the iniquity of the Jews, who to some extent competed with the Saxons as small traders. The Swabians were very largely peasants, but the Saxons were often small merchants and owned a good deal of industry, smallish textile and glass and sausage-making factories, for example. The Saxons are well aware of the privileged position they had held until 1867; these people, with their sedulously cultivated historic consciousness, are able to despise the Swabians as eighteenth-century newcomers, but, of course, until the Compromise of 1867 Austrian officials had given specially favourable treatment to all the German-speaking groups. The Saxons have inherited a very highly developed community life through the centuries; in the Saxon towns all the unmarried boys and girls are traditionally organized in brotherhoods and sisterhoods and the married people into *Nachbarschaften*. The traditions of these Saxons had also been very little affected by the feudalism of the social atmosphere of pre-war Austria-Hungary. With a racial caste feeling already strong among them it is easy to appreciate with what readiness the Transylvanian Saxons adopted National Socialist doctrine, a doctrine which has a special appeal *per se* to German minorities abroad. The Lutheran Church had long played an important part in their community life, and though it was eagerly, perhaps aggressively,

German, it mildly restrained the Nazi fervour of the elder generation. Among the Catholic Swabians a more definite split was created after 1933 between the old and the young; the latter mostly became enthusiastic Nazis and accused their fathers of being reactionary and place-greedy, anxious to keep their children out of well-paid posts—the old *Bonzen* indictment with which one had grown so familiar in the Reich. Each of Hitler's successes weakened the resistance to *Gleichschaltung*, the Saar plebiscite in 1935 was, for instance, sentimentally utilized among the Banat Germans, both in Roumania and Yugoslavia, who were supposed to have come from the Saar-Palatinate regions; visitors from the Saar were therefore despatched to the Banat to stimulate feelings about their common "Kultur" and about liberation from an "alien yoke." [1] The Nazi conquest of Vienna in February 1938 was in many ways decisive for people with Dual Monarchy recollections and pre-1867 traditions; Hitler, strangely enough the old Emperor (who detested the Pan-German ideas which Hitler had picked up) would have thought, had now become the heir to the Habsburgs, he had become Francis Joseph's successor. And then came Munich which implied that the new imperialism was irresistible. All opposition, even among the Swabians, disappeared. To all outward appearance the autumn of 1938 effected the complete *Gleichschaltung* of the Germans in Roumania with the Hitlerist Herr Fritz Fabritius as their local *Führer*. [2] For the first three or four years of Hitler

---

[1] For a description of a visit of this kind see, e.g., The *Banater Deutsche Zeitung*, April 12th, 1939.

[2] To be distinguished from the present German Minister in Bucharest whose name is also Fabritius.

in power, the myth had been honoured that, although
Germany had become a One-Party State, the German
Government was not identical in outlook and organization with the National Socialist Party; indeed, while
pre-Hitler diplomats remained and world opinion
could be deceived, it was more convenient to have a
Nazi party organization apart from the German
Legations and Embassies abroad. But as time went
on the Legations and Embassies expanded prodigiously and became the local Party headquarters both
for citizens of the Reich and for the German-speaking
citizens of the country concerned. The Bucharest
Legation showed a particularly elastic quality, and an
attaché called Arthur Konradi made himself conspicuous—and incidentally disliked by many Roumanians—for his ubiquitous activities. In spite of the
generally less tolerant attitude in Roumania towards
the minorities from 1936, the German leaders had
kept on ostensibly good terms with the Roumanian
Government and somehow acquired privilege rather
than penalty.

The position of the German Minority in Roumania during the mobilization period in March and
April 1939 was particularly odd. A Saxon in Braşov,
who, when the troops were collecting, presumably
thought that the Germans had arrived, was unfortunately killed by Roumanians for exclaiming "Heil
Hitler!" One had the impression that many of the
Germans might have made the same mistake. Those
who were called up did what they must—one or two
with war experience even acted as officers in command
of the companies billeted about the country. But they
seemed to have not the slightest feeling for Roumania,

and listened superciliously to Roumanian youths who boasted that they would know how to stand up to the Germans if they came. Indeed the minority Germans who were called up looked with obvious contempt at the (at that time) mostly unmechanized apparatus of the Roumanian Army; it was clear that they would have deserted to German invaders and they betrayed no enthusiasm about resisting a Hungarian advance. Shortly after this, on April 10th, Herr Fabritius issued an ominous announcement from Sibiu (Hermannstadt) to the effect that the rush for membership of his Nazi organization, the *Nationale Arbeitsfront der Volksgemeinschaft der Deutschen in Rumänien* (or N.A.F.), was so great that the N.A.F. would be indefinitely closed to new recruits from May 1st. Herr Henlein had taken an exactly similar step in Czechoslovakia a year earlier in imitation of the Nazis of the Reich. The device was becoming a traditional one for stampeding the last recalcitrants into the Hitlerist organization, by the clear implication that those who were then found not to be with it would be held to be against it—they would know what they had to expect. The reason actually given by Herr Fabritius was the strain upon his organization with the necessity of educating so many people in the N.A.F. "spirit" (*Geist*); it was noted and resented by many Roumanians that while they themselves were allowed no organization outside the Front of National Rebirth, the German minority was now permitted to set up a whole hierarchy of Labour Fronts and Youth Movements to cultivate an alien "spirit" of its own. The effect of the German-Roumanian Treaty of March 23rd was clear, and by way of underlining Roumania's sovereignty the German Minority newspapers began to write a little as if they had annexed the Roumanians,[1] not at all as if they were still the subjects of Roumania.

As between the Roumanians and the Hungarians it is really impossible to exaggerate the emotional importance of Transylvania to each side. To the Magyars of Hungary proper it is the great *point d'honneur* to win back Transylvania, which was ruled by St. Stephen though it afterwards became independent of Budapest for so many years. To most Roumanians, whose people form about 58 per cent.[2] of Transylvania's population, to lose that principality would be to undo history, to deny the entity Roumania. Anguish commensurate with that of the Czechs in witnessing the destruction of Bohemia's ancient frontiers is at stake. Social prejudice also plays its part, for many Hungarians still despise the Roumanians as belonging to the lower orders, while the Roumanians not unnaturally identify Hungarian aspiration with social reaction; Roumania's land reform, as in the case of similar measures elsewhere, seemed to the Roumanians to fulfil a belated social justice, while to the Hungarians it seemed to aim only at expropriating their estates. There was the further complication of the half-million Székelys, whose obvious differences from the other Magyars the Roumanians attributed with some justification to an admixture of Roumanian blood, but who in their own eyes were only different in being the most truly Magyar of all.

[1] See below, p. 95.

[2] According to the 1930 census figures Transylvania proper had a population of approximately 2,870,000, but with Crişana-Maramureş and the Banat the total was about 5½ millions. Of these 57·9 per cent. were Roumanian, 24·4 per cent. Hungarian and 9·8 per cent. German.

This is not the place to make a detailed examination of the treatment of the Hungarians in post-war Roumania.[1] It must suffice to say that, while Hungarian disabilities in Roumania seem strikingly great to anyone familiar with pre-Munich Czechoslovak administration, they are not unlike those of the minorities in many other countries; they are based upon the Roumanian feeling that Hungarians cannot be trusted, and this, from the Roumanian point of view, is mostly the case. One can discount the heavy taxing of richer Transylvania in order to develop the poorer Regat, since there is a good social argument in favour of this. But it is impossible to deny that the Roumanian state has ignored many of its Minorities Law obligations with regard to local government in general and education in particular. Though towns like Cluj (Kolozsvár) and Dej (Dés) unquestionably have a Hungarian majority (the Roumanians nearly always preponderating in the country districts),[2] there has never, since the *fin de guerre* alterations, been a vestige of a street name in anything but Roumanian; the Roumanians, of course, pointing to the falling Magyar birth-rate, intend to "win back" the towns. Cluj, by the way, had long been regarded as the intellectual centre for Transylvanian Hungarians, but its University became Roumanian with the post-war regime, and one and a half million Magyars were left with no possibility of a university education in their own language except in Hungary. As for the schools, all sorts of reasons were found why the state should

---

[1] See C. A. Macartney, *op. cit.*
[2] See Silviu Dragomir, *La Transylvanie roumaine et ses Minorités ethniques.* Bucharest, 1934. P. 89.

provide a minimum of Magyar schools, and many Magyar children, especially in Székely districts, were put to Roumanian schools on the grounds that they were Magyarized Roumanians. This kind of thing rather cancelled out the "local autonomy in scholastic and religious matters" which had been guaranteed to the Székelys as to the Saxons in the Roumanian Minorities Treaty (§ 11). Confessional schools were allowed to continue, and the Catholic and Calvinist colleges of, say, Cluj, provided the best possibilities for young Magyars to be educated in their own language. The amount of Roumanian required in the compulsory state examinations gradually necessitated, however, that most of the teaching in these colleges should be in Roumanian after all.

When M. Maniu came into power in 1928 it appeared that the rigid centralism of his Regat predecessors might be modified in the light of the experience of a minority leader in old Austria-Hungary, but unfortunately all his attention was gradually absorbed by other cares. Until the early 'thirties the rigours were in practice softened for the Magyars by a growing general prosperity, by the easy-going character of the Roumanians and the possibilities of corruption.[1] Gradually, however, bribing used up the Hungarians' resources, and then came the slump to harden intolerance all the world over and provide fuel for an Iron Guard mentality. It has been seen that the Bucharest Government more and more accepted the Iron Guard attitude towards the minorities from about the year 1936. From this time on, for example, Hungarians,

---

[1] "Corruption is our Geneva," a Jew in Roumania remarked to Mr. Macartney. See C. A. Macartney, *op. cit.*

and even occasionally Germans, whose knowledge of
Roumanian had hitherto been accepted as adequate to
equip them to work as state officials, were re-tested
and dismissed as unfit. The Nazi collaborators of the
Iron Guard were apparently only too content that
general tension should increase at the expense of a
few German salaries; they reported Alfred Rosenberg's anti-feudal-Hungary views to their Roumanian
friends, while other Nazi agents were hand-in-glove
with the wildest revisionists in Hungary. In 1938
Berlin was glad to observe a certain nervousness in
Roumanian official circles as to the likelihood of their
being faced with a situation like that which was being
induced in Czechoslovakia, though, as Roumanians
eagerly insisted in September, the Roumanian population was nearly everywhere so strong outside the
towns that a 50 per cent. line would be out of the
question. Many people felt that a centralist policy
had been justified and that it was clearer every day
that if the Hungarians had been given bigger opportunities they would, like the Sudeten Germans, be
breaking up the State, but the authorities thought a
conciliatory gesture should be made. The Hungarian
Government was pressing, the German Government
imperious and Roumania's alliances were perhaps
crumbling away. In August, therefore, the Roumanian Government published a Minority Statute
which was intended to reassure their non-Roumanian
citizens, and a benevolent Transylvanian professor,
Silviu Dragomir, was appointed as a Minister to care
for minority interests. The Hungarians, however,
complained that the Minority Statute was nothing but
the Minority Treaty without Article 11 which promised

cultural autonomy to the Székely; and in spite of Professor Dragomir they refused to believe that promises would in future be kept. Everything in Roumania now ultimately depended on the King, but the Hungarians believed that he was unfriendly to them on account of the cool attitude adopted towards him by the Transylvanian aristocracy.

It is obvious that Hungarian irredentism was very greatly stimulated by the events of the autumn of 1938, and that Transylvania in particular was necessarily disturbed afresh by Hungary's annexation of Ruthenia and the mobilization on both sides of the Hungaro-Roumanian frontiers. It is one of the disasters of a mobilization in a racially mixed country that, since the minorities live near the frontier and may have links with the unfriendly neighbour beyond it, it appears as an attempt to intimidate, and in any case it emphasizes all the possibilities of friction; this had been seen in Czechoslovakia in the previous May. But whereas the most rabid Sudeten German, if he complained that his chances of promotion were slight, admitted that he was well treated in the pre-Munich Czechoslovak Army, the Hungarian conscripts in Roumania, on the other hand, were often not trusted to handle a weapon and were kept in the background as orderlies. Now in March and April 1939 this attitude was re-emphasized, and, though there might be a Saxon or even a Bessarabian Russian officer [1] in command of troops, one never heard of a Hungarian. The mobilization inevitably brought unpopular billeting and requisitioning in Hungarian districts or on Hungarian estates, all old firearms were confiscated here and

[1] I happened to know of one.

Hungarians had their wireless sets taken away from them. There were incidents, too, when the Roumanian police dealt roughly with protesting crowds; on one occasion Roumanians fired a Hungarian pastor's house, but the Roumanian authorities quickly apologized and supplied compensation. In any case no one believed that the Hungarians in Roumania would be loyal to Roumania against Hungary if things became more acute.

It would, however, be extremely misleading to suppose that the Transylvanian Magyars as a whole wish to be re-incorporated with Hungary. They are very conscious of their separate tradition and infinitely proud of their unbroken history typified by the beautiful castles and the delightful Székely gateways which no Turkish invader has ever swept away. If the Székelys, therefore, regard themselves as more Magyar than the Magyars they have little desire to be ruled from Budapest. Old Transylvanian families like those of Count Bethlen and Count Paul Teleki are well aware of this and advocate a liberal autonomy for the old principality. This is the aspiration, also, of the distinguished group of Transylvanian Hungarian intellectuals who have been associated with the review *Helikon*, one of the pivots of post-war Transylvanian life. It is interesting that the leader of this group is Count Nicholas Bánffy, the political leader of the Hungarian minority. These people dream of Transylvania with its three million inhabitants as an Eastern Switzerland fulfilling the remarkable functions of that country, with Roumanian, Hungarian and German as its three main recognized languages. Though the Transylvanians live in wilder racial confusion than the

Swiss,[1] it is not impossible to believe that in happier times they will arrive at a solution of this kind—federation should suit the infinite local variety and diversity of the one country as of the other. If the Magyar peasants of Transylvania are far from envisaging the hopes of the *Helikon* writers and if they are strongly aware of their Magyarism and aware that in the old days they were an integral part of the ruling people, yet some of them, too, are doubtful about Hungary; most of them are not without land and the stories they hear from across the frontier are not always reassuring.

Autonomous ideas are not altogether distasteful to some of the Transylvanian Roumanians who feel all the dissatisfaction rife in the Old Kingdom with the additional annoyance that they, who in their own view at least have a more European tradition behind them, are left out of things, since everything is done from Bucharest—even to-day Professor Dragomir is the only true Transylvanian in the Cabinet, though one other Minister coming from Crişana is not a Regat man. The German whisperers at work in Transylvania have plenty of material in minority complaints, and can see to it that, if the Hungarians are not discontented about something, the Germans shall be, and *vice versa*. But while Nazi propagandists in the west attack the Swiss system as an offence against the racial *Zeitgeist* of the age, they have fanned the little flames of autonomous and federal desire in Transylvania. Would it not be altogether better, they can here insinuate, to be freed of the Balkan ways of Bucharest without falling into the feudal clutches of

[1] See below, Part II.

Budapest? Of course Transylvania could not stand alone, but Germany, the heir to the Habsburg Great Prince, would make an admirable protector, a mediator in any racial differences which might arise. The quixotic liberation of Slovakia was cited in the spring of 1939, and since neither the Roumanian nor the Hungarian papers may publish anything derogatory to Germany, the real fate of Slovakia was often only slowly appreciated, and people who are naturally befuddled by reference to good old days thought that the German plan was perhaps not a bad one. In many Transylvanian towns the German minority did everything to encourage the notion, and indeed presumed that this delightful project for protection was on the eve of materialization. To the Bessarabians, too, in their terrible poverty, it was easy to suggest that a German connection would bring them back the opportunities they had once enjoyed in Russia by re-associating them with another Great Power and one whose efficiency was proverbial—those who were opposed to the Soviet Government would welcome the new Germany in its stead.

(c) *The Economic Aspect*

Roumania, but particularly the Regat, is overwhelmingly agricultural in its economic structure, and from the reform of 1921 it emerged as a country essentially of small peasant farmers. In spite of post-war industrialization the Roumanian population remains about 80 per cent. agrarian. Grain production has if anything fallen as compared with pre-war figures [1] when there were a good many large estates,

---

[1] If one discounts the exceptional harvests of the last few years.

for the peasants' methods of cultivation are exceedingly primitive although the soil is extraordinarily rich. Both the agrarian reform and the relatively small amount of native capital and low degree of industrialization distinguish Roumania from Hungary. Before the war, thanks partly to the German tone of the Court and its pro-Central-Powers diplomacy, German and Austrian capital played a large part in the country, and it has been seen that Germans were already in those days concerned with the production of oil; during part of the war the Germans worked the oil-wells themselves, increasing production for their own war needs at the time. Actually the total production in 1913 had been 1,886,000 metric tons, and although this figure was not quite equalled in 1924, in 1925 it was up to 2,317,000 metric tons, and then rose steadily to the peak figure of 8,704,000 metric tons in 1936,[1] four times the 1925 figure. Even at this stage it is of interest that oil-production only employed about 25,000 workers.

The Roumanians had few capital resources of their own other than those so generously supplied by nature, and with the soaring interest in petrol after the war it was inevitable that foreign capital, this time British, Dutch, French and American, should be lavishly invested in the oil industry, although the dominant Liberal Party was unfriendly to this development. It was recently estimated that about half the foreign capital in Roumania is invested in oil and that this half is equivalent to about 85 per cent. of all the capital

---

[1] See Great Britain : Department of Overseas Trade, *Report on Economic and Commercial Conditions in Roumania*, May 1937, by Alexander Adams. P. 47, Table 8.

invested in the oil industry. The economic situation in Roumania to-day is, of course, the direct consequence of the World Depression and the Nazi Revolution in Germany. The breakdown of the international financial system, the autarchic ambitions of Germany and the frenzied war preparations which she has imposed upon Europe, forced Roumania to accelerate the tentative development of her industry and made her grain and oil supplies of cardinal importance to Germany at least.

When Hitler came to power the Czechs, particularly, were alive to the fact that he would revive economic as well as political Pan-Germanism—were they not by definition one and the same thing?—and that pre-war and war-time *Mitteleuropa* plans would reappear; though the word *Mitteleuropa* sounded more modest it had generally been interpreted to mean at the least a vast Customs Union to which Roumania should belong,[1] and by the Treaty of Bucharest in May 1918 the Central Powers had tried to enforce something like an economic annexation of Roumania. Czechoslovakia, therefore, exerted herself to build up close economic collaboration between the members of the Little Entente, and the Czechs themselves were at pains to supply, as far as they could, both the capital and the markets which Roumania and Yugoslavia needed more acutely than ever since the general slump; in their own highly industrialized areas the Czechs hoped to provide the peasant farmers of the

---

[1] See among other pieces of pre-war evidence about Pan-Germanism the despatch from the British Consul-General, R. Tower, at Munich, to Sir E. Grey, Jan. 24th, 1906 (F.O. 371-76, no. 14) ; in Great Britain : Foreign Office, *British Documents on the Origins of the War*, edited by G. P. Gooch and H. W. V. Temperley, vol. iii, chapter xxii.

Balkans with an alternative to the German market, in the hope of restricting Balkan dependence upon Germany. Thus Bat'a and Škoda factories multiplied in Roumania and Yugoslavia, and the tactical importance of arming one's allies with the same tpye of weapon as oneself was not overlooked in establishing concerns to compete with the products of Krupps. Among other undertakings Czech capital was invested in the Banat iron foundries at Reşiţa which had become Roumanian after the war. German interest in Roumania was none the less eager, and in 1936 the *I.G. Farbenindustrie* launched soya bean production there; towards the end of that year the German *Gutehoffnungshütte* undertook to construct a big steel-works at Hunedoara in south-west Transylvania. But for the time being things balanced up fairly well from the Roumanian point of view with vigorous competition for the goods Roumania so easily produced; she restricted her export both of oil and of wheat to Germany, in spite of the preferential prices offered from Berlin, by subsidizing exports to the free currency countries. By the use of this instrument Roumania, 63 per cent. of whose exports went to the blocked currency countries in 1935, reduced this figure to just under 50 per cent. in 1936 and 1937, keeping down what she sent to Germany to about 20 per cent. of all her exports.[1]

The critical year of 1938 opened with the Goga regime and the flight of several milliard lei of Jewish

---

[1] See V. Madgearu, *La Politique Économique Extérieure de la Roumanie* (1927-38), p. 42. Germany was also bound to provide some payments to Roumania in free exchange, but it became increasingly doubtful as to whether she fulfilled this obligation in practice.

capital. In spite of the extremely uncertain situation after M. Goga's fall, some of this capital subsequently returned, and a large part—perhaps nearly half—of the capital invested in Roumanian industry is still Jewish (at the time of writing), whether Roumanian-Jewish or foreign. The general result of 1938 and 1939, however, spelt the driving out of Jewish capital and the ever firmer entrenchment of German economic control. The fall of Austria brought into Nazi hands what was left of the shares of the once mighty Viennese banks in Roumania, e.g. at Reşiţa, and the Munich Agreement brought direct control of big Sudeten German investments like Schicht's and a great deal of influence over Czech concerns, or over those which had become almost wholly Czech, like the Aussig Chemical Company. Finally the German occupation of Bohemia and Moravia brought all the Czech interest at Reşiţa too, all the carefully planned Czech investments, directly into German ownership. Since Munich German representatives had been pressing that Roumania should mark off a far higher proportion of her exports for German consumption or for Germany to resell; indeed the idea of a German monopoly of Roumania's foreign trade was now broached, since Germany would be happy to resell what she did not consume in order to acquire free exchange. It was implied that Roumania would do well to close down most of the industry which the wicked Jews had imposed upon her solely for the sake of their own private gain and to concentrate on producing the corn and the oil which Germany lacked. The German negotiators, also, finding the Roumanians difficult to pin down, pressed for a long-term agreement, but the negotiations were broken off in the middle of November only to lead to four separate one-year agreements on December 10th, guaranteeing no more than that trade should not fall below its existing highest level between Roumania and Greater Germany and that the goods exchanged between the two countries should be of equal value. Even after Munich Roumania was exporting only on a scale of about 30 per cent. of all her exports to the new Reich.

It has occasionally been conjectured as to what extent Hitler's occupation of Prague was decided upon in order to break the insubordination being shown at the time by most of Germany's smaller neighbours to her east and south—a demonstration of Germany's remorseless strength should prove salutary. Certainly the Roumanians were helpless when Hungary was stirred up to threaten their invasion, while the Germans could now completely hold up the military supplies from the Škoda factories and imply that a German invasion was not impossible either—this was the German ultimatum at the time, reference to which the Germans did all they could to forbid. The Roumanians beat off the demand for a monopoly of their foreign trade and the threat to their industry and independence which this involved, but on March 23rd, 1939, they agreed to the remarkable German-Roumanian Commercial Treaty.[1]

This unprecedented agreement first of all accepted the long-term principle, for it was concluded for at least five years. Secondly, it provided for the all-round intensive exploitation of Roumania's magnificent resources through joint German-Roumanian companies.

[1] See above, p. 66.

Roumania's production of corn, timber, oleaginous and textile plants was to be intensified and the cultivation of new crops was to be introduced. Similarly the production of mineral wealth was to be stimulated— of oil, bauxite, chrome and manganese ore—and machinery and plant were to be provided for these purposes from Germany, to whom "free zones" in Roumania were to be allotted. A great many Roumanians, especially the more highly educated, were disagreeably startled by the publication of this treaty, and various efforts were made to explain it away. It was said that Roumanians were past masters at sabotage. It was said that the Germans would be disappointed; they could never squeeze the hides and the cotton they needed out of Roumania while the production of oil was falling off, from 8,704,000 tons of crude oil produced in 1936 to 7,153,000 in 1937 and 6,600,000 in 1938. Twenty-one years earlier, in May 1918, the victorious Central Powers had imposed a treaty upon Roumania which, if very much harsher in detail, was not dissimilar in principle. It had not only established a monopoly of the whole agricultural produce of Roumania for nine years, but it had also arranged for Austro-German companies to monopolize the Roumanian oil-fields and for the Central Powers to control the chief Danube ports.

In March 1939 Roumanian opinion as a whole appeared to be content. The Roumanians were amused to see the British and the French now hurrying to offer them favours. Many of them felt that they had always been exploited by foreigners and Jews who were willing to work harder than Roumanians, and that if the Germans wished to drive the others out

by working harder still, what did it matter to them?
Indeed some went further, and, quoting the inevitably
better days before the war, reminded themselves that
it was mainly the Germans who had been at work
among them then. It was not difficult to meet men
with patriotic reputations who frankly said, "Well,
perhaps my farm will be made to pay now, and I'd
have no objection to that." As for the poorer population, it is wretchedly, and in the towns increasingly,
poor, and can readily be induced to resent exploitation,
to whomever this may be attributed. In those circumstances German propagandists enjoyed a tremendous
advantage last spring, for they were able to present
the new commercial treaty as a benevolent anti-
capitalist plan to cut out middlemen and foreign
investors and to bring the natural wealth of Roumania
into the very homes of the people. Dr. Funk made
various declarations to this effect,[1] pouring scorn upon
the egoism of foreigners who lent capital in the old
conventional way; Germany (who in fact had no
available capital to lend) did not indulge in such sordid
financial transactions, she helped the direct exchange
of natural wealth, the product of labour. This kind
of talk delighted youthful circles; they forgot that
even in *Mein Kampf* it had been made fairly clear that
the natural wealth of countries like Roumania was to
be brought into the homes of the German people, and
inferior non-German races like Roumanians and Slavs
might have to be reduced to a "colonial" standard of
living.[2] In the minority districts like Transylvania,
Dobrogea, and Bessarabia, where people attributed

[1] e.g., on March 30th, 1939, in Berlin.
[2] See *Mein Kampf*, 1933 edition, p. 767.

their post-war poverty to their incorporation with Roumania, the inhabitants were still more inclined to hope great things from the new German activities; the economic stagnation of Bessarabia was such that anything which stimulated economic life seemed desirable.

However that might be, shrewder people now began to speak of the three types of German protectorate since March 15th. The first, in Bohemia and Moravia, had comprised the complete subjection of the Czechs; the second had provided the Slovaks with diplomatic representation and a territorial guarantee, which was promptly followed by a Hungarian invasion and the cession of Slovak territory to Hungary; the third was established by the commercial treaty with Roumania; what further type might yet be evolved? An honest Transylvanian Saxon journalist, Hans Kaiss, published an article called the "New face of Europe" in the *Siebenbürgisch-deutsches Tageblatt* at about this time, in which he consolingly explained that, whereas "the incorporation of Bohemia, of Moravia, and in a freer form of Slovakia, were a necessity for the German Reich's security . . .", the relationship between Germany and Roumania was not a physical thing but a matter of common destiny. For the Roumanian people, wrote Kaiss, the inevitability of the connection lay in the fact that if Roumania could not export her surplus production to Germany she would find herself in a desperate financial plight.

At all events, the Roumano-German treaty was a piece of German economic speculation. Where many foreign observers were wrong to make light of it was in their failure to appreciate that the Germans were willing to take wholly uneconomic risks which the old-established companies would never think worth while, and that these risks may lead to the successful boring of oil-wells whose possibilities would never have been considered by more conventionally minded business men; after all, it is the production of the established oil-wells of the big Ploeşti area which is falling off. The treaty of March 23rd, however, had other inconspicuous possibilities for the Germans, who quickly prepared to erect flour-mills at Braila, to build a big power station near Timişoara and to set up artificial textile factories in the Danube Delta. Within a few days of its signature German technicians were arriving in quantities to explore their new *terrain*, and the most technical expert is unlikely to slip out of Nazi Germany without propagandist training and safe-guards exacted that he puts it to good use. There had been a good deal of talk among the optimists of various kinds about the restrictions imposed by the Liberal administrations upon foreigners working in Roumanian concerns and, for example, the insistence upon State ownership of the sub-soil which might only be leased to companies not at work before 1925. What will help Germany to circumvent anti-foreign legislation is, however, the existence in Roumania of the now influential German minority, especially the Saxons with their interest in industry. In 1934 a law had been made in Roumania that 80 per cent. of the people employed in each category of any industry must be Roumanian citizens. In practice this law, like similar pieces of legislation in other countries, had for several years been a source of minority grievance, since it was often interpreted to mean Roumanian-speaking

citizens and had been used, especially in the anti-
minority atmosphere of 1936 and 1937, to turn out—
if not Germans so much—at any rate Hungarian
citizens of the State. Now, however, the Roumanian
Government can be sharply called to order if its
legislation should be used to the exclusion of the
German minority just when the real distinction between a Reich German and the member of a German
minority abroad has virtually ceased to exist. In any
case, with a Reich German or so at the head of a concern, and plenty of enthusiastically Nazi Saxons at
work under cover of the 80 per cent., and with the
Roumanian directors of the establishment not sorry
to leave exertion to others, it looks as if a great deal
of future activity on Roumanian soil will be to all
intents and purposes German. Moreover, in the free
zones mentioned in the treaty, Roumanian legislation
will not necessarily apply. The treaty among other
things provided for the development of communications and public utilities, and through these things it
seems inevitable that the Germans, whether Reich or
Minority, will exert a considerable influence upon
administration as a whole, and the German Legation
at Bucharest, with its enormous personnel, will make
sure of what kind this influence shall be. And so
much control with regard to key industries and roads
is enough in itself to give the German-Roumanian
Treaty of March 1939 strategic importance. It is true
that the next few months did not pass without friction
between the Roumanians and the Germans, who were
not able to buy up all Roumania's wheat production
as they wished. It is true, too, that the subsequent
commercial arrangements between Roumania and

Great Britain, by which the British provided credits to be spent on the purchase of British cotton and woollen yarns, did not fit into the Nazi plan. But Great Britain's efforts involved no British activity on Roumanian soil such as could counteract German activities effectually, and they were easily discredited by Nazi propagandists, at least in the eyes of the simpler-minded public. The British could be attacked on at least two points. They were only willing to offer world prices for the Roumanian wheat they bought, while Germany, it will be seen, appeared to be offering more. And they charged the relatively high rate (for Government guaranteed bonds) of 5 per cent. on the $5\frac{1}{2}$ million credit they put at Roumania's disposal, so that cries of Jewish usury were inevitably raised.

While the Nazis reap the advantage of Roumanian illogicality in suspecting foreign capital and yet wanting foreigners to do the work, they also make good use of the widespread poverty in the country—the Regat as well as the rest—and its Balkan characteristics. For nowhere more conspicuously than in Bucharest does starving degradation jostle with nonchalant wealth; in more "European" capitals the poor are at least kept more decently in their place. While a rich man like M. Manolescu-Strunga, who is strongly interested in the activities of the *I.G. Farbenindustrie*, despises the petty Kingdom of Roumania and would like it to be merged in the great and glorious Reich —he was arrested in a Night Club in Bucharest for the too frank expression of these views in March—the people as a whole are easily persuaded to feel, and to resent, that their rulers exploit them. Not only is

King Carol regarded as a foreigner, but also malicious rumours suggest that he makes financial profit out of his position; he, or at any rate Madame Lupescu, is said to be too friendly with M. Auşnitt, the Reşiţa steel king and a baptized Jew. Nothing, of course, would please the Germans better than to push M. Auşnitt out and strengthen their own hold upon the Reşiţa foundries; in the Malaxa locomotive works they also have material with which to incite xenophobia, since M. Malaxa is a naturalized Greek who is backed by considerable British investment.

A noticeable rise in prices has lowered the standard of life in the towns and increased discontent in general. The cost of living in Bucharest rose by 25·7 per cent. between February 1937 and February 1939 and by 49 per cent. between July 1934 and 'February 1939.[1] This increase is due in part, but clearly only in part, to a certain degree of inflation which resulted from the French and Swiss currency depreciation in the autumn of 1936. Another important contributing factor is Germany's policy of pushing up the rate of the mark in lei; in the November-December negotiations in 1938 she tried to put it up from 38 to 55, but 41 was adopted as the rate for the time being.[2] The ways of Roumania's currency are notoriously mysterious and it is difficult to gauge the relative importance of various factors. In order to increase her imports from Roumania and at the same time in order to reduce, if possible, Roumania's trade with other countries, Germany has paid preferential prices which have

---

[1] According to Central Institute of Statistics, Bucharest. Above figures quoted in *The Fight for Roumanian Trade* in *The Economist*, June 3rd, 1939.

[2] Actually 40·5 (buying) and 41·5 (selling).

temporarily raised the standard of life of the Roumanian peasant farmer, but by pushing down the value of the lei against the mark Germany herself pays less and less, while she pushes up prices inside Roumania. Even for the farmers the improvement is only temporary. As Professor Madgearu writes, "Certaines mesures, telles que les primes et les compensations, si elles ont pu améliorer momentanément la situation des producteurs agricoles et particulièrement des exportateurs, ont eu, par contre, comme effet durable, d'abaisser le standard de vie, en provoquant un renchérissement progressif des produits." [1]

While German policy has contributed to a temporary improvement in the Roumanian peasants' purchasing capacity which the post-war industrial development of Roumania is ready to meet, Germany is clearly determined to supply it herself through industrial products sent from the Reich or provided in the new German free zones in Roumania; recent Roumanian-British developments, while cutting across the German plan, may also hinder the development of Roumanian textiles. If the Germans can thus succeed in de-industrializing Roumania except for certain factories of their own, the social prospect for Roumania is at least as alarming as for Hungary, though naturally the circumstances vary from one country to the other. The Roumanian birth-rate is

[1] V. Magdearu, *ibid.*, p. 38. He calculates that the purchasing power of the Roumanian peasant farmer in 1937 was 27 per cent. less than in 1929-30. He also writes (p. 46), " . . . les mesures de protectionnisme indirect d'autres pays d'une part (en rendant plus difficile l'exportation des animaux et des produits animaux) et les primes économiques et monétaires d'autre part (favorisant la culture du blé et donc une culture extensive), ont contribué au maintien d'une capacité de consommation extrêmement réduite chez le paysan roumain."

high,[1] and with overseas emigration long ago prevented, the surplus peasant population needs to be
absorbed by industry or the peasant prosperity of the
moment—such as it is—will soon disappear and the
misery of the towns increase; in Roumania the possibilities of further agrarian reform are a good deal more
slender than in Hungary. The prospect of the intensification of the misery of Balkan towns is particularly
grim, for this is a cumulative misery—the inflowing
peasantry worsen poor urban conditions by their
unfamiliarity with them. And by taking advantage of
the administrative anxieties of those who have to deal
with growing destitution and unrest in backward
towns, totalitarian propagandists are able to instigate
unpopular high-handed "authoritarianism" against
"Communist agitators." It will be found that the
effects of German economic policy in Yugoslavia [2]
have been similar and even more complete.

[1] 11·7 per 1000 per year.   [2] See below, p. 163 *et seq.*

CHAPTER III

THE SOUTHERN SLAVS OF YUGOSLAVIA [1] AND
BULGARIA; THE EASTERN MEDITERRANEAN

(a) *Political Development*

To those who wish to fish in troubled waters, post-war Yugoslavia provides opportunities not to be equalled elsewhere. If the individualisms of Transylvania are unique, and if the diversity of its races and religions are intricate, it has a coherent historic tradition, and the unity of modern Roumania depends ultimately upon the one question of the possibility of a true Regat-Transylvania marriage. But Yugoslavia has many different histories to reconcile. And if Poland and Roumania are caught between the enmity of Germany and Russia, Yugoslavia is wedged between the ambiguous friendship of Rome with Berlin.

It is impossible to examine the activities of the Germans in Yugoslavia, since dynamic destructiveness became their *motif*, without a particularly careful analysis of the historical diversity and confusion which forms a considerable part of the material they use and which provides the only intelligible explanation of the rest. Yugoslavia was put together in 1919 from the two Balkan States of Serbia and Montenegro, which had won a perilous independence from Turkey during the nineteenth century, and from a considerable portion of

---

[1] Meaning, literally, Southern Slavia.

Macedonia which had been under Turkish rule until the Balkan Wars; the Voivodina was taken from Hungary proper together with Hungary's autonomous province of Croatia-Slavonia (the latter not, by the way, a part of the lands of St. Stephen) for the new state, and from Austria the provinces of Dalmatia, Carniola (or Slovenia) together with a portion of Styria; finally Bosnia (with Hercegovina), the scene of the Archduke's murder in June 1914, was transferred from an Austro-Hungarian condominium to be incorporated also in the new triune Kingdom of the Serbs, the Croats and the Slovenes.

Each of these provinces had a history of its own, while their frontiers coincided with no clear racial nor religious demarcations, and illiteracy, especially in the ex-Turkish regions, made it difficult to appreciate the distinction between language and dialect. The Serbs and Croats spoke the same language, though the former used the Cyrillic and the latter the Roman alphabet, while the language of the Slovenes, though very definitely South Slavonic, was distinct. The Slovenes were geographically the most orderly group, apart from the handful of Montenegrins who subsequently vanished from the census and other records. The Croats lived in Croatia-Slavonia, Dalmatia, Bosnia, and a few in Voivodina, the Serbs in Serbia, Croatia-Slavonia, Voivodina, Bosnia and in the Macedonian area in the south. Even the religious and the racial demarcation, as between, say, Catholic Croat and Orthodox Serb, sometimes failed to coincide, because in the fifteenth century both Croats and Serbs in Bosnia had become Mohammedan and had remained so ever since. The population of the new Yugoslavia may be estimated to have comprised: [1]

> $5\frac{1}{2}$ million Serbs, of whom about three million were Serbs of Old Serbia and the rest Prečani Serbs or ex-Hungarian.
>
> $3\frac{1}{4}$ million Croats.
>
> 1   million Slovenes.
>
> 700,000 Moslems (Serb and Croat) of Bosnia and Hercegovina.
>
> 600,000 Macedonians.
>
> $\frac{1}{2}$ million Germans.
>
> $\frac{1}{2}$ million Hungarians.
>
> $\frac{1}{2}$ million Albanians.

Perhaps the clearest line could be drawn between ex-Austria-Hungary and the rest, for, although both Austrians and Hungarians eagerly emphasized the significance of the Leitha, and although they were correct in doing so, the Dual Monarchy had a certain homogeneity and a certain occidentalism; it was beyond the Sava, not, as Metternich once said, beyond the *Landstrasse*, that Turkey in 1919 still began.

One of the ironies of the situation was that the ideal of Southern Slav unity was a comparatively strange one to the rulers of Serbia, who were now given Southern Slavia to direct; the Yugoslav idea,[2] on the contrary, was essentially a product of the later liberalism of Habsburg Austria, an idea which the Serbs of Hungary concocted together with the Croats and the Austrian Slovenes in the hotly Slav air of Prague and its Czech university.   The Serb peasants of Serbia

---

[1] Estimate based on the 1921 census.

[2] It had actually been formulated in 1848 before an independent Serbia existed.

itself dreamt, perhaps, of Southern Slav brotherhood, but to them it meant union with the also Orthodox Bulgars. But the authorities in Belgrade, both civil and military, were more or less Pan-Serb, even apart from the terrorists of the Black Hand who had helped to engineer the murder at Sarajevo. As Mr. Macartney has written:[1] "During their (the Serbs') century of gallant and extraordinarily successful national struggles they had increased their territory more and more, but always spreading outward from a central core. The expansion had always taken the form of a greater and ever greater Serbia, built up firmly round this strong core; and they did not believe any other system durable or even feasible." It is relevant, too, that Serb military men were not at all enthusiastic about the acquisition of Slovenia whose position was in any case so exposed to attack. Some Serbs, indeed, remained very sceptical about being too much involved with the Slovenes and Croats whom they regarded as over-softened by Habsburg rule, for they never distinguished at all clearly between what they regarded as decadence and what most West Europeans would consider as the pleasing effects of more civilized conditions.

It was in a sense fortuitous that so many non-Serb groups were now united under the rule of the Kara-georgević dynasty. The Slovenes and Croats of the Habsburg Empire thought in terms of the unity of the Yugoslavs of the Monarchy, and despatched the Slovene leader, Father Korošec, to represent them in Western Europe in the autumn of 1918. The Croat representative, Dr. Trumbić, had signed the Declaration

---

[1] C. A. Macartney, *op. cit.*, p. 364.

of Corfu with M. Pašić, the Serbian Premier, in July 1917, in favour of a united democratic and Parliamentary Kingdom of Serbs, Croats and Slovenes, but it had apparently never occurred to him that the ex-Habsburg territories would not be autonomous, that Belgrade, that is, would insist upon a unitary state. Towards the end of 1918, in view of the danger from Italy to Slovene and Croatian territory, it proved possible through the agency of M. Svetozar Pribičević and the Prečani or ex-Monarchy Serbs, to rush through a declaration of the unity of the new Yugoslavia on December 1st, 1918, and to place the authority over it in the hands of the Serbian Prince Regent, afterwards King Alexander, who, of course, solemnly affirmed that he would "always remain true to the great principles of Constitutionalism, Parliamentarism and the widest democracy based on universal suffrage."

From the very word "go" the Croats were filled with indignation against the fate which they had allowed to overtake them. From that day to this the Croatian question, even the Macedonians notwithstanding, has held the centre of the Yugoslav stage, and has supplied material for every manner of intrigue, Italian, Legitimist and finally Nazi. The problem in its essence has changed very little in the last twenty years—it remains a problem arising out of the deplorable subjection of a more civilized national group to a less civilized one with which the first had little in common but language, not even handwriting and script. On the other hand, one's initial sympathy with the Croats soon becomes restrained by greater intimacy with the question. For the Croats—it is not their fault—are incorrigible *frondeurs*. As far as history goes back they have been a small nation on the defensive, always against the Magyars, and sometimes and increasingly towards 1914 against Vienna as well, and they have, presumably in consequence, developed a genius for making life complicated or difficult—to which the Serb reaction for many years was simply—"Oh, hell."

The outlook and aspirations of the Croats have been for many years so closely associated with the Radić family that it will be best to try to examine the Radić point of view, to which Dr. Maček in 1939 is absolutely faithful. The Radić's were a brilliant peasant family with means and with the genuine educational avidity which is typical of the Croats and only some-times out-distanced, among mainly peasant communi-ties, by the Slovenes. Stepan Radić, who afterwards became the Croat national hero, studied in Prague in the 'nineties, where he not only married a Czech wife but moved to some extent in the Masaryk circle. It was rather his brother Antun, however, who formul-ated the ultimate values of Croatianism. It was true that Croat village life had ancient communal traditions; the community organization or *zadruga* had been highly developed at an early stage and had arrived at a remarkable form of village co-operation which had been partially perverted by Austrian and Hungarian feudal, and later bureaucratic, influences. Such in-fluences, according to Antun Radić, represented the force-values of the Graeco-Roman world which con-tinued to conflict with the true and unpolluted Christianity of Croat village life;[1] it emerges from his writing that the Croat peasants automatically regarded

---

[1] I am indebted to Croatian friends for this account, since the material has not, as far as I know, been translated.

aristocrats, middlemen and officials as immoral inter-
lopers to whom passive resistance was due. It is clear
that the servants of any modern state, however
civilized, would have been frowned upon by members
of the Croat Peasant Party, which adopted this point
of view as its own—even the most skilful administrators might have found a point at which they were
forced to impinge upon the co-operative organization
of the Croatian villagers for which the rough and in-
experienced new Serb officials were without all respect.

Štepan Radić founded and built up the Croat
Peasant Party upon these ideals of co-operative village
democracy. In the Croatian Parliament or *Sabor* of
1906 there were only three Croat Peasant deputies, but
this was primarily due to the strange inequalities of the
franchise in Hungarian days; in the elections for the
Constituent Assembly in November 1920, the Radić
Party was revealed as much the strongest in Croatia;
in 1924 it was represented by 70 deputies and it has
been gradually growing in strength ever since. Štepan
Radić immediately rejected the Serb authority as an
uncalled-for military invasion, and, although he was
conspicuous for his emotional, and sometimes for his
political, instability, he forthwith laid down a programme to which he thereafter remained faithful for
the fraternal federation of the Slav peasant states.
While Stambulisky lived Radić was his enthusiastic
friend, for he hoped to start with a Croat-Serb-
Bulgar Federation; within the federation each group
was to be completely autonomous and indeed nationalistic; in claiming what Radić regarded as the historic
frontiers of Croatia-Slavonia with Dalmatia the awkward fact that Croats and Serbs, or even Serbs and

Bulgars, lived in confusion over considerable areas was conveniently ignored.

In view of bitter divisions and of the illiteracy of the southern half of the Kingdom, it was not surprising that the attempt to introduce wholesale democracy on the western model proved unsatisfactory, the more so since King Alexander, whose Tsarist education and sympathies were manifest, can scarcely have been more than half-hearted in the matter. In Yugoslavia it required no economic collapse for the democratic system to break down; indeed it was in June 1928, at the height of the boom, that the Croat leaders were shot down in the Skupština itself by a desperado who had clearly had encouragement in high Serb places. The martyrdom of Štepan Radić himself was enhanced by the fact that he lived on for six or seven weeks, only then to succumb to his wounds. His tomb became a sacred national symbol to the Croat peasantry. To the Croats the murder summed up the brutal terrorization to which their peaceful and democratic community-civilization had most wrongfully been subjected. The Serbs, the Croats said, had been nurtured in the ways of Eastern despotism, and knew no better; under the menace of the Turk tax collector their villages had never developed an organic life of their own. More specifically the Croats complained that they were financially fleeced, their young men sent into exile, their children mistaught by an alien and barbarian regime which kept all diplomatic and large or small official posts in Serb hands. The financial difficulty was much the same as that between Transylvania and the Regat. The southern part of the Yugoslav Kingdom was very much poorer than the

ex-Habsburg lands and in far greater need of houses,
roads, schools and everything else; if the idea of a
Yugoslav territorial unit were accepted at all it was
just that the richer Slovenes and Croats should contribute to the greater needs of the poorer Serbs and
Macedonians. But in the Slovene, and particularly the
Croat, view, their carefully husbanded resources were
simply being stolen to finance the alien and militarist
rule which oppressed them. That there was corruption in Belgrade and that the young State spent a lot
on its Army were attributed solely to Serb original sin.
There were bitter complaints that Croats not only had
no chance of being officers of senior rank, but that
Croat conscripts were forced to languish in distant
Macedonia while performing their military service.
As for the schools, these, it was said, were filled with
half-educated Serb teachers who taught the children
to forget they were Croats and to think only in terms
of the expansion of Serbia; it was interesting, by the
way, that most Croat children appear to have been
completely immune to Great-Serb suggestion and to
have regarded the Serb teachers as their hereditary
enemies.

Declaring with some justification that Parliamentary
Government had hopelessly broken down, King
Alexander, on January 6th, 1929, inaugurated his own
dictatorship, and on September 3rd, 1931, he proclaimed a new constitution which did little but sur-
round the absolutism of the crown with a certain
parliamentary paraphernalia. For years January 6th
and September 3rd have been marked as black days on
the Croatian Calendar, and in café conversation the
visitor to Zagreb was lost if he did not know what

those dates implied. For Alexander foolishly attempted political mesmerism, and ignorant foreign
diplomats would tell one that there was no Croatian
question for the King had told them so; the Triune
Kingdom had turned into a unitary Yugoslavia over-
night. The Croats were outraged by, among many
other things, the administrative redistribution of all
Yugoslavia into Banovinas, districts whose boundaries
cut right across the historic frontiers of Croatia, and,
by dividing the Croats of the interior from those of
Dalmatia, preserved only one tradition, the hated
pre-war boundary between Austrian Dalmatia and
semi-Hungarian Croatia-Slavonia. If Serb police
methods had seemed rough and oriental before, they
were now allowed to become absolutely brutal; the
gendarmerie, incidentally, was almost purely Serb; if
a Croat took so much as an urban traffic-regulating
policeman's job in Zagreb he was subject to Croat
detestation as a renegade. The Serbian State Police
officials appear to have been told to eliminate the
Croat state of mind; if necessary elimination must take
the form of beating and torturing it away, and cruel
persecution occurred.[1] That other device of terroristic governments was naturally also resorted to:
armed bands of terrorists, known as Četnici, with
licence to do what they would without fear of punishment, were let loose all over Croatia. Foreign visitors
to Zagreb, incidentally, were incompetently, indeed
conspicuously, shadowed, and thereby encouraged to
champion the Croats.

[1] It would be unfair to the Serbs to imply that their police methods were
unique; though many people in Western Europe are unaware of such
things, terrible police methods are used anywhere in Eastern Europe—
particularly, since the Nazi regime, in the German Reich.

This state of affairs continued until the assassination of the King-Dictator at Marseille in October 1934 by a man generally supposed to have been a Macedonian associated with the Croatian Ustachis, as well as with the notorious Internal Macedonian Revolutionary terrorist Organization (the I.M.R.O.). Though the Croat Peasant Party had always taken up an attitude of non-violence and had avoided intrigues abroad, there were Croats who had strayed from the paths of pastoral innocence. Dr. Pavelić and Dr. Frank and other survivors of the pre-war pro-Austrian politicians in Croatia had undoubtedly schemed with Habsburg Legitimists for Croatia to join Austria on Kaiser Otto's return. They had used any accomplices they could find in Italy and Hungary, where a few Croat terrorists known as Ustachis were harboured and even trained in violence; such people would obviously have contact also with the Macedonians, who were, up to this time, still trying to disturb Serb authority in the valley of the Vardar. It seemed inevitable that the death of Alexander should cause the disintegration of post-war Yugoslavia, and there were Peasant Party Croats—not only Frankists—who boasted that they drank all night for joy after news of the murder had reached them. It is not altogether easy to say why the Yugoslav State nevertheless held together. It is incontestable that dissension within it was more bitter and more fundamental than in Czechoslovakia in 1938 where two-thirds of the Slovaks, according to the uninfluenced local elections in May and June, were in favour of fidelity to Prague. But in 1934 Germany's disintegrating activities had scarcely begun in Yugoslavia—rumours of German instigation of the Marseille assassination were never corroborated. Italy's behaviour at the time betrayed a guilty fore-knowledge, but after the murder of Dollfuss in July 1934, fortunately for Yugoslavia, Italy and Germany were still on bad terms.

The death of Alexander Karageorgević in fact marked the beginning of a change in the Serb point of view. Even officially a few gestures were made such as the release of Radić' successor as Croat leader, Dr. Maček, though the dead King's system was only gradually and slightly modified. Originally Serb opinion had regarded the Croats as factious and bothersome degenerates; they had been demoralized, the Serbs said, by the feudal standards prevailing in Hungary and Austria; under Habsburg rule they had become susceptible to pernicious anti-Semitic and clerical influence. To the Serbs, who made few fine distinctions between Austrians, Germans and Magyars, they had all represented something brutal and decadent which had almost strangled Serbia at birth, and, when she eluded Vienna's authority by destroying the Austrophil Obrenović dynasty, had stolen Bosnia from her, and then in 1914 prepared her total destruction. With Austria the Serbs almost identified the Catholic Church against which they entertained a furious hostility—they seemed to hate Catholics far more than Mohammedans. Most of the Croats and Slovenes were devout Catholics, thoroughly priest-ridden in Serbian eyes, and the average Serbian rather took the view that they could not help but be traitors and irredentists until at least the younger generation had been differently brought up. Though Maček was anti-clerical and personally on indifferent terms with the clergy, the Croats had, of course, underlined their

Catholic observances as an exhibition of anti-Serb sentiment. There were also Serb academic theorists like Dr. Cvijič who had discovered that the Serbs represented a particularly splendid racial type of Dinaric man with whose qualities the Croat, though also Slav, could by no means compete.

With the royal dictatorship, however, followed by the world depression, the Serbs, too, began to find the Belgrade administration oppressive. Village life may not have been so highly developed among the Serb peasants and they may have been used to all sorts of rough things, but they were simple, fair-minded people and proud of being a peasant State without social distinction and with a native peasant dynasty of its own. If they despised the feudalism of old Austria-Hungary their contempt was based on its military caste system; an officer in the Serb army had never been regarded as socially superior, and there were Croats and Slovenes who were certainly too slow to comprehend this. Now the royal dictatorship was exploited by some of its instruments to be socially pretentious at a time when the people were becoming disagreeably aware of the general impoverishment, and their indignation was often treated as brutally as if it were the supposed separatism of the Croats. In spite of the tremendously pro-Russian sentiment of the people, the King refused to recognize the Moscow regime even when his allies of the Little Entente did so, and he more and more tended to regard students or peasants who expressed discontent as dangerous Communist agitators. Elections in the 'twenties had been gloriously incorrect, but they were not so exasperating as the intimidating system of open voting

which now prevailed, and while there was a riot of
political parties people had not been made to feel that
they were not allowed to make any protest against the
powers that be, whereas under the dictatorship it was
just as likely as not that the gendarmes forcibly
prevented anti-Government people from voting
at all.

Indignation only arose slowly and gradually in
Serbia, but there were people with vision who already
felt that the Serb and the Croat, and still to some extent
the Bulgar, peoples were being brought into ruinous
conflict when all their interests were essentially the
same. The Left Wing Peasant Leader, Professor
Dragoljub Jovanović,[1] and his friends hailed the death
of the King as the occasion for a Serbo-Croat truce.
"Your Radić was killed," they said to the Croats,
"and now our Karageorgević—let us accept a death
for a death and let us begin again and fight together
against brutal and corrupt dictatorship." Though
Dragoljub Jovanović was penniless and powerless his
voice was heard—it was at about this time that I was
amazed to hear a Slovene Clerical in Ljubljana refer to
him as "the hope of the future"—and his proposition
was the beginning of the United Opposition which
was virtually victorious in the elections of December
1938. From the beginning an important element in
the new Serbo-Croat democratic alliance were the
Prečani Serbs, the ex-Habsburg Serbs of Croatia and
Voivodina who had followed M. Pribičević. Though
originally exaggerated centralists, more Serb than the
Serbs of the Kingdom, they had become the bitter
opponents of the policy of the King in spite of the

---

[1] Dragoljub Jovanović came from Pirot near the Bulgarian frontier.

advantages they had originally enjoyed as Serb by race and Orthodox by religion.

The relative success of the Oppositional groups even in the elections of May 1935, in spite of all the obstacles put in their way, was impressive. While claiming that no radical changes, and above all, no constitutional (i.e. decentralizing) reform, could be carried through during the minority of King Alexander's eldest son, young King Peter, the Regency, which was now responsible for the government of the country, appeared to appreciate the need for a change of policy, and continued to make conciliatory gestures. Of the three Regents appointed according to the late King's will, the senior was his cousin, Prince Paul, who also through family connections had lived in something of a Tsarist atmosphere. The popular attitude towards Prince Paul was that he should be given a chance to put things right—of the other two Regents one heard little, and, as time went on, less and less. Prince Paul got rid of M. Jevtić and his group of Radicals, who had been most thoroughly implicated in King Alexander's dictatorship, and chose a Radical banker, Dr. Stojadinović, to be Premier. Of all the dissident groups in the State, it only proved possible to persuade the Slovene Clericals, still led by Father Korošec, and the Bosnian Moslems under M. Spaho, to join the Government Party which was thenceforward known as the Yugoslav Radical Union. The Croats remained completely hostile and refused to take such seats as had perforce been allotted to them in the Chamber, as a protest against the centralist and anti-democratic constitution which they would never recognize to be legal.

By forbidding regional political parties, King Alexander had actually pushed together the Serb and Croat oppositions; [1] it remained for the Stojadinović regime to achieve what King Alexander had failed to do—the conversion of the naturally centralist Serbs to a policy of decentralization. They had rebelled against the earlier dictatorship as undemocratic, brutal and corrupt, but if they had therefore found some common ground with the Croats, they had continued to regard Croatian federal plans as fantastic and dangerous, as they possibly were. That Dr. Stojadinović brought about this remarkable change may be attributed, on the one hand, to his ill-concealed financial greed and, on the other, to his foreign policy. He was appointed ostensibly to bring about an internal *détente*, but it is generally agreed that, apart from keeping M. Spaho at the Ministry of Railways to satisfy the Bosnian Moslems, he was uniformly unsuccessful in fulfilling his task; even the Slovenes, in spite of Father Korošec's position as Minister of the Interior, were none too content. The Croats and their visitors found police activities rather more encompassed, but this did not impress them; it had become impossible, they said, to terrorize so superbly organized a nation which was 90 per cent. devoted to a freely chosen leader, Maček, while the Četnici had disappeared because they were too much afraid of the spontaneously organized Maček Guard. If police oppression was reduced and the press a degree freer in Croatia, financial tyranny, the Croats declared, had expanded.

---

[1] Since the Croat Peasant Party, for example, was not allowed to exist politically, even as the " Maček List," unless it had supporters all over Yugoslavia.

It has been seen that they had long ago protested against the proportion of wealth which they were expected to contribute to the State while receiving small benefit from it—it was calculated that in the decade from 1925 to 1934 (inclusive) 63 per cent. of all Yugoslav expenditure had been devoted to the Serbs of old Serbia, 23 per cent. of the population, and Croat statisticians worked out that while the Savska Banovina, i.e. roughly Croatia without Dalmatia, had contributed in all 60 milliards of dinari in taxation since 1919, only half that sum had been spent on the area which had produced it. Dr. Stojadinović was probably indifferent as to which part of the country he annoyed so long as he extracted as much as possible from the richer sections. It has been worked out that in 1936 the average amount of direct taxation paid per head in

Croatia	was	199	dinari,
Slovenia	,,	240	,,
Voivodina	,,	290	,,
Serbia	,,	112	,,
Dalmatia	,,	61	,,
Bosnia	,,	66	,, [1]

This annoyed the Croats, but showed a not uniformly bad assessment of the paying capacity of these provinces; and Dalmatia, where after all a high proportion of the population is Croat, was lightly let off.

Meanwhile police brutality and interference increased throughout old Serbia, and the Government further angered the peasants by super-imposing its

---

[1] Croat academic sources.

own quite unsuitable nominees to preside over the village councils through which it was hoped to influence peasant opinion by one means or another. During 1937 the struggle over the Concordat provided an indication of how feelings were developing. This Concordat had been arranged with the Vatican in 1935 and offered certain privileges to the Catholic clergy. Now some of the Croatian clergy had been showing strong pro-Italian and pro-Franco sympathies which were angrily repudiated by Maček and the Peasant Party. Croat opinion as a whole, therefore, regarded the Concordat which was sponsored by the Orthodox, but evidently cynical, Stojadinović, as an attempt to split Croatia and to buy over the clergy. In view of their traditional attitude towards the Roman Catholic Church the feelings of the Serbs at this treachery on the part of their Government need scarcely be elaborated, and the Bishops of the Orthodox Church gladly came out on the popular side. In the end the Government admitted defeat and the Concordat was withdrawn.

The Concordat had, of course, been interpreted, not perhaps correctly, as part of Dr. Stojadinović's general foreign policy, as in fact a gesture to Italy. With her exploitation of the breach between Italy and the Western Powers over Ethiopia which, among other things, led her to remilitarize the Rhineland in March 1936, Germany was now in a position to attempt the disruption of the whole European system in her own favour. The imposition of economic sanctions against Italy, according to her obligations to the League of Nations, imposed a heavy sacrifice upon Yugoslavia who had been accustomed to export a good deal to Italy;[1] when Germany showed readiness to increase her imports from the Yugoslavs Dr. Stojadinović was only too pleased. General Goering, it seems, had also been working with his customary vigour to bring about a Yugoslav-Bulgarian *rapprochement*, in order, presumably, to loosen the Balkan Entente concluded between Yugoslavia, Roumania, Turkey and Greece in February 1934 with a view to preserving the Balkan *status quo*. In fact Yugoslavia and Bulgaria signed a Pact of Perpetual Friendship on January 24th, 1937; although it was later regarded as an example of Dr. Stojadinović's generally irresponsible behaviour, since no assurances from Bulgaria were required, it was not in itself unwelcome to Yugoslav public opinion. In March, however, he proceeded to sign a Treaty of Friendship with Italy, in response, as it seemed, to Signor Mussolini's pro-Hungarian speech at Milan in the previous November which had obviously aimed at the loosening of the Little Entente. From this time onwards the indignation of Croats, Slovenes and Serbs, but particularly the latter, was constantly stimulated by Dr. Stojadinović's apparently light-hearted entanglements with the Axis Powers, and it was believed that he was by no means disinterested in their commercial relations with the Yugoslavs.

The Treaty with Italy was repugnant to the Slovenes and Croats on account of a long enmity dating from Habsburg days; the Dalmatian Croats hated Italy's Adriatic threats and of course her position at Fiume, Zara and Lagosta. Both Croats and Slovenes were sensitive with regard to the miserable conditions in which the Croat and Slovene minority (about 600,000

[1] See below, p. 154.

people) in Italy lived; in general they considered that the Belgrade Cabinets had been far too careless of Adriatic interests. The Serbs were a little less bothered by these considerations, but rather more anxious about the general implications of the Treaty. Their feeling as a whole was pro-Slav, pro-Czech and pro-Russian, and also pro-democratic, for the Serbs felt profoundly suspicious of a pro-Axis inclination—dictators were birds of a feather they feared; so long as Italy and Germany could be played off against each other there had been a case for a *rapprochement* with Italy, but now it appeared to them to be like nibbling the cheese on a mouse-trap. The curious situation now arose that when Dr. Beneš paid an official visit to Belgrade in the spring of 1937 the police provided fairly rough discouragement to the demonstrators who turned out to cheer the official ally of the Government.

The policy of Dr. Stojadinović facilitated a closer alliance between the oppositional Serb groups— Agrarians, Liberals and a number of dissident Radical politicians who disliked the existing Cabinet—and Dr. Maček; though some of the Croats, Clericals and others, were lending their ears to anti-democratic propaganda, Dr. Maček himself was untouched by it. His federal plans, it has been seen, were originally repugnant to Serb opinion, and in earlier days his Serb friends had hoped to dissuade him from insisting upon them, but they now began to take him very seriously. In October 1937 they invited him to Belgrade. The police got at least one machine-gun into position, but it soon became evident that the pro-Maček manifestations would be too tremendous to be suppressed without wholesale massacre, and so the little peasant lawyer from near Zagreb had a triumphal procession through the streets of Belgrade. This demonstration was the more remarkable in view of the paralysing censorship of the press, where nothing derogatory to the Government or the foreign governments it wished to flatter might appear. But news rushed round the bars and cafés of Belgrade all the more briskly—there is no oriental languor about the Serbs. Street demonstrations depended to a large extent upon the students of the University of Belgrade, who showed splendid courage in facing the weapons of the police. The primitive students of Belgrade not only kept up the traditions of their fathers who had fought so indomitably between 1912 and 1918, they were also the only group of students in all Europe east of Switzerland and west of Russia who rejected the obscurantisms fostered by post-war disillusionment. For they were neither anti-Semite nor the supporters of political tyranny; many called themselves Communists, but upon analysis this turned out to be mainly as a protest —the dictatorship of the proletariat meant nothing to youths so close to the peasantry, or if it did mean anything, it seldom won their applause. Russia, however, whatever her political colour, was dear to their hearts, something which had saved them from being helots to the Turks and to the Germans, and something which could save them from the Germans again. There were Serbs, of course, who were attracted by the egalitarian, no-nonsense, strong-man, anti-clerical line of Nazi Germany, and, until Austria disappeared, ancient prejudice caused the majority of Serbs to sympathize with Hitler rather than with Schuschnigg. Yet in spite of the vigour with which these feelings were encouraged, especially by Herr Franz Neuhausen,[1] head of the German Travel Agency and German Consul-General in Belgrade, in spite of free German publications, free German tuition, conducted tours to Germany, and in spite of a growing number of people who had an interest in increasingly close commercial relations with Germany, it was astonishing to observe how little Serb public opinion was won over to the Reich in 1937.

The far-reaching events of 1938 modified, but did not alter, this situation. One might have despised the Schuschnigg regime in Austria while complaining that it did nothing for its Slovenes, but it was ten times as disagreeable to have the Nazis on one's already weak northern frontier; the Nazi method, moreover, of dealing with the Austrian Slovenes was to denationalize them as quickly as possible.[2] During the summer young Yugoslavs got ready to fight for Czechoslovakia, and they were among the most enthusiastic visitors to the gathering of the Sokols in Prague. The Czech tourists had never been loved in Dalmatia, but the Dalmatians were eager to fight for the Czechoslovak Republic. In September Dragoljub Jovanović was probably expressing public opinion when he addressed an open letter to Dr. Beneš,[3] denouncing the treachery of Dr. Stojadinović, who had behaved with diplomatic docility towards the Powers of the Axis. After February and September the strategic position of Yugoslavia had greatly deteriorated and the Western democracies were immensely discredited,

---

[1] See below, p. 150.　　　　　[2] See below, p. 139.

[3] D. Jovanovic was immediately imprisoned for his audacity, and in April 1939 was tried and condemned to a fairly severe sentence.

while the Little Entente had in practice ceased to exist. Yet in spite of the fact that there was now a far better case for the Stojadinović foreign policy, and in spite of the possible cessation of all Russian interest in Europe, the popular Yugoslav view was unchanged, and his unpopular foreign policy contributed to his virtual defeat in the elections of December 1938.

The outcome of Dr. Maček's visit to Belgrade in October 1937 was a ratification of the Serbo-Croat United Opposition on a basis of constitutional revision along federal and out-and-out democratic lines. Later the Opposition gained the support of some new and rather unexpected, but not unimportant, allies. The old Radical leader, M. Jevtić, who had been turned out to make room for Dr. Stojadinović as Premier, joined forces with General Živković to form a Yugoslav National Party (the J.N.S.). Now General Živković had been a close associate of King Alexander, and as Premier in the early days of the royal dictatorship had then been identified with the attempt to suppress the Croat movement completely. Since then he had remained of some account in military circles, and gossip had often reported that he had been won over to the absolute necessity of conciliating the Croats and that he might soon emerge from behind the scenes to help bring this about. Jevtić and Živković disliked a pro-Axis foreign policy; they were regarded as the true political heirs of the late King, and this gave them influence in quite other directions from the other parties of the United Opposition; they were thought to be popular among the Bosnian Serbs.

In accordance with Stojadinović's tactics the police

were relatively mild with the Croats during the election, though some hundreds of small officials were afterwards dismissed, and some imprisoned, for having voted for Maček. But in Serbia the terrorization was tremendous. A certain priest in Niš, one heard, armed himself with revolvers and led the people to the polling-places to vote against the Government, but in many places the gendarmes easily prevented the opposition from voting at all. With the system of open voting introduced in 1931 it was absolutely impossible for the army of officials in Belgrade to vote against the Government, and it was therefore not surprising that the Government vote in the capital increased in 1938 as compared with 1935. The final result was announced as being 1,643,783 votes for the Government and 1,364,524 for the United Opposition —and it should not be forgotten that this was the Government estimate of the votes. Considering that Dr. Stojadinović had contrived to keep the support of Father Korošec and of M. Spaho, and therefore the votes of at least the simpler-minded Slovene peasants and Bosnian Moslems, the figures were an amazing confession of failure. Even now, however, neither the Prince Regent nor the Prime Minister felt constrained to abandon dictatorship and bow to the popular will. On the contrary, Dr. Stojadinović, like M. Imrédy, appears to have succumbed completely to the totalitarian contagion and to have begun to organize his own fascist movement complete with salutes for its Leader and with shirts—green for its Youth Movement and dark blue for adult performers. The Prince Regent must have had some idea of how unpopular he himself as well as his Prime Minister was becoming, and at last, on February 4th, 1939, he dismissed the Stojadinović Cabinet. Dr. Stojadinović himself was kept under house arrest for some time, but, since he remained the President of the Yugoslav Radical Union or Government Party for another five months, little confidence was inspired by Prince Paul in dismissing him. The fallen Prime Minister, who had made so many promises that he was really about to put through a solution of the Croat question this time and this time, had in fact caused the crystallization of Croat opposition into a highly organized national movement enthusiastically supported by the majority of the Serbs; this was the result of so dexterously playing them off against one another. Even before the events of the spring 1939 it was a perilous state of affairs for a small country wedged awkwardly between two closely allied and destructive Great Powers, and yet Yugoslavia still showed signs of incorrigible health.

The sequel to King Alexander's assassination had shown that Italy's attempts to break Yugoslavia had failed, and after that time they ceased to be important. But German intrigue then embarked upon the exploitation of the Croat question and developed every aspect of the situation with its customary zeal. While official Germany had more and more praised Stojadinović for his cold-shouldering of the Little Entente in favour of the Axis Powers, whisperers in Croatia had lavished sympathy upon the Croats in the oppression of their race by the alien Serb regime. The racial theories of a Croat writer named Sufflay were taken up since Sufflay had held that the Croats were not Slavs like the Serbs, but were the descendants of a settlement of

Goths. This notion was to be found in the paper *Nezavismost* (Independence) brought out by a certain M. Buć who was obviously dependent upon German funds. It was characteristic of the whole situation that *Nezavismost* furiously attacked Dr. Maček for his moderation in championing the Croat national cause against the pro-German Stojadinović regime though M. Buć was supported by money from Germany. Whereas in Belgrade there was no noticeable feeling against the few Sephardim Jewish families who had been settled there for centuries, in Zagreb the anti-Semitic traditions of Austria-Hungary had survived; indeed during the depression there was a great deal of talk at the expense of Jewish banking circles. Zagreb students thus took easily to anti-Semitism, which was stimulated by *Nezavismost* and by other more influential circles, Clerical and Frankist; the latter were easily brought into contact with German agents in consequence. The pro-Italian pro-Habsburg Frankists, like M. Budak who launched the *Hrvatski Narod* newspaper, attacked Dr. Maček because he carefully eschewed separatism, but there were separatist elements in his party which were certainly in relation with the anti-democratic pro-German and pro-Italian groups. During the winter 1938-39 German agents made great play with Germany's quixotic "liberation" of Slovakia from Czech "tyranny" and offered similar help to the Croats. All sorts of indirect offers came from Germany to Maček, but he managed to ignore them and to reject insinuations that he was the Hitler of Croatia, and yet to keep all his followers together.

In February 1939 Prince Paul appointed an ostensibly transitional Cabinet of ministers who were generally held to lack all distinction; he nominated M. Cvetković as Premier and charged him with the final solution of the Croat question. With the German action in Bohemia and Moravia in March and its hints to small Powers that Hitler stood no nonsense, the times seemed to the Yugoslavs earnest indeed, and there was more and more demand, especially in Serbia, for a democratic government of national concentration under Maček. Feeling in Croatia was exceedingly confused. Intransigeant Croats had observed the outcries of the German press against the appointment of M. Cvetković in Dr. Stojadinović's place and were inclined to say, if the Serbs have turned against Germany let us turn to her, but the fate of Prague disturbed them again. Just after March 15th the Buć people tried to stage a pro-German street demonstration in Zagreb, but only about thirty people participated and some of them afterwards confessed that they had been bribed with 60 dinari (about 5s. in English money) each. At the same time the windows of the local German Tourist Agency were broken and it had to be guarded by police. Meanwhile more than half the Frankists, who had been very much shaken by the disappearance of Austria, expressed their wish to be identified with Maček after all.

Conversations now began in earnest between M. Cvetković and Dr. Maček, and Italy's seizure of Albania on April 7th made the Belgrade Government all the more anxious to arrive at a settlement. War might after all, were one never so careful, be round any corner now, and it was vital to weaken the position of the most separatist Croats; the latter had long declared that what they needed was a war for they

would know how to fire at the Serbs once they had
arms. People of this kind now said that even the
Serb opposition only wanted Maček in office so as to
be sure of Croat loyalty in war-time. The Serb democrats meanwhile suspected M. Cvetković of working
to break up the United Opposition by his offers to
Maček. A marvellous opportunity had arisen, however, of using the hour of national danger to bring
about a real Serb-Croat reconciliation backed by all
the finest instincts of both peoples, which, in spite of
Munich, looked to the Western Powers with more
affection and less incredulity than did the Roumanians.
The danger to Axis policy was proportionally great,
and, while Western diplomacy looked helplessly on,
there were plenty of signs of the mobilization of
German influence to intimidate Prince Paul and to
press the Croats to make impossible demands; it will
later be seen that economic and German minority
pressure were in full play, too, to darken the hope of
Yugoslav consolidation.

A Maček Cabinet, certainly, would have left little
power in the hands of Prince Paul whom its members
might tend to regard as a snob and an idler with too
much money to spend on works of art, and it was easy
to whisper at Court that one might as well appoint a
Ministry of Bolsheviks. Diplomatic pressure was also
brought to bear upon the Yugoslav Foreign Minister,
when he visited Venice later in April, to the effect that
Yugoslavia's only hope was to make friends with
Hungary and Bulgaria and divert their appetite
towards Roumania—complete treachery, in fact, to the
Balkan Entente. No doubt the Prince Regent had the
same advice tendered to him with greater emphasis

when he visited Berlin in June. With the Croats, it has been seen, the Germans had lost ground since Prague, and, in spite of the pro-Axis censorship of the press, the Slovak example was no longer good bait. But centuries on the defensive had given the Croats—even the best of them—a narrowly nationalist point of view, and only a little pressure from outside upon the Croat Peasant Party's more separatist elements, whose sentences sometimes had an oddly Nazi twist, might react fairly strongly upon Maček at this moment. Coming from pro-Maček Belgrade to Zagreb in April there was something grotesquely unpleasant about finding supporters of Maček, who assured one that the Pan-Serb spirit was unrepentant and must be resisted to the last, for had not the Serbs always boasted that they would gladly have murdered Radić six times if necessary? And though the Frankists had mostly recanted, in Croatia, as throughout the ex-Habsburg Empire since Vienna had come under Hitler, it was easy here and there to stimulate an attitude of, "Well, wouldn't it be quite a good thing to be attached to Germany—wouldn't it be much the same as the pre-war state of affairs?" If the negotiations with the Serbs should fail, the Serbs would be branded as quite impossible this time, and the idea of association with a large and powerful Empire to the north could be relied upon to thrive.

The Croat leaders had all along demanded a full federal status in which Croatia should be completely autonomous; she would accept as institutions in common with the Serbs only the dynasty, the Foreign Office and the Ministry of Defence. Even finance was to be entirely apart except for the expenses of the three common institutions; in serving in the Army in future the Croat recruits were to be kept in Croatia. To this programme M. Cvetković agreed in principle. It then became necessary to draw the frontiers within which Croatia was to enjoy this extensive autonomy— until this was done Dr. Maček would not consider taking office, though he contemplated a coalition Government after that in conjunction with the various groups of Serb oppositionals. The frontier proposals Dr. Maček laid before M. Cvetković when the latter saw him in Zagreb on April 17th, were as follows:— Either a historical or a racial demarcation was demanded. If the historic criterion were chosen by the Serb negotiators the Croats would expect Croatia to be what Radić had claimed, the old Croat Kingdom of Croatia, Slavonia and Dalmatia stretching down to Kotor on the coast and to Zemun just across the Sava from Belgrade, and Bosnia like Slovenia would itself become a similar autonomous unit in the new Yugoslav Federation. If, on the other hand, M. Cvetković preferred the racial principle the Croats would drop the Zemun idea but demand the division of Bosnia between themselves and the Serbs. These demands, though in a sense reasonable, were as if directly inspired by somebody's malice. The Bosnians would almost certainly prefer autonomy, but the most conciliatory Serb would feel it to be grotesque that Zemun, whose population has always been Serb and which has more and more become an industrial suburb [1] of Belgrade, should cease to be Serbia; in pre-war days the Austro-Hungarian frontier officials at Zemun were bitterly resented when Belgrade was nothing but an over-

[1] There is an important aeroplane factory at Zemun.

grown village. But to propose the division of Bosnia with its confusion of race and its expanding mineral wealth raised a forest of difficulties. On April 27th it was nevertheless agreed between M. Cvetković and Dr. Maček that plebiscites should be held in Bosnia and in Syrmia—the district around Zemun—while the question of Kotor was to remain open. But this undertaking failed to receive confirmation in Belgrade, and on May 8th, when the Croats held their National Assembly in Zagreb, by stating that there was no difficulty between the Serb and the Croat peoples, Dr. Maček threw the blame directly upon the Prince Regent for the deadlock which seemed to have arisen. The times were troubled and the holding of plebiscites a tricky expedient, but the issue deserved that great risks be taken. The Western Powers, certainly, can only have desired Serbo-Croat reconciliation, but it was to Berlin that Prince Paul paid a State visit in June. If foreign influences were to blame, it can only be supposed that while German intrigue had pushed Croatia's terms up, German advice must inevitably have condemned an agreement which would bring a democrat like Dr. Maček into office—indeed a Maček Cabinet would probably be regarded as an affront to the Axis. The Serbo-Croat conversations, so vital to all Yugoslavs alike, were thus allowed to remain barren month after month, though at the time of the celebration of Dr. Maček's fiftieth birthday on July 16th it was hinted that agreement might yet be in sight. This birthday celebration in Zagreb was made particularly impressive by the active participation of the Archbishop,[1] who thereby identified the Church with

[1] *Times*, July 16th, 1939.

the Croat Peasant Party and emphasized Croatian unity.

Before considering the problems of Slovenia and the Voivodina, which economic circumstances and the presence of a German and Hungarian minority make particularly relevant to the theme of undeclared war, it may be as well to take up and dispose briefly of the difficulties facing the Serbs in the southern portion of their Kingdom. Though Italian influence was paramount in Albania before Good Friday 1939, the direct administrative hold upon that country which the Italians have now grasped materially increases their ability to disturb the *status quo* and loosen the Balkan Entente through propaganda and intrigue; there was talk at once of the drive they could now direct along the Tirana-Skoplje-Sofia line. It was unpleasant for Yugoslavia to be more definitely shut into the Adriatic with the Albanian ports belonging directly to Italy.[1] Her own half-million Albanian subjects were indignant, at first, against Italy's action, but they had enjoyed little enough consideration in the twenty post-war years and were by no means deaf to Italian suggestion. "There is a certain attraction about unification with Albania, even if it is only under another foreign despotism."[2] It was not, however, about Albanians that Yugoslavia felt primarily concerned. But "Tirana-Skoplje-Sofia" raised the Macedonian issue and the whole question of Serb-Bulgar relations.

[1] The Yugoslav Government was suspected by its subjects of all but conniving at Italy's invasion of Albania ; it certainly allowed one Yugoslav newspaper to accuse the Albanians of constituting a danger to Yugoslavia.

[2] See Hugh Seton-Watson, " Yugoslavia and the Axis," *Spectator*, June 16th, 1939. This Albanian reaction will be found to have its counterpart in Slovenia, see below, p. 142.

The Macedonians are generally regarded as a separate racial entity though their blood and their dialects have undoubtedly absorbed various Bulgar, Serb, Greek and Turkish admixtures. They are admitted to be closer to the Bulgars than the others, and until 1934 their Internal Macedonian Revolutionary Organization (the I.M.R.O.) [1] was frankly encouraged by Sofia against Belgrade. The Bulgars still dream of the San Stefano frontiers drawn for them by Russia in 1878, according to which Macedonia would be theirs. But the Congress of Berlin tore up the projected Treaty of San Stefano, and at the end of the Great War the heart of Macedonia was left in Serbian hands, the Serbs claiming the valley of the Vardar as a vital necessity. For years to follow the Serb authorities did their best to beat the Macedonians into good Serbs, while the Bulgarian Government provided encouragement and refuge for those Macedonians whose resistance was not worn down; the Serb-Bulgar frontier was usually closed between 1926 and 1933. Incidentally the Macedonian revolutionaries were just as remorseless as the Serb gendarmerie— each seemed to justify the brutality of the other. But in spite of this feud between the Belgrade and Sofia regimes, the Serb and Bulgar peasantry could never be cured of a deep sentimental attachment the one for the other, based upon their common southern Slav blood and Orthodox religion and the feeling they had of a common social interest. This sentiment had been represented in the years immediately after the war by the Bulgarian "Peasant Dictator," M. Stambulisky, who, with people like Štepan Radić, dreamt of the

---

[1] Founded in 1893 to free Macedonia from Turkey. See above, p. 112.

organization of the Balkans into a great federation of co-operative peasant communities freed from the tyranny of middleman exploitation; this was the goal of Stambulisky's "Green International." Though the conception of a Serb-Buglar Southern Slavia seemed actually more feasible than a Serb-Croat one, military and Macedonian influences brought about the murder of Stambulisky in 1923 and the reversal of his policy. It is remarkable how the peasants, Serbs as well as Bulgars, still cling to his memory.

During 1933 the King of Yugoslavia, uneasy perhaps over the obstinate refusal of the Croats and Macedonians to become Serbs, and over Italy's active encouragement to both of them, made gestures of friendship to Sofia. The practical outcome proved to be that the Bulgarian Government in the course of 1934 dropped the Macedonian revolutionaries, and their leader, Mihailoff, was driven into exile. Against the pro-Serb feeling of the peasants, nevertheless the revisionism of more chauvinist Bulgar circles still weighed heavily, and the more Italy supported Hungary's claims, the more Bulgarian revisionists looked to her too. Thus, in spite of King Boris' marked response to King Alexander, Italian influence was able to keep Bulgaria as well as Albania out of the Balkan Pact of February 1934; this pact, which had been intended to give expression to the slogan "The Balkans for the Balkan peoples," and to convey a warning to the still relatively embryonic Nazi expansionism of those days, was in this way robbed of its efficacy, for it now appeared as merely anti-revisionist. Already, unconsciously, Italy was working for Germany, and the improvement in the relations between Belgrade and Sofia in 1937 and in 1938 merely made it easier for Dr. Stojadinović to betray the Little Entente.

Bulgaria, small, weak and far away, with its over 80 per cent. peasant population of apparently incurably Slavonic and democratic sentiment, without a German minority or important mineral resources, might have seemed uninteresting from the German expansionist point of view. But thoroughness forbade the Nazis to ignore revisionism in Bulgaria, for this ambition demanded a return to the treaty dictated by Germany herself in Bucharest in 1918; it could make the Bulgarians a disturbing factor and minimize the security of each of the members of the Balkan Entente. It had happened, also, that when Bulgaria's foreign trade (such as it had been) was almost wiped out in 1933 by the world depression, her commercial relations with Germany were the thing that saved her. From that time on Bulgar-German trade developed prodigiously and became a factor which could not be neglected. Further, if there was no German minority as an outpost of Nazi Empire, Professor Tsankoff, the man who had succeeded Stambulisky as Premier in 1923, became the leader of a violently revisionist and pro-Nazi group known as the National and Social Movement. The Tsankoff people were exceedingly active in 1935 and 1936, and although they obviously failed to win over the Bulgarian people, they have usually been represented in recent Bulgarian Cabinets. Nor did it go unconsidered in Axis policy that King Boris was a Coburg whose father lived in Germany while Italy had provided his wife.

In July 1938 a friendly treaty was arrived at between

Bulgaria and the Balkan Entente, and the latter agreed that Bulgaria's right to rearm, like that of Hungary, should be accepted; it was hoped that if the Axis Powers had broken the Little Entente, the Balkan Entente, at any rate, had demonstrated its solidity and its realism. But the Munich Agreement and the Belvedere Award inevitably relit the fires of Bulgarian territorial desire, and tremendous revisionist gatherings took place to protest against the maintenance of the Treaty of Neuilly. Axis policy now crystallized upon the usual principle of "defeat your enemies by dividing them and crushing one at a time." The plan then revealed itself in spring 1939. German action in Bohemia created disturbance and anxiety; Italy seized the opportunity to occupy Albania. Yugoslavia found herself in a tight Adriatic corner with the Croat problem ripe for solution yet unsolved. It was of first-rate importance to Germany, if not to Italy, to keep the Croats rebellious and therefore the Slovenes in anxious isolation. The weakness of the Balkan Entente was the absolute lack of popular consciousness of a common Balkan interest, both among the Roumanians and among the Yugoslavs—the Yugoslavs had Pan-Slav feeling for the Bulgars and also for the Russians of whom the Roumanians were still so much afraid. It was possible then for the Axis Powers to press the Yugoslav Government, nervous before the large demands from Croatia and Dr. Maček's new popularity among Serbs, to see an alternative in a *rapprochement* with Bulgaria—let Serb-Bulgar enthusiasm compete with the United Serbo-Croat Opposition idea. The Bulgarian revisionists could apparently now be persuaded to shut their eyes to Macedonia and look only for satisfaction from Roumania in Dobrogea (Dobruja), and the Beliţa incident in May conveniently accentuated the tension between Sofia and Bucharest. The seduction of the Yugoslav Government went so far that it felt constrained to show signs of regarding the Anglo-Turkish Pact as irreconcilable with that of the Balkan Entente. It seemed possible that the coincidence of the Serbo-Croat *impasse* with the Italian seizure of Albania would achieve the disintegration of the Balkan Entente—after all, if Yugoslavia resisted the pressure of the Axis, a Tirana-Skoplje-Sofia drive could now in reality revive the whole Macedonian question. This was an efficacious threat, and it was observed that "When Yugoslav students visited Sofia for the university jubilee celebrations and joined Bulgars in singing the Pan-Slav hymn 'Hei Slaviani,' bands of young men usually supposed to be Fascists spoiled the occasion by singing Macedonian laments." [1] It was all the more unfortunate that the Belgrade Government had now adopted a policy of putting Macedonian Fascists encouraged from Italy, where Mihailoff had gone, into administrative positions.[2] Meanwhile Macedonian democrats, who wished to bring Macedonia into a democratic Southern Slav Federation with their Serb and Bulgar brothers, were persecuted by the Yugoslav authorities in just the same spirit as they persecuted the democratic pro-Maček Serbs.

Whatever may become of Bosnia and the Voivodina, it is taken for granted that Slovenia, the northern

---

[1] See *Times*, June 12th, 1939, "The Key to the Balkans." The writer strongly emphasizes the pro-Yugoslav feeling of the Bulgars.

[2] See Hugh Seton-Watson, *ibid*.

province of the Triune Kingdom of Serbs, Croats and
Slovenes established after the war, will enjoy the same
status as Croatia, if a future Yugoslav Federal State, in
spite of every obstacle, should yet be evolved. About
a million Slovenes live in Slovenia very neatly, so to
speak, for they are not entangled with other racial
groups to any extent. On the other hand, nearly half
a million Slovenes live in Italy (together with one or
two hundred thousand Croats), and in what was
Austria, and the Slovenes of Yugoslavia are intensely
conscious of the miserable status they enjoy. It seems
that no Italian promises made since the Stojadinović
rapprochement have been put into practice. As for the
Slovenes in Carinthia, who are estimated by Ljubljana
at about 80,000, there is much feeling against the
National Socialist attitude of virtually denying their
existence. At the time of the German census on May
17th, 1939, the authorities and the press informed the
Slovene population that even if they did talk an
indigenous Wend dialect—the Slovene language is
disposed of in this way—they spoke German too,
and should therefore register as German.

The Slovenes in general make the impression of an
unheroic, very sensible people. Their language, as
much as their history, divides them from the Croats
and the Serbs, whose common language history has
not been able to undo. Under long years of Austrian
rule the Slovenes never lost their South Slav identity,
but they learnt to adapt themselves to their own
numerical inferiority and to make the most of the
quarrels between Germans and Italians. They also
learnt to use every educational opportunity. Today
with their many bookshops they make the impression

of being a genuinely educated community; they are, at the same time, the most highly industrialized section of Yugoslavia. While the Serb and Croat populations are still about 80 per cent. agricultural, only 60 per cent. of the Slovenes live by agriculture. The Slovene Clerical Party, which was the backbone of Slovene nationalism before the war, is still politically dominant, though the industrial workers have recently contributed to an accession of strength to the Anti-Clericals. As between the Serbs and Croats, the Slovenes, profiting perhaps by their pre-war experience, turned the situation to advantage until their own position was revolutionized by the German conquest of Austria. Partly, of course, their geographical position before 1938 made it easy for them to keep in the background, but also it was true that where the Croats discovered and almost multiplied difficulties, the Slovenes just as naturally made little of them, and profited by the administrative and political experience they had acquired in old Austria, qualifications of which Belgrade was by no means sorry to make use. Indeed it has become a stock complaint, in Croatia particularly, that "the Slovenes are our Jews for they have all the jobs"; in Serbia, too, of late, the Slovenes have become unpopular, partly because of the dislike felt towards Dr. Stojadinović's Minister of the Interior, the Clerical Slovene, Father Korošec. The vitality of legend is well illustrated, however, by the constantly repeated assertion that the Slovenes have all the jobs, for it turns out to have little foundation in fact, if one examines the statistical evidence. Of the 656 Ministers who held office between 1919 and 1938, only 49 were Slovenes, i.e. almost exactly the number which popula-

tion proportions would dictate; it is true that there
were 452 Serbs in this number and only 137 Croats, of
whom Croat patriots reject 111 as renegades or
members of parties or groups which were willing to
co-operate with Belgrade. Early this year, out of
Yugoslavia's highest judges 8 were Serb, 2 Croat and
2 Slovene, while of the 170 generals, 167 were Serbs,
2 Croats and 1 Slovene, the feeling in the Army
against senior officers with Habsburg social traditions
being very strong. The Slovenes, on their side, have
not been without grievances against the Yugoslav
State. They have complained of the taxes they pay to
Belgrade and that they have been left without enough
money to make up their own Ljubljana streets. And,
of course, they have grumbled a little about the
"primitive" Serbs. Yet in view of the justice of such
and similar complaints, it was extraordinary how little
one heard of them before Germany had got the
undeclared war well under way.

To no people in Europe did the formation of the
Rome-Berlin Axis in 1936 and its corollary, the
German absorption of Austria, bring such a complete,
immediate and disagreeable change as to the Slovenes.
The two-thirds of their nation which lived in a
Southern Slav State more or less of their own choosing
were now wedged tightly between the two Great
Powers, collaborators in aggression, who ruled the
rest of the Slovenes. Further, once Austria was Nazi
the Nazis were full of plans for the "reclamation" of
all old Austria too, for among its various aspects the
Third Reich, it has been seen, claimed to have stepped
into the mantle of both Holy Roman Empire and of
Dual Monarchy at once. North-east Slovenia, in fact,

consisted of a portion of the old Austrian province of Styria, and this the Styrian Nazis intended to restore to the authority of their capital of Graz without the delay that other reclamations might necessitate; thus Slovenia from February 1938 was a scene of increasing agitation. Many of the young Slovenes were passionately eager to resist the German advance and followed Serb-Croat negotiations in 1939 with full realization that their very survival was at stake; the federal status which Slovenes and Croats were alike to enjoy would involve far less change in Slovenia where, partly on account of the language, the officials were mostly Slovenes already. It was interesting, however, that many older people now seemed to become more aware that the Serbs tyrannized over them and were without "Kultur." After Prague and Tirana had fallen the Slovene peasants wondered rather uneasily whether "this one" would come or "that one," preferring a little superstitiously not to mention Hitler or Mussolini. In their unheroic way some of them, and people in the towns too, wondered whether it might not be quite satisfactory to become part of the Great German Reich—after all they too repeated, in a slightly rehearsed way, it would not be so different from the prosperous old days before 1914. There were even others, a little more aware of the nature of the German danger, who whispered to one another that it might be as well, if changes were coming, to come under Italy because with over one and a half million Slovenes under his rule Mussolini, they flattered themselves, would be compelled to grant them autonomy; it was not unlike the Albanians' idea.[1]

[1] See above, p. 133.

(b) *The Minority Aspect*

The German minority in Yugoslavia as a whole numbers just over half a million, but relatively few of them live in Slovenia, whose population, for this part of Europe, has been seen to be unusually homogeneous. Although the Yugoslav estimate of the Germans in Slovenia is only 29,000, the German figure differs by a good deal more than the normal discrepancy between rival statisticians. This can be explained by the relatively high number of Slovenes who before 1914 found it convenient to accept Germanization—German, after all, was an enormously more useful language than Slovene, which was spoken and understood by so few people even among the Slavs. Nazi propagandists now find it extremely satisfactory to reclaim the Germanized Slovenes and to feed them with stories of the marvellous employment conditions in their true Motherland, Hitler's Great Germany. The actually small German groups in Slovenia—if racial criteria be preserved—have thus become an important asset in the circumstances, and the wealth still retained in their hands, owing to the status of the Germans as the ruling class in old Austria, adds to their "White War" value. Geographically, also, Slovenia lies on the German road to Trieste. It is therefore not surprising that the staff of the German Consulate in the Slovene capital Ljubljana (Laibach) has been expanding rapidly, and that early in 1939 it had been found necessary that it should establish a branch office (*Zweigstelle*) at Maribor near the German frontier. Pre-war Maribor (Marburg) made a German impression, and many of the elder

Slovenes here are of the ambiguous Germanized type. It was especially interesting to find that some of the important visitors to the Maribor *Zweigstelle* in spring 1939 were old collaborators of Henlein from the Eger headquarters of the old *Sudetendeutsche Partei*, men who were expert in Nazi intimidation in mixed frontier districts.

That some Slovene opinion is well aware of the Nazi drive and resents it has been illustrated by minor incidents of one kind or another. In September 1938 the windows of M. Miklič's hotel, the Metropol, opposite Ljubljana station, were broken, since the Metropol is known to be a Nazi headquarters, an easy gathering-place for the crowds of German tourists, genuine and otherwise, who swarm to the mountains of Slovenia. Soon after the German invasion of Bohemia, one Sunday about Easter-time 1939, the mainly German inhabitants of the small Yugoslav frontier town Apačo (Abstall) decided to celebrate the triumphs of Germany with an enthusiastically white-stockinged demonstration. As so often happened in pre-Munich Czech days, the police were instructed not to interfere since the Great Neighbour might feel provoked. On the following Sunday an attempt was made to repeat the demonstration. What was the surprise of the demonstrators when they found themselves attacked and beaten off the streets by apparently ordinary people who also spoke German: again the police were ordered not to interfere. Although the story of the second Sunday in Apačo was passed round with great satisfaction in anti-Nazi circles, the very much more serious result of Germany's new position after Prague was her request to the Slovene authorities to sanction the opening of about thirty new branches of the German *Kulturbund*[1] in Slovenia alone. These cultural organizations, which busy themselves with the circulation of German books, periodicals and newspapers, all, of course, vigorously expressing the Nazi, the only true German, point of view, and expounding the theories of Germany's vital necessities and her historic mission to rule (together with her peaceful intentions), provide a particularly effective method of influencing the Slovenes, whose older generations lived in a predominantly German state; even the younger generations, who have grown up so near to Austrian Styria, are relatively susceptible to *Kulturbund* pressure. Apart from Maribor and a frontier townlet or so, the Germans in Slovenia are only numerous in the district of Kočevje in the south, and for the thirty thousand Germans alone all this cultural organization would seem to be on a very vast scale. These Germans who, until recently at any rate, were only found in the towns in Slovenia, would not count for very much as a racial group were it not for the direct stimulus emanating from adjacent Austrian Styria which has always been aggressively German and makes their 100 per cent. Nazification a matter of course.

It is in the Voivodina and Croatia-Slavonia (including Syrmia) that the German population is considerable in itself, and, especially in the Voivodina, consists largely of Swabian peasants settled on the land.[2] The Voivodina, together with the Roumanian Banat, comprises an area recovered by the Habsburgs

---

[1] See below, p. 147.

[2] These are a different stock from the Germans in Northern Slovenia, who are Styrians claiming Bavarian descent.

from the Turks in the late seventeenth and early eighteenth century, and deliberately colonized in a multi-racial way, part of it being organized as a Military Frontier against Turkey until about 1870. The Austrian Emperor gradually handed these territories over to the Hungarian authorities; with the Compromise of 1867 this process was virtually completed. Thus Magyar settlers only arrived in the nineteenth century and were regarded as newcomers by the Germans, Roumanians and Serbs whose fathers had founded the eighteenth-century settlements. In the Voivodina territory, which was included in Yugoslavia in 1919, the population was composed approximately as follows:—

491,000 Serbs,
113,000 Croats,
385,000 Hungarians,
314,000 Germans,

together with 87,000 Roumanians, 63,000 Czechs and Slovaks and various other smaller groups (Census figures 1931). Novi Sad (Neusatz) on the Danube was a great cultural centre for the Prečani Serbs in pre-war Hungary; it was also a centre of German life. In the new Yugoslavia about 110,000 Germans in Croatia-Slavonia were only divided from the Voivodina by the Danube, indeed they mostly lived along its right bank. Thus the major German grouping in Yugoslavia consists of these, say, 425,000 people living along the banks of the Danube and the Theiss (Tisza); besides this there are only some 15,000 in Bosnia to make up the total Yugoslav computation.

In the early days the minorities in Yugoslavia undoubtedly had a rough time, though the Croats would claim that conditions were as bad for them, and for Macedonians they were unquestionably worse; as in Roumania the Germans were better off than the Hungarians, and if an ex-Magyar could not discover a true Yugoslav heart beating in his breast it was better to discover a German one. The Germans started a *Schwäbisch-deutscher Kulturbund* at Novi Sad in 1920; for a time the Serb authorities took exception to it but it was reopened in 1931 by arrangement with the King-Dictator, and from that time onwards the Germans of Novi Sad showed a knack for siding with dictatorship, and the German candidates for the Skupština always stood as supporters of the Belgrade regime. As in Roumania, the National Socialist Revolution in Germany split the German ranks in the Voivodina and Slavonia between the young and the old. The *Kulturbund* leaders showed a cautious conservatism in both social and religious questions, while the younger and wilder spirits complained that they only wanted to cling to their authority, having failed to appreciate the revolutionary meaning of the Nazi message. A young man named Awender started a Regeneration Movement (*Erneuerungsbewegung*), and in 1934 another "young" group seceded from the central *Kulturbund* to form the *Kultur- und Wohlfahrtsvereinigung des deutschen Slawoniens*, known mercifully as the K.W.V.D. This new organization was led by a retired officer in Osijek named Altgayer, who had always counted as Croatian in the past; he now found it necessary to abandon his Croat Christian name Branimir, and proceeded to sign himself Siegfried, and it was not long before he became a guest of honour at the Nazi Party Rally at Nürnberg.

In spite of youthful protest and the considerable success of the Altgayer movement, the old *Kulturbund* remained the centre of German minority life and the chief among the distributing centres used by the propagandists who streamed in from the Reich after 1933. The mountains of Slovenia and the coast of Dalmatia made Yugoslavia a more attractive country than Roumania for patriotic German tourists,[1] who combined pleasure with propaganda and an interest in *Auslandsdeutschtum*. One of the more remarkable but none the less frequent ironies of Nazi propaganda in Yugoslavia, as elsewhere, has been the enthusiastic applause provided for this anti-Christian tornado by members of both the Catholic and Protestant clergy. The most flagrant cases have usually been those of priests of German origin. Out of numerous examples that of the village priest of Bogdanovici near Vukovar may be cited, a Franciscan of German descent. His flock was only about one-quarter German but he took to celebrating mass in German, and finally enraged his Croat parishioners to such an extent that they drove him away. There was another strange case of a Protestant Pastor named Strumberger at Slavonian Brod; he was condemned in court for striking children who dared to answer in Croat during the religious instruction he gave them. And though true Lutherans in Germany itself were soon persecuted by the Hitlerist regime, Dr. Popp, the Protestant Bishop of Yugoslavia, was an enthusiastic visitor to Hitler's puppet Bishop-in-chief, Ludwig Müller, in 1934.

Through the *Kulturbund*, and in a lesser degree

[1] There were also more currency facilities for German visitors to Yugoslavia.

through the K.W.V.D. and all available organizations, the German minority was inflamed in Yugoslavia as in Czechoslovakia, Roumania and everywhere else; it was stimulated by revived German folk-songs, peasant costumes, folklore and the rest, by the "right" books in more and more libraries, by listening-in to the Reich-German wireless and so on, from a revived German consciousness into imperialistic Pan-German-ism. It is not without interest that Herr Bürckel himself brought the greetings of the Palatinate to Novi Sad in 1935, after his success in the Saar, but before his Austrian career. During 1937 the *Kulturbund*, which was itself on the defensive towards the "young" organizations, increased its membership by about 22 per cent. to 75,000. At the end of that year it controlled 143 libraries carefully purged of literature which might not be sufficiently Nazi, and amply supplied with all the new stuff. In this way or that the German minority was primed with instruction about the civilizing rôle of the Germans and the German Empire in the south-east, and its enthusiasm worked up for the Mother Country, which was strong enough to-day to demand not merely rights but privileges for its members, so that they should the more easily carry the Nordic Man's Burden. It became the job of the German minority to keep Yugoslavia straight, and they had instructions to support Dr. Stojadinović in his task of "regenerating" his country in return for which his indulgence towards them was sure to be complete. The German newspapers now led the pro-Axis press campaign, and, being in a language which many Yugoslavs could read, had potentially great influence, although, of course, no amount of journalistic admiration expressed for Nazi Germany has yet been able to convert most Yugoslavs to the German point of view. For all German propaganda unlimited funds were, as ever, available, and while the German Legation in Belgrade went through the usual process of *Gleichschaltung*, it was the German Consul-General, Herr Neuhausen,[1] also at the head of the German Tourist Office, who appeared to be the most powerful link between Nazi Germany, Yugoslavia and its German minority. He represents various German business houses as well as the German State Railways and *Lufthansa*, while the *Dresdner Bank* works in connection with his Travel Bureaux which are the centres of all German activity in Yugoslavia. Anti-Nazi circles greatly resent what they are convinced to be true, that Herr Neuhausen has successfully insisted upon the resignation of frontier and other officials in Slovenia.

While extremist Croats all but invoked Herr Hitler's aid against Herr Hitler's good friend, Dr. Stojadinović, the new German spirit involved an anti-Slav, and therefore in Slavonia, an anti-Croat campaign. The German birth-rate has been falling in the Voivodina but rising in Slavonia, and though the Germans in Slavonia have been slower to respond to the Nazi call —in 1935 they are thought to have voted solidly for Maček—they have done so at last. Positively Germanizing efforts are now being made.[2] The Germans of Slavonian Brod, for example, have now demanded that German schools be provided by the Yugoslav

---

[1] See above, p. 123.
[2] These had not been possible since before the war and then scarcely took place in Croatia.

State in every village in the district which contains
25 German children of school age.[1] The meaning of
German is liberally interpreted so that children who
know almost no German have been enrolled in Brod
itself, Vinkovci, Vukovar, Virovitica, etc.; moreover
the Yugoslav authorities will not be able to maintain
many parallel schools, so that the German demand
may often come to mean the maintenance of a German
school and nothing else. Meanwhile those Croats
who cannot be Germanized are to be despised, for
confidential instructions circulated in 1938, for instance, to the Germans in Valpovo, Ruma, Virovitica
and Garechnica, according to which the Croats are to
be regarded as half savage. Mixed marriages are therefore condemned. Among other recommendations is
one to avoid alcoholic drink but to sell it in as large
quantities as possible to the Croats; on occasion the
press of the Reich has supported an attitude of this
kind.[2] All this should be contrasted with the views
supported by the Nazis in Zagreb in the paper *Nezavismost*.[3] And while some Croat peasants have demanded
a boycott of the German minority,[4] it should not be
forgotten that if the Serbo-Croat negotiations of 1939
break down completely, the Nazis will renew their
campaign to enlist Croat indignation in support of
some project for German protection in (at first)
palatable disguise.

The events of 1938 naturally stimulated the arrog-
ance with which the Germans of Yugoslavia were

---

[1] The pre-war Austrian and post-war Czech laws which provided a school
for *forty* minority children were always considered generous.

[2] Quoted in the Croat paper *Hrvatski Dnevnik*, June 27th, 1938.

[3] See above, p. 127.

[4] e.g. the villagers of Račinovci.

being steadily imbued, and led, again as in Roumania and elsewhere, to the triumph of the out-and-out Nazi sections of the German community. After the disappearance of Austria Altgayer's K.W.V.D. declared itself to be the only National German Front; it proceeded to adopt Henlein's programme soon after his notorious speech at Karlsbad in April, and published the following demands in its paper, the *Slawonischer Volksbote*, on May 8th:—

1. Recognition of our national individuality and right to live to be expressed legally and constitutionally.

2. Recognition of our ethnic group as a legal personality.

3. The State to provide our national community with a status according to which all the problems which relate to us, national, social, economic and cultural, can be discussed and solved.

4. Recognition of the leaders of the national community as the sole qualified representatives of our national group in relation to the State and the authorities.

5. Recognition of our right to organize our people according to the national order inspired by the national ideology which is our own.

After Munich and the full accordance of these privileges to the Germans remaining in mutilated Czechoslovakia, with an almost ludicrous parallelism with German developments in Roumania, the *Kulturbund* opened its arms to the Altgayers and Awenders, and in fact allowed them to impose their programme upon it: a certain Herr Hamm has also become a prominent *Führer* in Yugoslavia now. The annexation of Bohemia, bringing nearer the promise of German East-European Empire over Slavs, encouraged these *Auslandsdeutsch* Nazis afresh.

As for the Hungarians in Yugoslavia, they number slightly less than the Germans; they, too, live mostly in the Voivodina. Until the stiffening up of the Roumanian attitude towards minorities, the Hungarian minority in Yugoslavia was probably the worst-treated group of Hungarians living outside Hungary; it, too, has lost heavily and not always justly through agrarian reform, and to-day consists mainly of landless agricultural labourers. The sufferings of a minority are, of course, irrelevant to the uses to which they will be put by the most eloquent neo-Wilsonians. Although the territorial gains of Hungary since Munich have aroused the Hungarians in Yugoslavia from something like apathy, Axis policy, in order to break the Balkan Entente, requires that Hungary, like Bulgaria, shall be reconciled with Yugoslavia in order to quarrel more forcibly with Roumania. This destroys interest in Yugoslavia's Hungarians for the present.

(c) *Economic Pressure*

Yugoslavia is another predominantly peasant State; at least three-quarters of her people depend on agriculture and forestry, and, thanks again in part to post-war agrarian reform, the land is mostly owned by small peasant farmers. Yugoslavia produces wheat and maize, timber, pigs and cattle, coal (mainly lignite) and a certain amount of copper, iron, lead, bauxite and other ores in increasing quantities. She is the most important ore-producing country in South-Eastern Europe and has long attracted Germany's interest on this account; Germany has recently imported all the bauxite she exports and has shown the greatest eagerness with regard to her iron. Until 1935, with the occasional exception of Austria, Italy was by far Yugoslavia's most important customer, sometimes buying upwards of 30 per cent. of her exports and always more than 20 per cent. The imposition of sanctions against Italy by States members of the League of Nations put an end to this situation [1] and gave Germany an easy opportunity to come to Yugoslavia's economic rescue. Already, on May 1st, 1934, Germany had made an important commercial agreement with Yugoslavia on a clearing basis. In 1936, in consequence, while Italy's imports from Yugoslavia had sunk to 3·1 per cent. of Yugoslavia's exports, Germany's had risen from 11·3 per cent. in 1932 to 18·6 per cent. in 1935 and 23·7 per cent. in 1936, bringing the total value of Yugoslavia's exports up from 4 milliard dinari in 1935 to 4·4 milliard dinari in 1936. But Germany had not been able to pay for what she bought except in not necessarily desirable German goods, so that Yugoslavia now found herself compelled to increase her imports from Germany which in 1937 indeed rose much more rapidly than her exports to Germany. Meanwhile a high level of trade with Austria was kept up, facilitated as it was by low freight

---

[1] Italy's imports from Yugoslavia would probably have diminished in any case.

charges on the Danube, while Czechoslovakia was exerting herself to give the Little Entente greater economic meaning. The consequence was that the absorption of both these countries into the Reich had put Yugoslavia into the position of sending about half all her exports to, and receiving about half all her imports from, Greater Germany.

It is almost platitudinous to refer to the metropolitan rôle played by pre-war Vienna in the economic life of South-Eastern Europe, a rôle which was only partially destroyed by the World War and which survived even the collapse of the *Oesterreichische Creditanstalt* in 1931. Though Croatia had been attached to Hungary, the banks of Zagreb, like the less important banks of Ljubljana, had been far more closely associated with Vienna than with Budapest. Thus after the war Austria's financial holdings, in Yugoslavia especially, remained considerable, and through a bank like the *Länderbank* Vienna was still the clearing-house from which Western capital was passed on to the south-east. Some of the Habsburg financial inheritance passed automatically to Czechoslovakia, and Czechoslovak investment in Yugoslavia was then greatly increased, partly as a matter of Little Entente policy, but also because Sudeten German and Czech industrialists were impelled by new tariff walls to plant their own factories across the new frontiers. It thus came about that there was a great deal of Czech capital in the Yugoslav sugar industry and in textiles in Slovenia as well as in heavy industry concerns; there was a considerable amount of Czech capital in the Trebovlje lignite mines in Slovenia, and the Aussig Chemical Company had important affiliations in Yugoslavia. In 1937 foreign investments (combined capital and credit) in Yugoslavia were as follows:—

1. France	1,056,152,687	dinari
2. Great Britain	873,636,369	,,
3. Czechoslovakia	741,237,943	,,
4. Switzerland	707,365,346	,,
7. Austria	366,186,029	,,
8. Hungary	247,064,367	,,
14. Germany	54,655,578	,,

During 1937 (and subsequently too) Germany energetically invested capital in Yugoslavia particularly in mining undertakings—indeed investments of this kind, often in the form of industrial equipment, for instance for the Yugoslav State steel-works at Zenica, helped to explain the rise in Yugoslav imports from Germany in 1937. In that year a company was formed in Berlin with a capital of 500,000 Reichsmarks to explore and buy mining properties abroad and especially in Yugoslavia. This group, which seems to have been closely connected with Dr. Schacht and the *Deutscher Wirtschaftstag*, appears to have financed the buying of the *Risanjski Rudniki* antimony mine from the French; the Germans already owned the Montania antimony mining company, and were now, therefore, involved to the extent of 25 million dinari in the working of Yugoslav antimony. Germans were already interested in gold and chrome exploitation, and now silver and lead concessions in Bosnia were acquired. Germans have also been active in boring for oil in Northern Croatia; it is thought, though information is difficult to obtain, that the borings are fairly successful. Mean-

while the French and the American-owned Standard
Electric Company was acquired by a Berlin company,
while it is of interest that Siemens have obtained the
concession for the construction of the telephone connection between Belgrade and Sofia and Belgrade and
Athens. The German motor-car *Exportgemeinschaft*
has been supplying extremely cheap cars with all kinds
of favourable terms for replacement and repair financed
by the *Dresdner Bank*; it has become increasingly
difficult for anyone in Belgrade who is unwilling to
buy a German car to find an alternative, and all mechanical fittings in Belgrade seem to be German. In
1937, also, the *I.G. Farbenindustrie* bought up two firms,
the *Jugoslavenski Serum Zavod* at Zagreb and the *Patria*
at Subotica, both producing pharmaceutical goods;
in 1939 the *I.G.* started the *Adir* company in Yugoslavia for the exploitation of non-ferrous metals. In
addition, the German nitrogen trust, Pauling, has been
considering the opening of a factory in Serbia.

All these activities involved relatively small sums,
and, of course, the transference of cash was reduced to
a minimum. The absorption of Austrian and Czech
capital in Yugoslavia by Germany, however, brought
tremendous consequences with it; the Czechs had had
nearly half a milliard dinari invested in Yugoslav
industry alone and about a quarter of a milliard of
banking capital in Yugoslavia. After March 1939 it
was calculated that the new Reich held about 1,500
million dinari in Yugoslavia and was therefore well
ahead of both France and Great Britain; the British
had increased their holdings slightly, but still neither
of the Western Powers held very much more than
one milliard dinari in the country. That Greater

Germany should control nearly a fifth of the foreign investments in Yugoslavia constitutes one of the striking results of the establishment of the German Protectorate over Bohemia and Moravia. Nor is this all, for a considerable part of Slovenian industry is in the hands of German citizens of Yugoslavia, and what they own can to-day be simply written down as a Reich German asset. The most important person concerned is Herr Westen, who owns the heavy industry of Slovenia, the foundries of Jesenice and Celje. This man is known to have strong Nazi sympathies and to be in close touch with Herr Neuhausen on the one hand and Nazi Party circles in the Reich on the other; his employees are subjected to the kind of Nazi pressure which became familiar to workmen in the factories of Aussig or Komotau in Bohemia from about 1936.

There is yet another economic use to which the German minority in Yugoslavia has been very systematically put, and which, while it relates to the direct economic interest of Germany in the country, has a peculiar significance of its own. This is the matter of the acquisition of land. It should first be observed that in the ex-Habsburg territory of Yugoslavia, particularly in Slovenia where the upper classes before the war were German or Germanized, the big landed estates belonged to Austrian aristocrats of the usual kind. Of these the Auerspergs held the widest possession in pre-war days, something like 22,500 hectares, which, though reduced to about 5,500 hectares by Yugoslavia's agrarian reform, still leaves them with extensive estates around Kočevje and also in Northern Croatia. Until at least 1938 the Auersperg family was Nazi in sympathy and in the considerable influence it exerted; there have been indications, however, that its Nazi enthusiasm may recently have waned. It is also worth noting that a number of Slovenian forests and the vineyards around Ptuj and elsewhere are in German hands, some Reich German and some minority German.

That the German minority was systematically buying up land became visible early in 1937. It had been a tenet of the Pan-Germans of old Austria that capital, but particularly land, in non-German or disputed districts, should be got into German hands; "he who has land has power," and the Germans in those days, too, organized "Defence Societies," among other things, to help their individual members to buy land which then magically turned into "sacred German soil." It is no secret that the Successor States carried out their agrarian reforms with the idea of a counter-attack in the minds of some of their administrators, but in Yugoslavia as in Roumania it was Hungarian not German land which was sometimes too freely expropriated. From about 1936 the acquisition of land by Germans, by Reich Germans but mainly by Yugoslav citizens belonging to the German minority, was most evident in Slovenia, but the Slovene authorities placed obstacles in the way. In 1938, however, leaflets appeared in German houses in Slavonia, in Osijek and the neighbourhood, with the legend "wo der deutsche Pflug zu pflügen anfängt, hört er nicht mehr auf" (Where the German plough begins to plough, it will never cease to do so), and it was noticed that Germans from the Voivodina, particularly, were buying up land in Slavonia, especially

around Vinkovci and Vukovar. In the latter district
the estates of the Eltz family were for sale, and it was
observed that Croats, offering just the same prices as
the minority Germans, were refused. In one case a
landowner, Adam Prokop of Raćinovci, bought up all
available land and resold it to small German farmers.
In other cases the co-operative organization "Agraria"
at Novi Sad or Herr Neuhausen provided the necessary
credit. Whereas in Slovenia the talk had been of buying up the road to Trieste, in Slavonia the plan was
apparently to be contiguously settled along the Danube,
the Sava and especially the Drava, which, flowing
down from German Styria via Maribor and Ptuj, could
be made into a German chain linking Styria, Carniola,
Slavonia and the Voivodina, provinces which contained the main railway lines from Vienna and Budapest
to Belgrade. The German settlements in the Danube
valley in South-west Hungary could also be regarded
as part of this strategic plan.

A good deal of anxiety was expressed by those
Serbs and Croats who were aware of the German
minority's land-buying campaign, and the Yugoslav
Government was induced to decree that transfers of
land in frontier districts required official approval. So
long as Dr. Stojadinović was in power, however, it
was felt that the official approval was bought at the
low price of a German smile. Indeed in October 1938,
when a German minority deputation led by the old
German senator, Herr Grassl, waited upon the Prime
Minister to indicate that German voters would vote
for the Government in the December elections, the
Völkischer Beobachter [1] was able to report that Dr.

---

[1] October 16th, 1938.

Stojadinović had promised to revise the decree which put restrictions upon the buying of land. If M. Cvetković's Cabinet did something to call a halt, especially in the atmosphere created by the annexation of Bohemia, the Prince Regent's visit to Berlin in June 1939 may have made resistance to this form of pre-war invasion more difficult.

The effect of the recent increase of industrial and agricultural property and activity controlled by Germany through Reich German companies or by members of the now wholly docile German minority is not unlike the probable effect of the German-Roumanian Treaty of March 23rd, 1939. It means that the exploitation of Yugoslavia's resources is more and more in Nazi hands. The employment of foreigners has hitherto been more difficult in Yugoslavia than in Roumania, as it has been necessary to prove that no Yugoslav was available for the job, but it may now be found that German companies easily furnish the proof. Thus the post-Schacht plan, which one associates with Dr. Funk's journey to the south-east round about the period of the Munich débâcle, is unfolding in Yugoslavia too. Here also the Germans, by dumping cheap industrial goods, are happy to discourage Yugoslav industry, and in 1939 the demand for a long-term, i.e. three- or six-year agreements, first put forward by Dr. Funk in Belgrade in October 1938, has been persistently heard. In the trade talks at Cologne in May 1939, however, it was still not accepted.

It was with regard to Bulgaria that Dr. Funk's journey perhaps attracted most attention. In 1933 Germany performed a really sensational economic

rescue of Bulgaria, whose exports in that year fell to
the value of 2·8 milliard leva as compared with 6·4
milliard leva in 1929, and her imports from 8·3 to 2·2
milliard leva.   But her exports to Germany in 1933
were 36 per cent. of all her exports as compared with
26 per cent. in 1932 and similar percentages in previous
years, and her imports from Germany rose to 38·2
per cent. of all her imports as compared with 22 to 26
per cent. in the previous four years.   This was the
beginning of a steady development, so that after the
disappearance of Czechoslovakia it is estimated that
Bulgaria is sending well over 60 per cent. of her exports
to Greater Germany and is receiving at least as much
from the new Reich.   But already in October 1938, in
the days following the Munich Agreement, Dr. Funk
actually proposed to Sofia a purchase of all Bulgaria's
exports for twelve years at prices fixed beforehand,
Germany to provide machinery, expert advisers and
so on, in return.   Though the suggestion was made
informally and has not as yet borne fruit, it is an
extraordinarily interesting revelation of what spiders
may offer to flies when the time seems opportune.
Bulgaria with all her tobacco has nothing like the
importance of larger and richer countries for Germany,
but she would do to try out the Funk plan, and a
German quasi-colony on the Black Sea could be put to
many uses—"already it is scarcely an exaggeration to
say that the Bulgarian currency system is under
German control." [1]

Perhaps the most efficacious of all the weapons in
Germany's economic armoury will, in the long run,

[1] See Professor Allan G. B. Fisher speaking at Chatham House, Jan. 31st,
1939—lecture printed in *International Affairs*, vol. xviii, No. 2,

prove to be the preference and currency policy she has adopted towards the south-eastern countries. It is possible that this expedient was fortuitously adopted, but it would be inconceivable that its advantages, once observed, are not being used to the full. Though its effects are bound to emerge slowly, it is in Yugoslavia that this currency policy has hitherto had the most conspicuous results. For several years now Germany has been buying Yugoslav agricultural products at prices at least 25 to 30 per cent.[1] above the world price level. The preferential offer first made in 1934, when Yugoslav agriculture appeared to be hopelessly ruined by the slump, was irresistible from the Yugoslav point of view, but for some time it was difficult to explain Germany's apparent generosity, even if reselling a certain amount of Yugoslav produce at a loss brought her in a little much-needed free exchange. Gradually, however, she has pushed up the rate of the mark in dinari—it was on this point that the Yugoslav negotiators gave way to Dr. Funk in the German-Yugoslav Agreement of October 23rd, 1938 [2]—so that the prices Germany herself is paying to Yugoslavia have been steadily reduced. The result in Yugoslavia is a gradual rise in all prices in the country. No doubt other factors contributed to a rise in 1937, but it is noteworthy that in other countries exporting agricultural produce, such as the United States, Argentine or Holland, agricultural prices fell in 1938, in the first

[1] See P. Pejčinović, *Le Dinar a-t-il une parité?* in *Service Économique Yougoslave*. Série II. Jan. 1939. No. 29.

[2] In October 1938 the Yugoslavs agreed to abandon a fluctuating mark-dinar exchange, stabilizing at 14·30 to 14·70 dinari to the mark. By January 1939, however, the mark fell back to 13·80, owing to the exhaustion of the blocked marks fund, but at Cologne, in May 1939, the Yugoslavs were persuaded to accept the 14·30 to 14·70 valuation again.

two cases below the 1936 level. In Yugoslavia, however, 1938 prices were higher than 1936 prices by 19·1 per cent.[1]

Both abroad and at home the rise in Yugoslav prices, thus primarily due to the German preferences, is having exceedingly important results of a kind which fit perfectly into the German plan. Her high prices make it difficult for Yugoslavia to sell to countries other than Germany. Already in April 1936 the Yugoslav authorities were compelled to restrict their imports from the free exchange countries because their exports to Germany brought them only goods by way of payment, goods which did not help them to pay their free exchange bills. The result of the restriction was that they bought more from Germany.[2] Already it was true, as Dr. Grdjić was to write later,[3] "Les prix terriblement tentants que l'Allemagne offre à ces pays (in South-Eastern Europe) deviennent de plus en plus fatals à l'indépendance de leur politique commerciale." Then came the events of 1938 and early 1939; with the disappearance of Austria it is calculated that Yugoslavia lost a further 300 million dinari in free exchange annually.[4] In the case of the Czechs Yugoslavia was in the spring of 1939 in their debt (in clearing terms), and by Germany's seizure of Bohemia and Moravia her own "passivity" towards Yugoslavia at the time was, roughly speaking, cancelled out. But it has been seen that from this time at least half Yugoslavia's foreign trade has been with Germany.

---

[1] P. Pejčinović, ibid.

[2] See rise of Yugoslav imports from Germany (referred to above) in 1937 ; these also coincided with the first rush of German investment.

[3] See Affaires Danubiennes, Mars 1939, No. 3.

[4] See P. Pejčinović, ibid.

In this way she is more and more identified with Germany's economic system, with the high prices of the Reich and concealed inflation, and she is therefore increasingly cut off from freer world trade. Germany, by the way, according to current trade agreements, has hitherto been under an obligation to pay in free exchange for Yugoslav copper and one or two other products, but there is reason to suppose that this obligation is not always strictly observed.

A further disadvantage to Yugoslavia of the success of Germany in cutting her off from world markets and free exchange is the distaste felt by individual foreign investors for dividends which might have to be paid in kind. Actually British investments at Trepča slightly increased during 1938, but French and American capital tended to withdraw, and some Yugoslav economists believe that foreign (apart from German) investments are discouraged in circumstances which should otherwise be attractive to capital, the increasing value of Yugoslavia's ores, for example. As against this, political uncertainty, especially to Germany's south-east, accounts for a good deal of reticence on the part of investors to-day. Actually Yugoslavia last borrowed freely abroad in 1931, and to-day a free foreign loan would be extremely advantageous to her. There are, however, tremendous protests in the press, and wherever else German influence successfully makes itself felt, against any idea of foreign loans from the West; they are violently condemned as involving (of all things) political pressure, but they are mainly abused as *démodé* capitalism, a device by which the people makes payments for nothing to affluent greedy foreign usurers, either Jews or men imbued with Jewish ideas. German credits and investments, on the other hand, are lauded as good honest barter, and it is mostly implied that nothing so capitalistic as interest is charged or paid upon them. As a matter of fact it is extraordinarily difficult for even technical experts to check up on this kind of assertion. A German credit nowadays may involve simply the quick supply of a batch of Škoda goods; in Belgrade one heard a good deal of talk in April of a 10 milliard dinari credit from Germany to Yugoslavia, but by the time various exchanges of goods had taken place it seemed that in fact only some 3 milliard dinari worth of Škoda munitions, etc., were being delivered without delay to the Yugoslavs. Whether the goods which Yugoslavia will later send to Germany as repayment will include an amount equivalent to the payment of interest will really depend, again, on the exchange rates fixed; [1] in any case the financial calculations around barter of this kind are probably never revealed to the public, which is therefore able to believe that something pure and simple, and therefore, according to the Nordic code, something noble has occurred. When Yugoslav wheat or maize are promptly delivered to Germany, and Germany only provides the compensating goods much later, one does not seem to hear of a Yugoslav credit to Germany, though in fact forced loan would best have described several transactions of the kind. In the case of the many German investments in Yugoslav industry referred to above, it has been seen that the investment usually took the form of German industrial plant while

---

[1] This credit was later announced to have been granted for ten years at 6 per cent., see *Times*, June 14th, 1939.

the interest upon it is generally taken in the shape of the factories' produce; the Yugoslavs have not found themselves supplied with capital sums to spend as they themselves wished on their industries.

It would be inaccurate to deny that the earlier and short-run results of Germany's preferential prices for Yugoslav products proved advantageous to Yugoslavia. Agriculture was rescued, and for a time the country was better off in every way, with a noticeable improvement in the standard of life. One certainly had the impression in Belgrade towards the end of 1936 that the German aspirin which crowded old and new chemists' windows would be enough to cure all the headaches the Serbs were likely to have for a generation, but, with some exceptions, it is considered that the Germans supplied goods of reasonable quality and which were in demand. Since they wished to supplant local industry as well as to oust foreign competition, they had an interest in delivering and indeed dumping such goods. Speaking of the possibility for Germany to have charged very high prices for her industrial goods sold to Yugoslavia, Dr. Grdjić[1] wrote early in 1939, "La constatation contraire pourrait plutôt se faire, car l'Allemagne exerce une politique de dumping et met en danger, par des prix inférieurs, le niveau des prix à l'intérieur du pays (mais uniquement ceux des produits industriels). Ce fait ne paraît pas avoir été constaté uniquement sur le marché yougoslave. Cette politique coûteuse de l'Allemagne peut être interpretée différemment. Suivant les explications allemandes, elle ferait partie d'une politique à vues larges, ayant pour but de renforcer l'économie

[1] See *Affaires Danubiennes*, Mars 1939, No. 3.

des pays de l'Europe du sud-est, pour qu'à l'avenir les relations commerciales de ces pays avec l'Allemagne puissent s'effectuer à un niveau encore bien plus haut. Suivant d'autres opinions—qui à mon avis ne sont guère en contradiction avec la première—il s'agirait seulement du désir allemand de chasser les autres fournisseurs de ces marchés, pour tenir ces derniers dans une dépendance toujours plus grande." One increasingly gains the impression that, in Yugoslavia as in Hungary and Roumania, German economic policy dictates the shutting down of all but those specialized sections of the country's industry which the Germans intend to organize themselves—Slav and other non-German colonial territories must not be allowed to compete with the industrial production of Germany's own factories. That Yugoslavia, whose industry has developed very appreciably since about 1929, is as unwilling as Hungary to be de-industrialized was shown by her insistence in the German-Yugoslav Agreement of March 1937, that the proportion of agricultural to other goods exported to Germany should be maintained so that Germany should not take only agricultural produce. Since then the position has become complicated by Germany's acquisition of so considerable an interest in certain Yugoslav industries.

With every allowance for the initial advantages gained by Yugoslavia in the early days of German preferences and for the enjoyment provided by cheap German motor cars, the stage now reached in Yugoslavia is a socially painful one. It has been seen that the German preferential payments have played at least a main part in bringing about a rise in Yugoslav internal prices though there has also been a certain degree of official devaluation. If the corresponding German pressure towards the depreciation of the dinar has partially or slightly restricted the rise of Yugoslav prices expressed in other currencies on the world market, the effect upon internal prices has been doubly unfortunate. Retail prices in Belgrade in October 1938 showed an increase of 6·5 per cent. as compared with those in October 1937, and an increase of 19·9 per cent. as compared with those of October 1936. According to certain estimates the cost of living rose by 34 per cent. between January 1936 and October 1938,[1] and it has continued to rise since then.[2] There is no need to labour the social consequences; in agricultural countries like Yugoslavia where trade union organization had scarcely begun before authoritarian interference arose to ensure that its strength remain negligible, wages lag miserably behind prices. In the Balkan peninsula, where a few peasants' sons have suddenly found themselves in possession of a money-wealth whose unfamiliarity has sometimes induced in them a slightly intoxicated greed, it is particularly easy for those with an interest in social unrest to play up a rising-prices situation; they can stir smouldering indignation into flames by pointing, in these circumstances, to the corruption which undoubtedly exists here and there. The relatively long premiership of Dr. Stojadinović, with his banking connections, was a disaster from this point of view, for whether they were right or not, the Yugoslav public was increasingly convinced that he made particularly good use of all his opportunities, and that

[1] P. Pejčinovič, *ibid*.

[2] Belgrade retail prices—with 1930 as 100—rose from 94·9 in October 1938 to 97·1 in March 1939.

he reaped material reward for his Germanophil policy. The good name of Prince Paul also suffered on account of the general view that Stojadinović was "the Prince's man," the Prince had discovered him. The truth may merely be that it is indiscreet for Balkan Princes to collect Old Masters, for they provide subversive whisperers with too many chances. These same propagandists, who stir up feeling against a man like Stojadinović and pro-German diplomacy and economic policy, may, however, not be disconnected with others who are busy at court. To someone with a background half Tsarist, half British upper-class, like Prince Paul, the news of growing social unrest easily suggests "Bolshevism" and induces a readiness to suppose that friendship with the Axis Powers and imitation of their governmental technique is the best safeguard, the more when he observes the Western Powers positively courting the U.S.S.R. which has never yet been recognized in Belgrade. It is a cardinal feature of the German campaign to play everywhere upon the difficulties between Government and governed, and by alarming rulers to impel them to take unpopular measures. They then become more and more afraid of really representative Ministers, such as a Maček Cabinet would contain, and, having divorced themselves from the most useful servants they could find within their country, they are constrained to look abroad. It is evident that in such circumstances authoritarian friends seem most consoling. If by any chance a ruler like Prince Paul should think for a moment of appealing frankly to his people, the Axis Powers will have made it plain that they may feel affronted by a democratic regime where the press would be free to criticize them.   At any moment, then, they are likely to intervene and, by "restoring order," to destroy independence completely.

(d) *The Axis and the East Mediterranean*

Greece is of direct concern to National Socialist Germany even less than Bulgaria.   She is even more unproductive except for luxury products like tobacco and currants.   She has no German minority to be played up.   Nor are the Greeks Slavs.   The old tradition of German versus Slav is so powerful in Eastern Europe that wherever Slavs live the Nazis feel themselves directly concerned either to suppress and denationalize as they are doing in Bohemia or Carinthia, or to make a great show of magnanimous friendship as they did, for a time, at any rate, in the case of the Ukrainians.   Of course, heroic Greece is claimed to have been the child of a Germanic ruling caste from the North, which, however, failed to keep its blood pure and was consequently submerged, while inferior mixed races replaced it.   This easily explains the Greeks of modern Greece who, with their incorrigibly Western outlook,[1] are clearly bad material from the Nazi point of view.   It is, of course, satisfactory to Germany that Greece is ruled by a dictator like General Metaxas with markedly German tastes, and Germany has deliberately offered high prices for Greek tobacco, as she has for Roumanian and Yugoslav grain; German-Greek trade has therefore increased, but by no means to the same extent.   Of course, the extensive international trade and mercantile marine of Greece are of great potential interest to

[1] See Elizabeth Monroe, *The Mediterranean in Politics*, 1938, p. 22.

Germany, but geography combined with the Anglo-Turkish treaty prevents this interest from materializing for the present.

The naval harbours of Greece create her political importance, for their control may well be decisive in any Mediterranean conflict. It is therefore from the Italian point of view that the Axis Powers are concerned with Greece. Backed by the Anglo-Turkish Treaty, the Franco-British guarantee of April 13th to Greece became a serious "No Further" spoken to Italy after the rape of Albania; it is said that signs of extraordinary Italian activity at Rhodes spurred the Turks on to their agreement with Britain.[1] The question must now be considered of Italy's rôle in Germany's game. In 1936 Italy conquered Abyssinia at the price of becoming a German dependency. Apart from official declarations the Germans and Italians, each using a rather different tone perhaps, are more and more willing to admit this to be true. Whatever their censored newspapers may say, the Italians know that anti-Semitic legislation was forced upon them from Germany. They dislike large numbers of German officers and technicians in Italy instead of tourists from the West with money to spend. Many of them, especially those in North Italy, believe that Mussolini betrayed their interests when he condoned the German occupation of Austria. Among other things the *Anschluss* diverted nearly 200,000 tons of Austrian exports from Trieste and led to a state of affairs in which nearly 80 per cent. of the trade of that port is now under German control, and Ger-

---

[1] See W. Duranty, "The Soviet Standpoint," in the *Spectator*, May 26th, 1939.

many is about to operate a free zone there.[1]   In any
case the North Italians know perfectly well that a
Pan-German heir to the Habsburgs is almost bound to
claim Trieste for the Third German Reich some day.
Thus the usual evolution has occurred in Italy too.
Except among the very fiery young men the pro-
German policy is unpopular; the Mussolini regime is
more and more afraid to discard something which is
rapidly becoming its only strength; its pro-German
enthusiasm is therefore likely to grow.

This situation has become another trump-card in
Germany's hand as she plays it in Europe east of the
Axis.   Wherever one goes, and very markedly in
Hungary, Roumania and Yugoslavia, people assure
one that Italy is really working against Germany and
that they themselves are able to exploit this to the full.
The Hungarians have already forgotten that Italy
could not get Slovakia and Ruthenia for them in
November 1938.   Above all, the Yugoslavs are convinced that they can exploit the clash of German and
Italian interests in Slovenia and Croatia including
Dalmatia.   That this clash is real there can be no
possible doubt.   It is very probable, too, that various
signs of vigorous Italian economic activity this year,
the attempt to stimulate Italian-Yugoslav commerce
and the offer of credits by Italy to Yugoslavia,[2] are
actuated by a genuine Italian desire to stand up to the
economic majesty of the new German Empire.   It
is perfectly convenient to Germany that this should
be so.   The Yugoslavs, and the other small nations,
without being pro-Italian, hasten to accept Italy's

---

[1] See *The Economist*, "Germany Comes to Trieste," July 19th, 1939.
[2] See *Times*, June 14th, 1939.

offers in the hope of playing Italy off against Germany. But Italy, too, is a closed currency country and an economic dependency of Germany. By economic agreements with Italy the other countries cut themselves off from the free-exchange world and entangle themselves more completely in the Axis world of barter. And if at any moment Italy should betray any positively anti-German interest or feeling, Germany could immediately call her to order; it has been seen that the present Italian regime cannot afford to dispense with the only strong factor upon which it can rely. Thus whispers all over the Balkans that one should come to terms with Italy in order to beat off Germany suit Germany well; they are a means of winning anti-German support for the expansion of the new German *Mitteleuropa*. Italian racial maps have been coming out claiming about a quarter of France as Italian by race and, of course, the whole Dalmatian coast. If Italians do not take racialism very seriously they have never, since the war at least, been allowed to suppose that Dalmatia should not be theirs. Since this means trespassing upon the soil of the good "Gothic" Croats,[1] it is always possible that it will be necessary to restore order in the Adriatic too. Trieste is just as much an "old German town" as Prague; indeed Germany's policy has been admitted to be, "as it was recently—and most tactlessly—expressed at a semi-official dinner, the restitution of the *ur-deutsch* provinces of Trentino and Trieste."[2]

Early in July 1939, a few weeks after these words had been spoken, it was uneasily revealed that the

[1] See above, p. 127.
[2] See *The Economist*, "Germany over Italy," June 17th, 1939.

German-speaking population was to be removed from
the South Tyrol, or, as the Italians called it, the Alto
Adige. This German minority, transferred from
Austria to Italy after the war, lived so compactly that
ethnical frontier revision would just for once have
been easy. The South Tyrolese Germans have all
along felt intense bitterness with regard to the unquestionably bad treatment Italy has given them.
They have until now entertained a childish confidence
in Hitler as their liberator-to-be, whatever his public
pronouncements about the "eternal" Brenner frontier;
when in February 1938 the *Führer* became master of
Innsbruck, the South Tyrolese felt certain that he
would soon join the South and North Tyrol again.
It is impossible to over-emphasize the extraordinary
attachment of these peasants to the mountains and
valleys among which their ancestors have lived for so
many centuries—if ever soil was German, if ever soil
was sacred, it is here. The early mediaeval songs of
Walther von der Vogelweide are traditionally associated with Bozen (Bolzano) and the South Tyrol.
Andreas Hofer, who led the Tyrolese peasants in their
War of Independence in 1809 and was shot by the
French in Mantua the next year, came from the
Passeiertal in South Tyrol. He became the hero of all
Tyrol and a national hero of Germany, and the
Hoferlied, which Mosen wrote some twenty years after
his death, became a German household-song, with the
ringing words,

> "Da rief er aus: Gott sei mit euch,
> Mit dem verratenen deutschen Reich,
> Und mit dem Land Tirol." [1]

---

[1] Then he (Hofer) cried out, " God be with you, with betrayed Germany
and the country of Tyrol."

Hofer's country is now to become a centre of Italy's war industries, and the German-speaking population is to be driven away to Calabria, perhaps, or into Germany; foreigners have been removed first so that they shall not be witnesses of the coercion which will become necessary.

To have agreed to this evacuation is the most cynical piece of opportunism the "Blood and Soil" National Socialist leaders have yet perpetrated, a corollary to the occupation of Prague; for why should not the other German groups outside Germany be dispersed and sent back to the Reich? If the Tyrolese people north of the Brenner understand what has happened, their Nazi enthusiasm will die. No doubt Berlin and Rome have made a common-sense plan, no doubt it was time Germany gave Italy something, and it is even possible that the German Alliance will now be more popular in Italy. Whether this is so or not, Signor Mussolini and Count Ciano are likely to feel more pro-German than ever, while Germany will still be able to turn Italian intrigues in the Balkans to her own advantage; and, later, if necessary, her claim to a completely Italianized Bolzano can still be made as good as her claim to the capital of the Czechs in March 1939.

CHAPTER IV

POLES, UKRAINIANS AND BALTS

EVEN in Poland the illusion died hard that Italy could be used against Germany. In February 1939 when the Polish students, egged on by influential Army people, were demonstrating in Warsaw and elsewhere against Germany, they were ready to cheer the pro-German Italian Foreign Minister, Count Ciano. Only in the early summer of 1939 was the Polish boycott of Italian newspapers, because they had perforce taken Germany's side against Poland, established.

Until the Munich Agreement National Socialist technique appeared to prosper as well in Poland as elsewhere in Eastern Europe. In the first place Poland had a tremendous Jewish problem. Where Germany's Jews at the beginning of 1933 were usually estimated at less than 1 per cent. of her other population and were on the whole assimilated and often patriotically German in outlook, Poland has over three million Jews or about 10 per cent. of her population, massed in the towns; *qua* Jews in Poland they had a thousand years' tradition behind them, and many of them were Polish enough in sentiment but considerable numbers were by no means assimilated. Industrial wealth, as distinct from the landed wealth of the aristocracy, was, unlike that of Germany, almost exclusively in Jewish hands. It was therefore inevitable and indeed natural that the simpler chauvinists of Poland should be

177

violently anti-Semitic and ready to applaud Adolf
Hitler's treatment of the Jews and the anti-Semitic
note in all Nazi propaganda.

In the second place, Poland, like any of the three
Baltic States, was economically a new country, fresh
from foreign invasion, backward and poor. To
Poland, as to Lithuania, Latvia and Esthonia, Germany
was a tremendously important market, large and easily
reached, for agricultural, and especially for dairy,
produce and for livestock; for Finland's timber the
same thing was true; indeed, with the world depression, the German market became a matter of life and
death. When Poland and Germany made their celebrated Ten Years' Agreement of January 1934, the
path was cleared for closer economic co-operation
between Poland, Germany and Danzig, a goal at which
wiser instigators of the Treaty, such as Dr. Rauschning,
then President of the Danzig Senate, had aimed.

The German-Polish Treaty of 1934, never popular
in Germany, was regarded with some suspicion by the
Poles, but they were consoled by the fact that Marshal
Pilsudski was responsible for the reversal of policy
involved. From now on, however, the old Marshal
lost control of affairs, and his death in 1935 left the
somewhat notorious Colonels' clique as rulers of the
country. Without Pilsudski's prestige, Colonel Beck
and Colonel Koc and even Marshal Smigly-Rydż,
could do little to meet the rising discontent of the big
democratic Peasants' Party which had been banished
from power by the Pilsudski *coup* of 1926. The
Peasants' organization probably represented the main
feeling of the country; at all events it became increasingly clear that the dictatorial regime had the merest

fraction of public opinion behind it. The result, for a time, was similar to that which has been observed elsewhere. The regime clung to and fostered its German connection because it feared to be weakened in the face of its domestic enemies without it; it pointed to the generosity of Hitler in letting the "Corridor" question drop; it borrowed, where it could, from Nazi methods in muzzling the unrelenting opposition. Seriously afraid of the proximity of Communism and Russia, the Polish pseudo-dictatorship did all it could to exploit the traditional hatred of the Poles for the Russians; here, too, the Colonels found the Nazi propagandists to be ingenious and useful, and the friendship between Berlin and Warsaw was richly decked in "Salvation from Russia and Communism" catchwords.

The Polish industrial workers were Socialist rather than Communist, and the great peasant masses were anything but Bolshevik. Indeed Polish, like Roumanian, feeling was primarily against Russia, whatever her rulers might be. Though they were Slavs the Poles felt even more strongly than the Roumanians; they had always, for instance in old Austria-Hungary, been the dissident Slavs. This was mainly due to the subjection of the majority of the Poles to Russia from the late eighteenth century until the World War. The resentment between the Poles and the Russians had become more and more violent; the Poles, Western in their Roman Catholic religion, Latin script and their susceptibility to French and Italian influences, had regarded Russian rule as barbarous oppression, and, as the Tsars took more and more openly to russification, the situation became desperate. The Bolshevik invasion of Poland in 1920 had done nothing to bury the past. When the Russians were admitted to the League of Nations in 1934 the Poles, officially at any rate, took up an attitude not wholly unlike that of Germany; they stayed at Geneva, but they insisted upon renouncing their Minorities Treaties, thus repudiating in advance any future claim to international control, lest it should please Russia to ask awkward questions. Further, they followed Germany's example in making difficulties over the Barthou-Litvinoff proposals for an Eastern Pact.

Pro-German policy in Poland was strengthened at this time by a feeling of disillusionment towards France; rightly or wrongly the Poles believed the French, who had financed much of Poland's economic enterprise, including the new railway line from Katowice's industries up to Gdynia, to have behaved ungenerously towards them. When in May 1935 the Franco-Czech-Russian alliance was arranged, German propaganda reaped a rich harvest in Poland. For the Czechs, also, were something of a bugbear to the Poles. This was a legacy from old Austria, where the Czechs had always championed Slav solidarity and encountered Polish irritation as their chief difficulty apart from the hostility of the non-Slav races. In 1920 during the Russo-Polish war the Czechs had not only betrayed their sympathy for Russia by holding up munitions in transit to Poland, but in the now traditional Polish view at any rate, had exploited the situation by occupying most of the important mining and heavy industry district of the Duchy of Teschen in ex-Austrian Silesia. This area was something of a racial jungle, many of the working-people not knowing nor caring what they were and talking a mixture of Polish and Czech with a few German words thrown into it. Actually the Czech and German Tescheners together were numerically not very far short of the Poles, and the Germans here much preferred the idea of Czech rule. In November 1918 there had been a provisional agreement to divide the territory between the Poles and the Czechs. Later the Czechs did drive out the Poles from districts to which they had no very good claim, and it was then to the Czechs' advantage that the Poles were involved in conquering Eastern Galicia and that Pilsudski marched off to Kiev. It was in July 1920, just before the Poles defeated the Russians outside Warsaw in August, that the Conference of Ambassadors finally divided the Teschen territory between Poland and Czechoslovakia, giving the latter a larger share than had been indicated in 1918, both of territory and therefore of industrial wealth. Many Poles nursed an undying grievance against the first Czechoslovak Republic for this and chose to make Dr. Beneš personally responsible for their annoyance. Difficulties between Poles and Czechs were partly a matter of conflicting temperament, for, where the Poles were romantic and picturesque, the Czechs were clumsy, matter-of-fact and reliable. When the Slovaks, who, superficially at least, shared the temperament of the Poles, began to bicker with the Czechs, the Poles were full of sympathy for them, the more since the Slovak autonomists were a clerical party and Roman Catholicism so cherished an element in Polish nationalism.

The Polish Peasants, who, in spite of the highly developed industries of Warsaw, Katowice, Lódż,

Piotrków and so on, formed the big majority of the nation, did not feel any particular antipathy towards the Czechs; indeed their political leaders like M. Witos were on very friendly terms with Czech Agrarian leaders. But in the 'thirties M. Witos was in exile in Czechoslovakia and his party in bitter opposition to the Colonels' regime, which therefore played up anti-Czech feeling in order to weaken its political opponents at home. This again pushed Colonel Beck and his friends into greater dependence upon Germany and a pro-German policy. Then came the long-drawn out Czechoslovak crisis of 1937 and 1938, throughout which the Germans were able to take advantage of Polish anti-Czech chauvinism and the indignation of the Poles over the supposed sufferings of the Polish minority in Teschen (only about 80,000 people). Many Poles belonging to the democratic oppositional parties were uneasy at the policy of their government and the pro-Nazi tone of its press, but Polish intellectuals were always at pains to point out that Herr Hitler was a pre-war Austrian Pan-German naturally impelled to march into Austria and Bohemia on his way to the Balkan pensinula, and that Poland did well to encourage him to take the south-eastern route and leave her unmolested in the east and in the Baltic. Thus in Poland, too, the illusion, so helpful to the Nazis, was nursed that National Socialism had single-mindedness of purpose and was not a many-headed hydra of opportunism, and the Poles, like the Hungarians, found themselves unable to resist German encouragement to indulge their anti-Czech prejudice. In the view of many Czechs Poland's friendly attitude towards Germany during September 1938 was decisive, for it supplied the final incentive to Herr Hitler to defy the world; it also forced the Czech General Staff to abandon their intention of offering resistance to Germany, since without Polish neutrality it was sheerly suicidal for the Czechs to fight.

Once the Czech question was disposed of by the Munich Agreement, the fundamental antagonism between Poland and Germany was inevitably revealed. The first unmistakable sign of it was the Polish seizure of Bohumin (Oderberg), the important railway junction near Teschen in the industrial area near Moravská Ostrava, a strategic point which the Germans had certainly not intended should escape their own control. Then came the first period of uncertainty over Slovakia and Ruthenia when the new Polish-German conflict of interest was sharply revealed by Poland's pressure for a common frontier with Hungary. The Belvedere Award,[1] though it gave a few more towns to Hungary than the Germans had originally intended, yet represented a humiliation inflicted by Germany upon Italy, Hungary and Poland. Though March 1939 saw the Hungarians in full occupation of Ruthenia and the common frontier with Poland was in so far achieved, yet the Germans were now, to all intents and purposes, the masters of Slovakia, which meant a very disagreeable lengthening of the German-Polish frontier and a German advance to outflank and encircle the Poles along the Tatra mountain-range. Thus Czechoslovakia's destruction inevitably put an end to the diplomatic attachment between Poland and Germany, though the 1934 treaty was not actually repudiated until Herr Hitler's speech to the Reichstag on April 28th, 1939.

[1] See above, p. 21.

The post-war situation in the Baltic had also supplied National Socialist Germany with admirable gunpowder to be used when the time should seem ripe. The economic difficulties of Danzig and Memel, which had not been prosperous in the years preceding 1914, were not to blame, but, as ever, the grotesque inapplicability of the principle of self-determination to the countries on the Baltic. The peacemakers perhaps achieved their happiest compromise in the matter of Danzig, for given goodwill in the place of malevolence there was no reason why the arrangement they made should not have worked. Danzig was a city and a territory inhabited by Germans, but its position at the mouth of the Vistula gave it military control of Polish Pomorze and Poznania, and, as originally the only seaport of Poland, Danzig could control Polish export overseas. Thus if Germans were not to be coerced by Poles nor Poles by Germans a compromise was essential, and the political autonomy of Danzig with Polish control of her customs and railways and of her foreign relations seemed to meet the case if, as it was intended, the League of Nations kept such control within unaggressive limits. If, however, propagandists could obscure the strategic dependence of the Polish "Corridor" upon Danzig they could maintain with great plausibility that the Germans of Danzig had unjustly been cheated of their self-determination. Later, when Poland built Gdynia, the propagandists plausibly discovered that the justification for the Danzig arrangement had disappeared, though actually Gdynia made the "Corridor" more important to Poland, not less so, and Poland was perfectly able by now to feed two big ports.

In the complicated questions of Vilna (Wilno) and

Memel the peacemakers simply bowed to *force majeure*. The Polish, like the Lithuanian case, in the matter of Vilna, was backed by serious contentions, since the district was another area of racial confusion, and Memel-land, if the Nazi blood-test were accepted as valid, was predominantly Lithuanian by descent, though most Memel-landers wished to remain attached to East Prussia. That the Poles should seize Vilna and the Lithuanians Memel seemed to provide an easy way out, but one *fait accompli* can always be taken to justify another, and, if the Lithuanians had seized Memel in January 1923, this gave the Germans all the justification they desired for doing the same thing in March 1939, even if the Allied Powers had subsequently persuaded Lithuania to agree to an Autonomy Statute for Memel-land. In the Nazi view, the Vilna situation worked out most successfully of all, from the time of Hitler's rise to power until it was drastically resolved by the Poles in March 1938. Lithuania and Poland had had a long historic connection, Polish patriots like Pilsudski himself had been of Lithuanian descent, and the Poles, through all the eighteen years during which the Lithuanians refused to be on speaking terms with them, took up rather the attitude of an elder brother, half annoyed but half amused by the tantrums of a child. They were glad enough, nevertheless, to be on good terms with Germany from the beginning of 1934 because of the inevitable pressure exerted upon Lithuania by the Polish-German *rapprochement*, and the Lithuanians, who, like the Latvians, Esthonians and Finns, loved Russia as little as the Poles did, were constrained to be much more cautious towards Memel and Germany than they otherwise might have been. Thus the big neighbour, Germany, reaped a double advantage, rather as she did in the quarrel between Roumania and Hungary, and the Germanophil elements in Warsaw and Kaunas profited.

The questions of Danzig and Memel, while providing an aspect peculiar to these two harbour towns, merge into the whole question of German minorities in North-eastern Europe. To North Germans, as contrasted with Austrians, Germany's eastern and north-eastern, rather than her south-eastern, mission is her true imperial task, clearly traced out for her as it was in the Middle Ages. The Prussians believe in Germany's necessary march to the east to restore and expand the old mediaeval empire of the German Knights, who had established their rule far into Poland and around the Baltic until that unfortunate accident of history, the defeat of the Order by Polish and Lithuanian forces at Tannenberg in 1410. The great red-brick fourteenth-century fortress of the Knights at Marienburg typifies the Germany also of to-day. There, in the person of the Grand Master of the Order, reigned the leadership principle, and there prevailed the Spartan equality of those who obeyed him. The Teutonic Knights lived to subject the land to the east; their methods were remorseless, but they were somehow covered by the morality of the age. Just as the Nazis have vindicated their actions in the name of the modern principle of national or racial self-determination, so the Knights kept up the myth of the Crusades that they served Christianity.[1] The rise of Hohen-

[1] Cf. R. L. Buell, *Poland—Key to Europe*. "Lacking whatever idealism had originally inspired the Crusades, the Knights resorted to great brutality, regarding their campaign against the pagan Slavs as man-hunts. After reading the history of this Order, one understands the fanaticism and sadism of the German Nazis."

zollern Prussia in the seventeenth and eighteenth centuries, and above all, the career of Frederick the Great, together with the partitioning of Poland, had turned the tide of history again after Tannenberg, until the—in Prussian eyes—superfluous rehabilitation of Poland in the World War. Perhaps even more than in the south-east the Germans established beyond Germany eastwards have regarded themselves as a superior class, basing its privilege upon the heritage of the *Ordenstaat* of the Knights and their pioneer work of so-called civilization. The Baltic Barons, the Germans who remained as the landowning class in the western provinces of Tsarist Russia, expected to enjoy not merely a local prestige, but also regarded themselves as the potential civilizers of Russia. From the time of Peter the Great, or even earlier, the Russian Government had looked to Germans for technical progress, and in the years prior to 1914 the Civil and Diplomatic Service of Russia were to a considerable extent in the hands of Baltic and other Germans; this fact has been emphasized in such different books as Leon Trotzky's *History of the Russian Revolution* and Adolf Hitler's *Mein Kampf*. The position of these Germans in Russia was not unlike that of the Magyar-ized German Civil Servants in Hungary [1] and aroused a good deal of indignation in Russia, especially in Pan-Slav circles; one need hardly recall that the fall of Tsarism was partly due to resentment against the strength of German influence at the Petersburg court. The intention of National Socialist Germany to divide and rule Russia [2] is partly based upon a claim to carry on the work of the Baltic Barons; in the economic

---

[1] See above, p. 19.　　　　[2] See below, p. 223.

sphere she intends to follow up the German merchants, who probably did most to develop Russia's wealth before the war.

It would be tedious to recall in detail the effect of the establishment of a Pan-German authority in Berlin in 1933 upon all the German and partly German communities to the east and north-east, since in the main the Nazi Revolution had similar results all over Eastern Europe. At first it brought division, and especially in Danzig, the most German district of them all, it met with serious opposition; from 1936, however, the defeatist behaviour of the West combined with Colonel Beck's policy to facilitate the progressive success of the Nazis in the Free City. In districts adjacent to Germany like Danzig and Memel the Nazis were helped first by their good fortune and skill in abolishing unemployment, the news of which made a great impression, and secondly, by the intimidation they were able to practise. In districts farther away from the Reich, in Esthonia, or in Latvia where some 60,000 Germans lived mostly in Riga, the Germans did not hear so much of the disagreeable discipline imposed in the Reich, but were readier to accept romantic accounts of how splendid everything had become, and particularly enjoyed the idea that they themselves constituted, not a dissident minority in a tiny State, but the advance posts of a mighty empire, and that, as such, they had a claim to hitherto unformulated privilege.

Poland herself, apart from the 400,000 Danzigers in the north who, for tariff and diplomatic purposes, are attached to her, has a considerable German minority of her own in the "Corridor" and in Upper

Silesia, but also scattered about the whole country. The 1931 census gave 741,000 Germans in Poland. While the Germans inevitably claim more, it is safe to suppose that the number is just about three-quarters of a million; of these about 45 per cent. live outside the former German provinces and about 20 per cent. in and around the great textile centre of Lódź.[1] The Germans in Poland consist of the old Prussian land-owning class, of professional men, industrialists, technicians and industrial workers in towns like Lódź but especially in Katowice, and of fairly prosperous peasant farmers in Pomorze and Poznania but also farther to the east. Those of the Germans here who had been accustomed to Prussian rule have complained without cessation since 1919 of their subjection to the *Sau-Polaken*, and landowners like Prince Henry of Pless were particularly bitter over the Polish expropriation of portions of their estates; when the German-Polish Agreement was first signed they felt themselves to have been grievously betrayed. Actually what happened was that press hostility was called off on both sides, official personages in Berlin and Warsaw became very civil towards one another, and many Polish students and others, who were easily attracted by the ideas of determined leadership and anti-Semitism, were delighted to observe Adolf Hitler's magnanimity towards racial aspirations other than his own. But if a few less frontier incidents were recorded there was no real change in the attitude of the Poles and Germans on the spot, either on Polish territory or in East Prussia or Silesia or the *Grenzmark Posen-West Preussen*; they still regarded each other with dark suspicion. Nazi

[1] See R. L. Buell, *op. cit.*, p. 239.

propagandists seemed a little taken aback to begin with, but they soon adopted slightly more caution and continued their activities busily; for a time the V.D.A. and even the *Bund Deutscher Osten*, which existed mainly for an anti-Polish purpose, diverted their attention towards the Sudeten German question. Whatever was said by Berlin to Warsaw, there was no question but that irredentism was fervently preached; it was explained to the Germans in Poland that Hitler had only made a treaty with the Poles in order to hoodwink them until he was ready to take action and it would be wise to be on good terms with the local Nazis before then. The official friendship between the countries thus won over a section of Polish opinion to a pro-German view and facilitated Nazi propaganda among the Germans as well, partly because the anti-Nazi Germans who were reasonably loyal to Poland found themselves without protection from the Poles, while in the eyes of Berlin they had become politically pernicious and traitors to their race. The distress in the industrial district of Upper Silesia was still very great at this time, and the stories of employment in the Reich worked wonders; indeed many Polish working-men who could not speak German were persuaded to join Nazi organizations on this account, and forthwith indulged in the activities which led to the big Katowice treason trial. It thus appeared for a time as if National Socialism might be successful exploiting the German-Polish Treaty in order to undermine Polish authority throughout West Poland, the more since the Upper Silesians were followers of the Catholic democrat Korfanty, and particularly hated the Colonels. As Korfantists, however, the Upper Silesians, like the rest

of West Poland, had vivid recollections of Prussianization before the war, and they kept their heads clearer
than Croats in comparable circumstances, resisting
Warsaw primarily because Colonel Beck's policy was
pro-German. Graczynski, the Voivod of Upper
Silesia, if disliked for his centralism, was approved for
his fighting spirit towards Germany, and the Polish
Western Society, with his tacit approval, continued
activities the reverse of consistent with Polish diplomacy; early in 1937, for example, it was publicly
supporting Polish claims to further cession of German
territory. When the Geneva convention safeguarding
Upper Silesian autonomy lapsed in July 1937, Polish
feeling pushed on the Government to make the most
of the new state of affairs; it was now possible to carry
expropriation of German estates further, and to modify
provincial administrative boundaries so as to weaken
the German element. The German-Polish position in
1937 was really an absurd one. Both countries were
complaining of Czechoslovakia's treatment of their
minorities when each of them knew that the other
behaved far less correctly; in Germany the Poles were
already finding their position more and more difficult;
though they numbered something between a million
and a million and a half they were a poor population
and it was harder for them to defend themselves; as
time went on the Nazi authorities were less and less
willing to provide them with education, so that in 1938
they had only ten elementary and two secondary
schools, while the Germans in Poland had respectively
75 and 26. It was, however, an essential part of
the new German technique to crush one enemy
before falling out with the next one. The Polish

liaison must be maintained until after Czechoslovakia had been crushed. Common interests were therefore underlined, and a mutual declaration signed on November 5th, 1937; according to this, both countries abjured forcible assimilation, promised to provide enough minority schools and to guarantee perfectly free use of the minority's language in speech and writing and full freedom of association. Why could not the Czechs behave sensibly too, Poles and Germans asked at the time, though on the whole Czechoslovakia was organized in accordance with the German-Polish Declaration and Germany and Poland certainly were not. The Nazis at home, except for one or two naïf and innocent spirits, regarded a non-German minority in Germany as a dissident group which should hasten to fit into the German totalitarian State by devoutly embracing that German *Kultur* to which it so fortunately had unhampered access.

The declaration of November 1937 remained nothing but a pious aspiration of questionable sincerity. Within a year the undoing of Czechoslovakia had unmasked the relations between Germany and Poland, not merely with regard to the Germans in Poland or the Poles in Germany, but also with regard to the Ukrainian minority in Poland. Germany's attitude towards this problem is distinct from the use she makes of German minorities all over Europe. The Ukrainians in Poland, moreover, constitute only a fraction—perhaps one-seventh—of the sum-total of Ukrainians in the world. It should be worth while to examine the whole Ukrainian question in considerable detail in order to estimate its potential value in Germany's eve-of-battle campaign.

It is singularly difficult even to formulate the Ukrainian problem; it is certainly impossible to do so without some attempt to consider Ukrainian history, yet this again is made more obscure by its fragmentary nature. It is known that Eastern Slavs settled around the lower Dnieper in the sixth century; their home came to be known as Little Russia and their town of Kiev was the centre of the life of early mediaeval Russia in the ninth and tenth centuries; for this reason Russian patriots regard Little Russia as the cradle of their national civilization. Then came the Tartars and the Turks, and the greatest days of historical Poland, whose expansion not only united her with Lithuania, but with wide territories to the east inhabited by a Little Russian or what would now be called Ukrainian population. But no one, in the fifteenth century, was at all aware of a Ukrainian nationality in the modern sense. The word Ukrainian simply meant frontiersman, since *Ukraina* meant frontier, and was vaguely applied to the borderlands between Russians, Poles, Tartars and Turks after the subsidence of the mediaeval Mongolian invasions. Settlers from Volhynia, the Western Ukraine, Podlesia etc., had gradually wandered into the rich eastern—or to-day Russian—Ukraine; they came to be known as Cossacks and developed a military organization in the sixteenth century to defend the country against the Tartars; their elected assembly, the *Rada*, chose their Hetman or chief.

During the seventeenth century Poland was constantly at war with the Princes of Moscow, around which city a new Russian State had developed. In

1654 the Cossack chief or Hetman seceded to the Moscovite Tsar, but in 1667 Poland and Russia divided the Cossack territory between them, taking the Dnieper as frontier; a Cossack Hetman still officiated east of that river. The rise of Peter the Great followed the earlier signs of chaotic devolution in Poland, which, already in 1676, in spite of the military prowess of the heroic John Sobieski, was forced by the Peace of Zurawno to abandon some of the Ukraine west of the Dnieper to the Turks. When Peter defeated Charles XII of Sweden at Poltava in 1709, he not only dealt severe blows at Sweden, Poland and Turkey, he also defeated Charles' ally, the Cossack Hetman, Mazeppa, and in 1710 in consequence the Cossack community east of the Dnieper accepted Russian rule; Catherine the Great later did away with Cossack autonomy. With the partitioning of Poland in the late eighteenth century many of her Little Russian or Ukrainian subjects were annexed by Russia. Since 1596 Poland had been forcing the Orthodox Little Russians to join the Uniate Church, but Polish fanatics were not satisfied with the retention of the Russian rite and Cyrillic script which this allowed. One of Catherine the Great's justifications for invading and seizing Polish territory was indeed the religious persecution of the Little Russian peasants by the Poles. With Galicia Austria at this time also acquired a mainly Little Russian population around Lwów (Lemberg), adjacent to the Ruthenian territory of Hungary, and to the Bukovina which Joseph II had acquired in 1775. Thus from 1815 onwards the big majority of Little Russians or Ukrainians were united under Romanoff and Orthodox rule, while a few millions were the subjects of the Catholic Habsburgs; the latter were known as Ruthenes, meaning Russian too, and, like the Roumanians in Transylvania, were able to insist upon their particular quality mainly by their adherence to the Orthodox ritual through the Uniate Church.[1] Few people still, and least of all Nicholas I or Metternich, had the remotest conception of a Ukrainian nationality. The vast majority of Little Russians or Ukrainians or Ruthenes were poor, illiterate peasants speaking a variety of dialects related to Russian rather than Polish; in the different valleys of Hungarian Ruthenia, the dialects varied the most on account of the mountain barriers between them. It was only with the Russian Ukrainian poet, Chevchenko, that the idea of a separate Ukrainian nationalism was really formulated, round about the middle of the nineteenth century.

To the Tsarist authorities and the Russians to the north the distinction between Great Russian and Little Russian was absurd and was simply not recognized; only the use of the Great Russian, from which Ukrainian was actually distinct, was allowed in the schools and elsewhere. Although the Ukraine was famous for the richest soil in all Russia, the Ukrainians were most of them peasants upon whom wealth might fortuitously descend, but for whom social or political advancement thus depended upon the acceptance of complete russification. The big landowners of the Russian Ukraine were Russian or Polish or completely russified Ukrainians, while trading was in the hands of the Jews, though the populations of the towns of Kiev, Kharkov and Odessa were largely Great Russian.

[1] Unlike the Roumanians, they retained their Cyrillic alphabet.

The Ukrainians, incidentally, developed a particularly savage anti-Semitism of their own;[1] inter-marriage with Jews was virtually unknown, and the Russian police agents found it easy, when they wished, to instigate ruthless pogroms in the Ukraine; later, in 1919, the atrocities of this kind at Kiev were notorious. The Tsarist regime not only did all it could to eliminate Ukrainian feeling in Russia, it used the Ruthenes in Austria-Hungary, so far as it was able, to embarrass the Habsburg authorities with directly pro-Russian Pan-Slav, and pro-Orthodox agitation.

Austria-Hungary, however, was able to take an ample revenge. Indeed the Russians complained that the Ukrainian idea was a Viennese pedant's invention, for Austrian professors took up the Ukrainian language and history, and exiles from the Russian Ukraine were welcomed to Galicia. In the middle nineteenth century the Austrian authorities had protected the Ruthene peasants against the Polish landowners, but in 1868 the Poles became, after the Germans, the most privileged nationality in Austria, and it was convenient to encourage the Ruthenes in another direction. Though the Galician Ruthene leaders soon began to think in terms of the complete liberation of Greater Ukrainia, the Austrians positively fostered the idea of an autonomous Great Ukraine within Austria-Hungary; it is said that the Archduke Francis Ferdinand was interested in plans for conquering the Russian Ukraine. In view of the economic importance alone of the whole Ukrainian area to Russia,[2] the

[1] In the seventeenth century the Cossacks had always been on the worst of terms with the Jewish stewards of the Polish aristocracy.
[2] See below, p. 202.

indignation of the Russians is easily imagined. Late in the century the Hohenzollern Reich joined that of the Habsburgs in baiting the Romanoffs in this way. It is historically interesting that during the Crimean War a group of Prussians led by the Prussian Ambassador to London, Count Bunsen, had urged upon King Frederick William IV that he should pose as the champion of Ukrainian independence against the Tsar and even annex Russian territory. Since Frederick William IV was the Tsar's devoted friend, this had, of course, led to no result. Later, in the feverish year 1887, Bismarck was willing enough that the Ukrainian question should be thrown, among other missiles, at St. Petersburg, and an article in *Gegenwart* in 1888 in favour of the partition of Russia was more or less inspired by him. It was not, however, until the last fifteen or twenty years before the World War broke out that the Germans became systematically concerned for the persecuted Ukrainians, through the activities of their anti-Polish *Ostmarkverein*.

The outbreak of war led naturally to a tremendous intensification of intrigue and propaganda. Russia stood for Pan-Slavism, a slogan of oppression in East Ukrainian ears. The Austrians busily championed Ukrainianism, petting Ukrainian deserters and refugees from Russia and schooling them in their separatism. The mass of the Ruthene and Ukrainian peasants were probably still unaware of these issues, but through their very small middle and professional classes a slowly growing number of people were affected by one or other nationalism. German publicists, like Paul Rohrbach, who pressed for a more vigorous exploitation of the Ukrainian situation, were finally rewarded by the

Treaty of Brest-Litovsk, or rather by the "Bread
Peace," an agreement signed there on February 9th,
1918, between Germany and the representatives of the
new independent Ukrainian Republic, three weeks
before the German-Russian Treaty of March 3rd.
For, after the fall of the Romanoff regime, the Ukrainians were the first people within Russia to claim
autonomy, and they set up a radical but anti-communist
Rada at Kiev whose representatives arrived at Brest-
Litovsk in January 1918. The "Bread Peace," as the
main Brest-Litovsk Treaty may well have done,
created an interesting precedent, a precedent for the
bulk purchase treaties which Dr. Funk is advocating
to-day, and the German-Roumanian Treaty of March
1939. The Ukrainians, who were certain to find
themselves politically dependent upon Germany,
were allowed to annex the predominantly Polish
territory around Cholm only just south of Brest-
Litovsk itself, and received a promise of autonomy for
the Ukrainians left in Austria-Hungary. "In return
the Ukraine undertook to place its surplus of foodstuffs and agricultural produce, computed to be at least
a million tons, at the disposal of the Central Powers,
who agreed to co-operate with the grain producers
in the exchange of wares of which they stood in need,
and in the improvement of the transport organization." [1] The Bolsheviks had, however, driven out
the *Rada* from Kiev twenty-four hours before this
treaty was actually signed, whereupon, in March 1918,
the Germans and Austrians occupied the whole
Russian Ukraine until defeat in the west compelled
them to withdraw in the following November. The

[1] See John W. Wheeler-Bennett, *Brest-Litovsk*, p. 220.

Germans established a local *protégé* of theirs named Skoropadski as Hetman, but they could do relatively little against the hostility of the peasants, and a silent war culminated in the assassination of the German General in command, von Eichhorn. The memory of this German occupation has died hard.

New Year 1919 was the moment of Great Ukrainian hope. The East Galician Ruthenes had set up a Republic under Dr. Petrusziewicz, which, in January 1919, proclaimed its union with the Republic of the restored Kiev *Rada* now dominated by M. Petljura. But neither the new Poland nor the new Russia was willing to renounce the ambitions of its Kings or its Tsars. To the Russians these people were Russians, and Kiev "la mère des villes russes"; if the peasants in the villages talked a dialect of their own what did it matter? Pilsudski dreamt in his magnificent way of a federation of Lithuania, Poland and the Ukraine; Russia would no longer threaten the independence of Poland if the Ukraine with all its riches were cut away from her. As for self-determination, it made no more sense than usual. There were millions of Great Russians in the Ukraine towns and plenty of Poles in Lwów and the East Galician towns—why should self-determination ignore the more alert urban populations and only consider the backward peasantry? So the Ukrainian question resolved itself into a Russo-Polish war and eventually brought the Soviet troops up to the walls of Warsaw. The Poles were successful at first. They had occupied all Eastern Galicia by the summer of 1919, and Petljura, preferring their friendship to that of the Russian Communists, accepted their alliance and brought Pilsudski with Smigly-Rydż to

Kiev. But the Russians drove both Petljura and his Polish friends out and were only defeated at Warsaw in August 1920.

In post-war Europe, then, Great-Ukrainian nationalism had failed to find political expression. When Poland and Russia made peace they both recognized the old Russian Ukraine as an independent Republic, but it was in Bolshevik occupation at the time; in July 1923 this State became a constituent member of the U.S.S.R. Russia in 1920 and 1921 had recognized the sovereignty of Poland over Eastern Galicia and Cholm and, on condition of consideration for minorities, over the Ukrainian districts of Volhynia and Podlesia. It has been seen that Bukovina and Bessarabia had meanwhile become part of Roumania,[1] and Hungarian Ruthenia had been attached to Czechoslovakia. With a not fully developed nationality like that of the Ukrainians or Macedonians it is literally impossible to estimate population figures with any exactitude, even apart from the scope which a situation of the kind provides for propagandists. It is approximately true, however, to say that of the not quite forty million Ukrainians in Europe, over thirty million were now under Russian rule, over six million under Poland, rather more than half a million under Roumania and rather less than half a million under Czech rule. Not all the Ukrainians in Russia live in the Russian Ukraine; they are scattered across Siberia, and something under a million of them live in what is called the Green Ukraine near Vladivostok.[2] Since they had been poor and without opportunities in

[1] See above, p. 50.
[2] See B. Paneyko in *The Nineteenth Century and After*. January 1939.

Europe, many Ukrainians had emigrated before 1914 to the United States and especially to Canada, so that there were about a million and a half in North America.

The mass of the peasants in the Russian Ukraine had been glad enough to be rid of the Tsarist land-owners, and they had preferred the Bolsheviks to the Liberal intellectuals who had brought the German Army into the country in 1918. But the Communist military occupation which followed led to insurrection, deliberate reduction of output and consequently to the famine of 1921-2. The Bolsheviks now gave up russification as a mistake, and from 1923 to 1929 the Ukrainians got on well with Communist Moscow, which accepted the fact of the separate existence of the Ukrainian language and even strongly favoured its use. From 1926 onward Bukharin declared that to fight against Ukrainization would be to do a service to Pilsudski and to all the enemies of Communism. At the Tenth Congress of the Soviets of the Ukraine, Kaganovich announced that "they must fight at the same time against Great Russian chauvinism, which considers the civilization of the Ukrainians to be an affair for backward peasants, and against Ukrainian chauvinism which is inspired by bourgeois ideology and looks to the bourgeois of the west in order to detach the Ukrainian peasants from the Russian prole-tariat and from Moscow." [1] Though a number of posts remained in Russian or Russian Jewish hands, Ukrainians received a good many important positions, the most prominent among them being the Ukrainian

[1] See André Sidobre, *Les Problèmes ukrainiens et la paix Européenne* (1939), p. 39.

Communist, Skrypnik, who became Minister of Education in the Ukraine.

From 1929, however, the picture changed again. " . . . bien que les réformes scolaires et administratives introduites par la Révolution aient incontestablement hâté l'ukrainisation du pays, le Bureau politique du Parti communiste en est progressivement revenu, par la force des choses, à l'esprit de centralisation dont tous les gouvernements russes, quelle que soit leur couleur, seront toujours naturellement imbus: qu'il s'appelle Staline ou Milioukov, Alexandre ou Nicolas, qu'il règne à Moscou ou à Saint-Pétersbourg, comment le maître de la Russie laisserait-il échapper 45% des céréales que son empire consomme, 50% de l'acier et du charbon, la quasi-totalité du pétrole qu'il produit?" [1] The Russian Ukraine, which contains about one-fifth of Russia's total population, is not only famous for its rich soil and its corn production, for the Donetz coal-mines and the iron ore of Krivoi-Rog; it also provides about 70 per cent. of Russia's sugar production, as well as fruit and salt on a large scale, has begun to grow cotton and contains at Dnieprostroy on the Dnieper probably the largest hydro-electric power station in Europe. With the industrialization of Russia the natural wealth of the Ukraine has become ever more important, and with the development of industry and mechanics the oil of Southern Russia [2] has become vital, while centralized control has seemed to Moscow a *sine qua non*. The Ukrainians had long complained that their national wealth was exploited for the rest of Russia, while they themselves were left,

[1] *Ibid.* Many estimates are higher than those of M. Sidobre; on the other hand, quite recent developments in the R.S.F.S.R. have reduced the economic importance, relatively, of the Russian Ukraine.   [2] See below, p. 238.

as, for instance, in the early 'twenties and again a decade later, to starve. And now in 1929 came the campaign for the collectivization of peasant agriculture. The Great Russian *mir* village organization was semi-collective, but the Ukrainian peasantry was more individualistic and thoroughly hated the new system; their sabotage helped to bring back famine in 1933 and many of them were deported to other parts of Russia. Already in 1930 mass trials and purges had begun for the nationalistic "deviation" of the Ukrainians from the true proletarian path. At Kharkov in that year forty-five so-called intellectuals were tried and condemned for membership of the League for the Liberation of the Ukraine; they were said to have received money from Poland, and with this allegation all the blackest suspicions between Russians and Ukrainians were released. The Ukrainian Communist leaders gradually disappeared, for Skrypnik committed suicide and others were shot or removed. Thus the Bolshevik regime found itself fighting that very Ukrainianism upon which in the 'twenties it had so benevolently smiled. In the middle 'thirties the standard of living began to rise again and returning prosperity [1] helped to relax tension. And yet tranquillity was not restored. This is one of the most obscure scenes on the European stage upon which no West European has hitherto thrown much illumination. The younger generation was perhaps more inclined to believe in Moscow than its parents; it was probably impressed by accounts in the Soviet press of the sufferings of the Ukrainians in the fascist grip of Poland. Yet the Great Russian

---

[1] See Hugh P. Vowles, *The Ukraine and its People*, Chambers, 1939, for an account from the pro-Soviet point of view.

press complained that Russian was boycotted in the Ukraine, and in May 1937 it angrily drew attention to the defacing of the Poltava monument in Kiev.[1] Poltava [2] was the symbol for the conquest of the Ukraine by the Tsars, and the incident provided one pretext for the series of purges in 1937. It would be rash to try to determine how far the trials and executions in the Ukraine at this time were part of Great Russia's party political troubles and how far they were the dead fruit of the hostility between Russians and Ukrainians. They resulted, however, in the suicide of Liubchenko, President of the Council of Commissars in the Ukraine, and the disappeareance of all the intellectuals including the well-known historian, Hruchevsky, who had originally thrown Ukrainia's lot in with Great Russia's. There would be plenty of reason to suppose that skilful propaganda, if it could be got through the G.P.U. barrage, could play upon old anti-Semitic prejudice and tremendously stimulate Ukrainian separatism. It is said that Japanese agents have busied themselves with the Green Ukraine for some time.

.   .   .   .

If the Russian Ukraine has lived tumultuously since Brest-Litovsk, the Ukrainian situation in the post-war Republic of Poland has been an unhappy one. The Ruthenes of old Austria hated the Poles as a harsh ruling class from which the Austrians had partly protected them; only in 1908 a Ukrainian student had murdered the Polish Governor of Galicia, Count Andrew Potocki. The ex-Russian Ukrainians of Volhynia and Podlesia, if in the old days they had

[1] See *Krasnia Svezda*.   [2] See above, p. 194.

made any distinction between the Russians and themselves, may not have loved the Russians particularly,
but their feelings were mainly a matter of peasant
dislike of officials. But there was an old tradition
among them "Rather with the devil than with the
Poles," [1] and yet the Polish-Russian peace had handed
them over to the Poles. The Polish attitude to the
Ruthenes and Ukrainians was one of impatient contempt; the Poles would not admit the undoubtedly
close relationship between them, and insisted upon
treating them as two different groups of unrecogniz-
ably backward Poles, or in the worst case as little better
than Russians. It was true that the Ruthene and
Ukrainian dialects varied and that they lay somewhere
between Polish and Russian, but every Slav language
expert with any claim to impartiality will agree that
there is one distinct Ukrainian language, which is
closer to Russian than to Polish. The ex-Russian
Ukrainians, who were Orthodox, were a great deal
more backward, socially, than the ex-Austrian Ruthenes of the Uniate Church. The Uniates, however,
were far closer to Orthodoxy than to Roman Catholicism, and they, too, used the Cyrillic script, which, to
the Poles, was a symbol of enslavement to Russia.

It was the more advanced Eastern Galicians who
resisted Polish annexation most stubbornly. At Stanis-
lawow in February 1920 they proclaimed unrelenting
opposition to Poland, and two years later their attitude
was unchanged and they boycotted the Polish elections. On September 26th, 1922, the Polish Sejm
passed a law for the three East Galician voyvodates to
have more or less autonomous diets in two years' time

[1] See *Neue Zürcher Zeitung*, Das Ukrainische Problem II, Jan. 4th, 1939.

from then, and in 1923 the Conference of Ambassadors
therefore at last assigned East Galicia to Poland on the
understanding that "it is recognized by Poland that
. . . the ethnographical conditions necessitate a regime
of autonomy." Autonomy, however, remained a dead
letter. While the Ukrainians claimed to number well
over six million, the Poles only admitted four million;
even in the 1930 census only 3,222,000 Ukrainians and
1,219,600 Ruthenes were officially counted. The best
argument against autonomy was, as ever, the extreme
confusion in which these various Slav people lived;
the Ukrainians were not so over-crowded as the Poles
and claimed over a third of all Poland as their territorial right. In the towns everywhere the proportion
of Poles was high; and, of course, in predominantly
Polish areas like Cholm or Western Galicia there were
also Ukrainians. At all events the Ukrainians of
Poland were now subjected to centralized administration carried through only by Poles. Polish colonists
were settled on expropriated aristocratic estates. The
old Ukrainian schools, which the Austrian Government had provided in Eastern Galicia, gradually
became utraquistic, i.e. bilingual, but there had been
relatively few of these schools and the rest of the
education now provided by the Poles for the Ukrainians was in purely Polish schools. As for the old
demand for a Ukrainian University at Lwów raised in
the years before the war when some subjects had come
to be taught in Ukrainian, it was accepted in the 1932
law but consistently ignored in practice; all teaching
was Polish and the number of Ukrainian students was
limited.

The Ukrainians took to self-help; they also looked

across the new frontiers of Poland. As far as the Polish police allowed them they organized educational associations, while agricultural co-operation was developed in Eastern Galicia with striking success. Their largest and most moderate political party was the National Democratic Party (or U.N.D.O.) which stood for autonomy but not by violence; it was represented in the Polish Sejm from 1922. The other parties were more violent and readier to carry on intrigues abroad. The Polish authorities, frightened of Communist Russia as they were, easily suspected their Ukrainians of Russophilism. Conditions were never very good on the Polish countryside, least of all near the Russian frontier, and in the Skrypnik period it was inevitable that Kiev should attract the sympathy of the Ukrainians in Poland; there were agents from Russia, of course, who were far more numerous and active in Poland than Polish agents in Kiev and Kharkov. But it was not only to the east that the Polish Ukrainians looked. The Weimar Republic was on relatively good terms with the U.S.S.R. but always on bad terms with Poland; Skoropadski had retired to Berlin more or less with the German Army, and the Ukrainian exiles in Germany were encouraged to work against Poland. When it came to Ukrainian terrorist incendiarism and sabotage in Eastern Galicia in 1930 and the undoubtedly brutal Polish "pacification" campaign which ruthlessly suppressed it, the German Press probably provided the most indignant foreign comment, though the Kharkov trials also embittered Russo-Polish relations in that year.

For the next four or five years relations between the Poles and the Ukrainians in Poland reached their nadir.

To some extent the Ukrainians were intimidated by the beating-up and imprisonment which many of them experienced. But in the long run the "pacification" helped to unify Ruthene and Ukrainian sentiment; the peasantry, which, as distinguished from the small but mostly ardent middle class, had scarcely been conscious of its equivocal nationality in the past, was now much more aware of Ukrainianism. The only active answer which could possibly be made to the "pacification" was more terrorism, and the farms of Polish colonists still sometimes burst into flames. The chief terrorist band was the Ukrainian Nationalist Organization or O.U.N., which was organized from Berlin by the Ukrainian Military Organization or U.W.O. directed by an ex-Austrian officer, Konovalec. Another group of terrorists was the *Unakor* (National Ukrainian Cossack Movement),[1] led by an old associate of Skoropadski; this was active in Volhynia until dissolved in 1937. The O.U.N. murder of M. Pieracki, Polish Minister of the Interior, in June 1934 seems to have had something of the desired effect in Warsaw, for the Polish authorities came to the conclusion that something must be done. Meanwhile German-Polish relations had become so critical after Hitler came to power in 1933 that Pilsudski had said to Berlin in so many words, "Do you want war or peace?" This was the prelude to the German-Polish *rapprochement* of January 1934 which survived its unexpected birth by five years and three months, and which should be attributed partly to Herr Hitler's Austrian attitude towards Poland, partly to Marshal Pilsudski's fear and

[1] See "The Ukrainian Problem" in *The Bulletin of International News*, Jan. 14th, 1939.

hatred of Russia, but partly perhaps to the Ukrainian question. It suited Herr Hitler to have a truce with his neighbour immediately to the east until he had rearmed and refortified Germany, but it suited the Poles, too, that Berlin should be less encouraging towards people like Konovalec. There were, of course, a large crop of rumours that the new German-Polish Agreement contained secret clauses in favour of German-Polish co-operation to the east at the expense of Russia, and, as Ukrainians hoped, a plan to detach the Russian Ukraine from the U.S.S.R. On the German side many people hoped that Poland would ultimately be persuaded to give up Pomorze (together with her rights at Danzig) and Poznania in return for compensation to the north of the Black Sea. But it has been seen that the Poles regarded the "Corridor" as all the more vital to them since Gdynia had been built, and it is unlikely that they ever contemplated military co-operation with Germany towards the east; the recollection of Poland's partitions was so intensely bitter that no Pole would consider a project whereby any foreign troops, were they German or Russian, should ever cross the frontiers of Poland, lest they should wish to remain; neither did the Poles at any time encourage the Germans to invade Russia via Roumania. It had been different when Pilsudski and Smigly-Rydż went to Petljura's aid in 1920, for the Germans were helpless at that time. But the U.N.D.O. leader, M. Mudrij, now urged the Ukrainians to forget their quarrels with the Poles in order to further German-Polish co-operation against Moscow. "The Soviets," wrote *Dilo*, the U.N.D.O. official organ, "are threatened with the partition of their

Empire. Poland is therefore faced with a dilemma; she must either observe passively the interplay of forces which are bringing about a change in the territorial *status quo* of Eastern Europe, or she must associate herself with those who rightly wish to establish a new equilibrium. As for us Ukrainians, we are determined and intransigeant revisionists. Our whole interest impels us to wish for an international agreement which will eliminate the Soviets."

Thus the events of 1934 made it seem possible to emerge from the Polish-Ukrainian impasse, and towards the end of 1935 the U.N.D.O. leaders came to some kind of understanding with M. Koscial-kowski, the Polish Prime Minister, who agreed to consider their demands. The latter included what one might expect:—Civil Service jobs for Ukrainians, more Ukrainian schools and the University at Lwów, the dropping of the distinction between Ukrainians and Ruthenes, and the prohibition of Polish coloniza-tion in Ukrainian areas. This protest against colon-ization was typical of the meaner side of nationalism and of minority grievance, for it has been seen that the mainly Polish countryside was more overpopulated and suffered accordingly with the ban on overseas emigration. The attitude of the Ukrainians, but perhaps also the assumption made even by the Polish Peasant Party that Poles are superior, prevented the co-operation of the U.N.D.O. with the Witos Party. This was a deplorable mistake on both sides, for the interest of the Ukrainian peasants was fundamentally the same as that of the Polish peasants and the outlook of both groups was opposed to the Colonels' dictator-ship. Had they been able to work together they might have dictated democratic terms to the Warsaw regime. As it was, the 1935 understanding with the Prime Minister led to satisfactory negative, but no positive, results; Ukrainians were freed from imprisonment, the police left their independent organizations alone, they were represented by eighteen of their own people as members of the Sejm—M. Mudrij even became its Deputy Speaker—, but no administrative or educational reform was achieved. As the talk in the world about German minority grievances was made to grow from 1936 until the critical period of 1938, the Ukrainians, too, were stirred by the call of "self-determination." They knew that few minorities lived under worse conditions than they who had no independent "Motherland" to back up their claims; they were thus inevitably affected by the large demands sponsored by Germany on behalf of the Germans in Czechoslovakia. Early in 1938 the Executive Council of the U.N.D.O. repudiated its truce with the Government and came out in the Sudeten German manner with a frank demand for complete territorial autonomy.

. . . .

It has been seen that the Ukrainians in Roumania lived in fairly uneventful obscurity except for those of them who thronged into the front ranks of the Iron Guard [1] and there reaped sensational reward. The history of the Ruthenes of Subcarpathian Russia or Ruthenia, who were, according to the Peace Treaties, transferred from Hungarian to Czech rule, was a very different one. From the beginning of the post-war period these Ruthenes had two main grievances against the Czechs, one that some of their territory with

---

[1] See above, p. 71.

some of their co-nationals had unjustly been incorporated in Slovakia, the other that their promised
autonomy never materialized. This promise was not
merely a vague implication; in the Czechoslovak
Minority Treaty of September 10th, 1919, a second
chapter was attached in which Ruthenian autonomy
was defined; there was to be an autonomous diet
exercising legislative power in local administrative and
cultural affairs; officials were to be chosen as far as
possible locally; there was to be a Governor nominated by the President of the Czechoslovak Republic
and responsible to the Ruthene Diet; finally Ruthenia
was to be equitably represented in the Czechoslovak
Parliament.[1]

It is true that the Czechs more or less administered
Carpathian Ruthenia themselves, allowing little say to
the Ruthene diet which was constituted with twelve
elected members but six Government nominees. But
the Czechs had two good excuses. Under Hungary
the province had been utterly neglected, and the
Ruthenes were mostly illiterate peasants living in
lamentably primitive conditions with a very high
birth-rate, which in itself made their education a
serious problem from the point of view of the less
prolific Slovaks and of the far more western Czechs.
Ruthenes who were fit to be officials scarcely existed,
for they had always been dealt with by Magyars if a
few of the Magyars were of Ruthene descent. Indeed
the province seemed, as it were, doped with Magyarism. There were something less than 500,000

---

[1] See text of the Minority Treaty in *History of the Peace Conference*, vol. v,
p. 461. The Czechoslovak Constitution of 1920 afterwards modified the
Treaty to some extent.

Ruthenes and something more than 100,000 Hungarians, but it was typical that the Ruthene priests of the Uniate Church, unlike the Roumanian priests in pre-war Transylvania, were only too eager to forget their Ruthenianism and to be mistaken for Magyars. It was not unreasonable, since it had been decided to take Ruthenia from Hungary, to hold that time must be allowed for so backward an area to emerge from the alien, but the only cultural, influence it had known, and the Czechoslovak Minority Treaty had only required for Ruthenia "the fullest degree of self-government compatible with the unity of the Czechoslovak State."

If the administration was Czech, it was also efficient, and, on the whole, remarkably liberal according to East European standards; Ruthenian, incidentally, appeared, among the languages of the Republic, on Czechoslovak paper money. Schools, hospitals and roads were built, and, if Ruthenia had lost a valuable market for her timber in Hungary, the Prague Government spent generously on her behalf. The education of the Ruthenes raised the intricate question of what their language really was, since it consisted of a mountain peasant dialect sometimes varying in the way it was spoken from valley to valley and scarcely recorded in writing. The Czechs by natural inclination had a good deal of sympathy for the Great Russian view that Ruthene was essentially Russian and that it would be foolish not to educate their new subjects in the language of a huge nation with a remarkable literature. When in 1921 a considerable number of Orthodox priests, who had fled from Russia, were allowed to take refuge in Ruthenia they induced a wave of conversion from the Uniate Church to Orthodoxy; an inevitable corollary to this was the increased use of Russian, for the Orthodox Church, to Russian priests, was essentially an expression of Russianism. But Ruthenia was also a natural refuge for Ukrainians flying from the Poles in Eastern Galicia, Ukrainians, that is, who were particularly conscious of their Ukrainianism as something distinct from the quality of either Russians or Poles. These Ukrainians were naturally eager to make full use of liberty in Czechoslovakia to reclaim their Ruthene brothers and prepare them for the Great Ukrainia of the future. Local particularist feeling, which might have attempted to insist upon the thesis of a Carpathian Ruthene language, was for a long time too much entangled with the feeling of allegiance to Hungary to make much progress. If the Czechs provided ample schooling for the children of Czech officials and did not discourage non-Czechs from enjoying it too, they exerted no real pressure upon the local population to desert its Eastern for its Western Slav studies—there was only the consideration, which weighed particularly with the local Jews, that advancement in Czechoslovakia would be greatly facilitated by attending the Czechoslovak schools and learning in the chief State language. Though the Great Russians produced the two main autonomous groups, those of M. Fencik and of M. Brody, they were not on the whole successful; they represented reactionary Russia and had little appeal to youth. On the whole it was the Little Russian or Ukrainian movement which flourished. Until at least the later days of the independent Czechoslovak Republic the Czechs were inclined to encourage the Ukrainians because Prague was usually on bad terms with Warsaw. The Uniate Theological College at Užhorod prospered under Father Vološin, the Ukrainian cultural society, the *Prosvita*, was energetic and successful, and Ukrainian gained fairly steadily in the schools. Even the relatively numerous Ruthenian Communists were pro-Ukrainian—they were bound to be opposed to the Russophil conservatives. It is important, however, to record that in Mr. Macartney's expert view:—"If a census of the whole population were taken to-day, probably the vast majority of the peasants above whose heads the whole controversy had really passed, would still describe themselves either by some local appellation such as 'Hutzul,' or as 'Rusins,' meaning thereby their own local brand of Carpatho-Ruthenes." [1] This was written about two years before the Munich Agreement and the Belvedere Award. Another distinguished authority, M. Beuve-Méry, wrote more recently, "Le peuple ruthène est en effet aussi primitif que sympathique. Son vocabulaire le plus courant est très proche de l'ukrainien, mais beaucoup d'intellectuels préfèrent employer le russe. ... Au total, c'est par son particularisme étroit que se distingue le mieux cette population, et, si l'on veut voir dans ce particularisme un nationalisme, il est sage de ne pas le prendre pour une aspiration naturelle et profonde vers la grande Ukraine." [2]

In their anti-Czech campaign, the Sudeten Germans made full use of all the opposition to Prague that they could find in Slovakia and Ruthenia as well as in the Historic Provinces of Bohemia and Moravia. As many

---

[1] C. A. Macartney, *op. cit.*, p. 240.
[2] See *Politique Étrangère*, Avril 1939.

as possible of the thirteen or fourteen thousand
Germans of Ruthenia were organized in the Carpathian German Party, which worked energetically for
Henlein. There were German-Hungarian intrigues,
of course, and to Ruthenia Berlin could already send
emissaries well-equipped to stimulate Ukrainianism.
The encirclement of the Czechs in 1938 weakened
their authority at Užhorod (the capital of Ruthenia in
those days), and immediately after Munich, early in
October, they agreed to extend the very extensive
autonomous rights now acquired by Slovakia to
Ruthenia as well—complete home-rule with a Czechoslovak authority only in foreign, military, and some
financial, affairs. In the middle of October a Ruthenian
Cabinet met for the first time; it consisted of the three
Russophils, MM. Brody, Fencik and Bacinsky, who
were known to be in touch with Hungary and Poland,
and of two Ukrainophils, Father Vološin himself and
M. Revay. Ruthenia by now was throbbing with
Hungarian intrigue, and the activities of the Hungarian
"volunteers" were facilitated by the uncertainty in the
minds of the authorities, such as they were. M. Brody
and the Hungarians soon felt sure enough of themselves to press for a plebiscite, but on October 26th
the Ruthenian Cabinet split on this point, and German
influence, exerted through the unhappy Czech Government, saw to it that Brody was arrested and that
Father Vološin should be appointed as Prime Minister.
Exactly a week later came the Belvedere Award, an
amputation which cost Ruthenia her southern district,
her only territory which was better than poor forest
land and which included Užhorod and Mukačevo, her
only noticeable towns. Indeed the frontier now

drawn seemed to make no sense at all. It would quite clearly fail to satisfy Hungary in the least, while it left Ruthenia attached to Prague on paper, yet without any means of communication with the Czechs. The latter had just lost much of their forest land to Germany and could have made good use of Ruthenian timber, but Ruthenia was left with no internal main railway connection except for a few kilometres from the small country town of Chust eastwards into Roumania, while the rivers of Ruthenia ran from north to south, several of them now meeting on Hungarian territory. The pre-Munich shape of Czechoslovakia had often been ridiculed, but post-Munich Czechoslovakia with its attenuated corridor towards the south-east *across*, not along, the mountain ranges and valleys, at first seemed almost impossible to explain. It had apparently been preserved, not as Dr. Goebbels had once professed to be afraid, as a corridor for a Russian invasion of Central Europe, but as a corridor for a German experiment in propaganda, and the rest, a pre-war campaign directed from post-Munich federal Czechoslovakia eastwards, to bring about the disintegration of Russia.

．　　．　　．　　．　　．　　．　　．　　．

There is a Ukrainian idea, to which Chevchenko among others gave expression, that the fate of their nation and of the other non-Russians in Russia is "Promethean." Prometheus, who brought fire to Man, is yet chained to a rock in the Caucasus and tormented by the vulture, the Tsarist—or to-day the Soviet—Government. But his body heals and his spirit is immortal, and the Caucasus and all the peoples of Russia will be free; Prometheus, then, is the symbol

of the Ukrainians' just revolt against tyranny. It is
not without interest that an eminent Ukrainian
exile, M. Choulguine, launched a new review
in Paris on October 1st, 1938, called the *Revue de
Prométhée* and dedicated to this theme. In Poland,
too, there is a group of "Prometheans," [1] the advo-
cates of Polish-Ukrainian understanding and co-
operation; they too wish to dismember Russia in
order to set up a united Great Ukraine, which, as
Pilsudski envisaged it, would depend upon the
leadership of Poland.

The possible uses of the separatism of the Cossacks
of the Ukraine appear to have crossed the mind of
Louis XIV, and it would have been extraordinary if
Napoleon had failed to consider the disruptive possibilities of the Ukraine in his duel with Alexander I.[2]
But it is, not unnaturally, the Germans who have
concerned themselves most in more recent years with
what they might gain by freeing Prometheus from the
vulture and turning his gratitude to their own advantage. Bismarck himself was almost certainly too
socially conservative, too much concerned with the
preservation of both a social and international equilibrium—he did not believe the two aspects could be
separated for long—to use the question of the Ukraine
except as a diplomatic pin-prick. Under William II,
however, the Bismarckian *Kleindeutsch* attitude was
already at a discount. The Emperor was stimulated
by magnificent ideas; *Weltpolitik* was the order of the
day, and William expressed his personal admiration
for the flatulent writings of a man like Houston

---

[1] See R. L. Buell, *op. cit.*, p. 272.
[2] See R. Martel in *Politique Étrangère*, December 1938.

Stewart Chamberlain. When Germany's neighbours showed uneasiness at the boundless imperialism expressed by the ever-expanding *All-deutsch* movement, William II and Bülow and the rest [1] condemned, not the Pan-German programme, but the frank folly with which it was revealed. But Germany's ruler at that time was intensely susceptible to the suggestion that his was the task of restoring Germany's mediaeval glory, above all that he, the Hohenzollern,[2] was the heir to the Teutonic Knights; if the Tsar turned against him he was ready enough to claim more living space for Germany along her Eastern frontiers. During the World War men like Paul Rohrbach denounced the whole idea of Russian unity as a gigantic illusion which Germany in her own interest should expose. In the Treaty of Brest-Litovsk they seemed to have reaped their reward. Not only did Germany recognize the independence of the Ukraine, she took over the Russian territory contiguous to her up to a line drawn from Narva to the Ukrainian frontier beyond Homel. Behind this line Germany intended to see a Poland dependent upon Berlin, and Baltic principalities under German rulers. And since conquerors must always seem to free those they conquer, and since Wilsonianism was already in the air, it was stated in Article 3 of the Treaty that "Germany and Austria-Hungary purpose to determine the future status of the territories in agreement with their population." It was, of course, only the small upper class of German

---

[1] See, e.g., Count Bernstorff from London to Prince Bülow, April 16th, 1904, in *Die Grosse Politik der Europäischen Kabinette*, vol. 20, part 1, No. 6376 (an interesting despatch much approved by the Emperor himself).

[2] He was descended from Albert of Hohenzollern who had become the last Grand Master of the Knights in 1512.

Barons which welcomed the prospect of German rule over the Baltic littoral. In conformity with the principle of disintegrating Russia, the Treaty of Brest-Litovsk was followed by a German expedition to "liberate" Finland, and General von der Goltz captured Helsinki on April 12th, 1918.[1] There were no German Barons to be championed here, and it is as likely as not that the Finns under Mannerheim could have liberated themselves, but von der Goltz believed he was saving Finnish *Kultur* from Bolshevism. "These Eastern soldiers had ethical imperialism in their bones," wrote Prince Max of Baden, but Ludendorff wrote in his memoirs, "Not Finnish but exclusively German, interests, took the Germans to Finland."

When the Pan-German drove out the *Kleindeutsch* point of view from Berlin in 1933 it brought into power disgruntled *Auslandsdeutschen* like Adolf Hitler and Alfred Rosenberg, men whose vanity would only be satisfied when Germans should dominate old Austria and the Baltic States from which they respectively came; it was the dominant position now enjoyed by a number of *Auslandsdeutschen* which helps to account for the success of National Socialist ideas among the Germans living in other States, since they suddenly found themselves in possession of a new imperial prestige in practice, not only in theory. In the so-called racial ideology of the Nazis there was nothing new at all. But Hitler and his associates made the old Pan-German talk immensely more potent than it had ever been before through their appreciation of

[1] See J. Hampden Jackson, "German Intervention in Finland" (1918) in the *Slavonic Review*, July 1939.

the uses of propaganda. On the one hand they "infected" the masses with the aggressive notions which had hitherto been the monopoly of irascible professors and the so-called *Intelligenz*, and, through the technical discoveries of the twentieth century, they could not only disturb the German working-man at home, but also the peasant in the plains of Hungary or even perhaps of the Russian Ukraine. On the other hand, at least until March 1939, they could at the very same time successfully ridicule the notion that Nazi Germany harboured aggressive designs. Unlike Bismarck, they were not afraid to play with social revolution, and they therefore defeated Socialism everywhere by taking its own words out of its mouth and by using its own weapons against it. And all this was done, not solely as Dr. Rauschning [1] believes in the Loki spirit of "Let the Gods die," but also with a certain genuine belief in the glories of German vitality; this capricious beast is powerful and at large and the Nazi leaders intend to ride it while it lives; they thirst for power rather than destruction; perhaps they are too ignorant to know that history scarcely distinguishes between the two.

Among the prominent Nazis Alfred Rosenberg is perhaps the most sincere; for this reason he has often been kept in the background. He was born at Tallinn (Reval), the capital of modern Esthonia, and fled to Munich after the Russian Revolution. As a Baltic German he feels himself to represent the formerly oppressed nationalities of Russia, and as a Balt he still regards Russia as Germany's necessary colonial space. It was from Rosenberg that Hitler learnt to write, "But if to-day in Europe we talk of new land, we can

[1] See *Die Revolution des Nihilismus*, 1938.

in the first instance think only of Russia and the border states subject to her. . . . Our mission is the industrious work of the German plough, to which the sword only has to give the soil." [1] This attitude is justified by a glorification of the Teutonic Knights' tradition and by an ingenuously elaborate racialism. In the eyes of Alfred Rosenberg the Nazi return to the heroism of force, of *Kriegslustigkeit*,[2] may yet save the world from racial degeneracy. Once Germany is purified of Jewish contamination, other countries must be saved. The French Revolution of 1789 he regards as the lamentable interruption of the rule of a superior Nordic caste by a rabble of Jews and Marseillais; French imperial policy in more recent times has only continued the bastardization of France to which the German crusading spirit will one day have to put a stop. "During the French Revolution," writes Rosenberg, "a man only had to be fair to be dragged to the scaffold by the Marats; in Russia he needed only to represent the tall, slim, upright human type to be murdered by the slant-eyed leaders of the Red Guard in the Cheka." [3] The Russian *status quo* means to him the deplorable subjection of the Nordic Ukraine, the land of the *Kriegslustig* or war-loving Cossacks, to the Mongolian savages of Moscow who have long been in league with the Jews. Versailles-Poland he believes to spell racial nonsense, and he has long taken her dismemberment for granted, for he has consistently advocated a German *völkische Imperial-*

[1] *Mein Kampf*, 1933 edition, pp. 742-743.
[2] Literally "a condition of exulting in war."
[3] Alfred Rosenberg, *Der Zukunftsweg einer deutschen Aussenpolitik*, p. 88. It was, of course, true that the early mediaeval Kingdom of Kiev was set up by Scandinavian invaders.

ismus which will seek *Lebensraum* contiguous to Germany in the East.[1] But it is the Ukrainian question as leading to the break-up of the U.S.S.R. which he has felt to be the really vital thing. "Russia," wrote Rosenberg in 1927, "was, then, not a national state, but a nationalities state,"[2] a phrase which was borrowed daily by the German press some ten years later in order to be applied to Czechoslovakia, while to-day it is cast at Roumania and Poland. "Once we have grasped that Germany's first requirement is to clear away the Polish state, a treaty between Kiev and Berlin and a common (German-Ukrainian) frontier becomes a racial and political necessity as Germany's future policy."[3] When one discovers that Rosenberg is also interested in Caucasian separatism[4] without giving any racial excuse, and that he speaks frankly of supporting the Ukrainian revolution against Moscow to ensure to Germany "Space, Freedom and Bread,"[5] the attitude of German Imperialism towards the Ukrainian question becomes fairly clear; all the evidence suggests that, while it varies with circumstances, it remains fundamentally unchanged. Though the Russia of to-day no longer rules over Finland, Esthonia, Latvia, Lithuania nor Congress Poland nor Bessarabia, an article of Rohrbach's about the lie of Russian unity was published in a German review in February 1937. For National Socialism is the apotheosis of the imperialistic Pan-Germanism of men like Rohrbach, striving to build up a greater and greater unity of its own by denouncing and destroying that of all other States. The geographical position of

---

[1] *Ibid.*, p. 20.   [2] *Ibid.*, p. 86.   [3] *Ibid.*, p. 97.
[4] *Ibid.*, p. 93.   [5] *Ibid.*, p. 98.

the Czechs caused them to become the first victims, but it has been seen that most States in Eastern Europe are disagreeably susceptible to minority agitation. In the *Sportpalast* speech of September 26th, 1938, Adolf Hitler referred to the "Ukrainians" among the suffering nationalities of the Czech Republic, and the subsequent dismemberment of Czechoslovakia, in detaching Ruthenia from Prague, could be made to challenge the unity of Russia, indeed to initiate her disintegration. In due course Russia could be revealed as another Czechoslovak Republic, another nationalities-state, on a grand scale. In Rohrbach's view, Germany might have won the last war in 1916 if she had proclaimed herself to be the liberator of old Russia's oppressed nationalities.

.   .   .   .

With the Belvedere Award of November 2nd, 1938, Ruthenia was forced to find a new capital town, and Chust, a very primitive place with some 25,000 inhabitants, had to be chosen for lack of any alternative. For four months, however, Chust in all its simplicity enjoyed something like a metropolitan glory, for it was the capital city of what Herr Hitler had now designated as the Carpatho-Ukraine. The Ukrainian Uniate priest, Father Vološin, was now the Prime Minister, and the authority of Prague all but disappeared; it was, nevertheless, presumed that the greatly impoverished Czechs would give financial help to the economically helpless rump of Ruthenia. It appeared, then, that a virtually independent Ukrainian State, laughably small and poor and unworkable though it was, had arisen, and Ukrainians from Poland and sometimes from Roumania or Russia, and of course from Germany, frequently arrived and were appointed to official positions. The most important of the new arrivals, probably, was Colonel Mylnik. This man, during the World War, was employed by the Central Powers to enrol Ukrainian legionaries to be used against Russia. After the Armistice he withdrew to Lwów and lived in retirement, occupying himself merely, it seems, with the care of the property of the Uniate Primate of Lwów, Mgr. Szeptycki, who is incidentally a great Ukrainian patriot, though his brother is a Polish officer. Immediately after the Munich agreement, Colonel Mylnik set out on a journey around Europe, and during October he was therefore able to get into touch with various groups of Ukrainian exiles. Konovalec, the head of the terrorist U.W.O., had been murdered in Holland in June 1938, and it appears that in November Mylnik was appointed to succeed him; at about the same time he settled in Chust and joined in the recruiting and organization of the S.I.Č or Ukrainian National Guard.

At about the same time Germany opened a Consulate-General at Chust, and from this time onward it seemed as if, not Father Vološin and his colleagues, but Colonel Mylnik, together with the German Consul-General, were the veritable rulers of Carpatho-Ukraine. A number of Germans, journalists, even one or two *Wilhelmstrasse* officials [1] and others, also took up their position in Chust, and were surrounded with a patron's prestige. Indeed a Carpatho-Ukrainian Minister now mostly received non-German foreigners only in the presence

[1] See Alexander Henderson, *Eye-witness in Czecho-Slovakia*, 1939.

of a German, and was liable to refer them for
information to the representative of the *Völkischer
Beobachter*. Meanwhile the liberated Carpatho-Ukrainians, who were to be trained to free their brothers in
Poland, Roumania and Russia, must first be taught to
enjoy their own preliminary freedom. This involved
their complete Nazification. They were organized
into one political party, the Ukrainian National Union
or U.N.O., with the S.I.Č.—soon known simply as
the *Sič*—as its S.S. and S.A. and National Army in one;
funds for the purpose were said to be provided from
Germany on a not very adequate scale, and a number
of *Sič* officers were Germans.[1] Elections to the first
autonomous Diet of the Carpatho-Ukraine were then
announced for February 12th, 1939. Mr. Alexander
Henderson, who witnessed the election campaign in
Chust, has described how the whole Nazi ritual of
ascertaining the previously induced wishes of the
people was imitated by the Carpatho-Ukrainians with
the necessary local variations. "Loudspeakers installed on the balcony of the *Sič* headquarters amplified
to the crowd of villagers standing in the mud below a
number of gramophone records of Ukrainian folk-
songs, which were interspersed with speeches by Dr.
Komarinskyi (the Propaganda Chief) and M. Voron
(Secretary-General of the U.N.O.). This latter gentle-
man laid a curse upon all who did not vote for the
U.N.O. They would be traitors, he said, and when
they died they would not lie quietly in their graves,
for the earth would cast them forth and reject them
for ever and ever. It seems that one of the greatest
dreads of the superstitious Ukrainian peasant is this,

[1] See above, p. 23.

and M. Voron's audience was deeply impressed by this threat." [1]   There had never been anyone other than a Jew who was able or willing to run a shop in places like Chust, and it was easy to stir up ugly feelings against the local shopkeepers.   And before and during the election campaign those known for their Great Russian sympathies were roughly removed from the scene.   The outcome of the voting was, then, a 95 per cent. vote for the U.N.O. although the results at the uninfluenced communal elections held in the previous May and June had been totally different.

In spite of the laughable primitivity of this national conversion, the U.N.O. and the Germans on the spot were prepared to follow up the election, and German experience has shown how a relatively sceptical public opinion can be frightened, hypnotized and convinced into acquiescence and perhaps even into active support. Moreover, the existence of a *soi-disant* Ukrainian Government and a Ukrainian Diet—however unreal its independence—even in this poor little town to rule over this strange strip of territory, in the expectant atmosphere of post-Munich Europe, had had a tremendously stimulating effect.   All politically-minded Ukrainians were probably aware of it, especially those of adjacent Eastern Galicia, where Mylnik's O.U.N. people were perpetrating outrages again.   The Chust regime already felt independent of Prague and was schooled to regard itself as the nucleus, the Piedmont, of the future Great Ukrainian State.   A Ukrainian journalist from Poland said to Mr. Henderson, "We don't need a war.   All we need is plenty of radio propaganda, an irredentist campaign, such as the

[1] *Op. cit.*, p. 281.

world has never yet seen. Then arms-smuggling, a little help from Germany, and the Ukrainians everywhere will do the job themselves. . . . Next year we may be sitting in Czernowitz (Cernauţi in Roumania) as we are here now." He expected an internal collapse in Soviet Russia, and referred to the discontent of her Ukrainian population now provoked afresh by post-Munich events. "He concluded by saying, as all Ukrainians do, 'We know we shall have to pay for Germany's help, but rather than have no help at all we are prepared to pay'." This man, at any rate, can scarcely have realized the price which Germany intended to demand.

The passage from *Mein Kampf*[1] where Hitler speaks of two hundred and fifty million Germans living in the twenty-first century in lordly prosperity across Eastern Europe was once regarded as fantastic, but Adolf Hitler is a realist and the Nazis see no reason why German expansion should fail to achieve this. One of their favourite messages with which they have worked to win over their own masses has been *Volk ohne Raum*, and its corollary that the people must help to conquer its *Lebensraum*. In the very heyday of the German-Polish entente it was a regular practice for the Nazi educational authorities to take school-children, students or teachers from the big German industrial cities to camps on the Polish frontier. There for a week or so they would be constantly told that across that frontier to the east there was space, not the over-crowding which they knew at home; alternating with this came instruction about higher grade German culture and lower grade Slav culture, and about the

---

[1] 1933 edition, p. 767.

sufferings of German brothers across there in the space to the east at present under Slav rule.[1] It is only when their liberation is advocated, because it will disintegrate Russia, that the Slavonic Ukrainians become a precious bastion of the Nordic race.

The educated Ukrainians themselves traditionally hope for a Great Ukrainia stretching from the River San to the Caucasus. Recent German maps of the future Ukrainian State, ostensibly dictated by the principle of self-determination as interpreted by the Nazis, have, however, portrayed it as the territory from Warsaw to Baku with a population of some 48 million inhabitants; it has been made to include non-Ukrainian territories not only in Poland and on the Caspian Sea, but those of Crimea and Kuban. It is of incidental interest that whenever National Socialism emphasizes its Ukrainian plans, it part company with its Tsarist Russian friends; there were loud protests from the Tsarist Russian exiles in Paris in the winter of 1938-9.

Now what, more precisely, do the Nazis intend to make of the Great Ukraine of the future? It will be found to be a thoroughly familiar theme. Clearly Ukrainia is, for all its size, to become another vassal State; its rulers with less tradition or experience than the new states of Poland, Roumania or Yugoslavia, will necessarily depend upon their liberator, Germany. If the new country stretches to the Caspian, the Germans, whose ancestors were settled on the Volga by Catherine the Great, might even be included within

---

[1] See accounts in a number of issues of *Nationalsozialistische Erziehung* (Gau, Berlin) in 1936, in which the theme of the necessity to conquer space, especially to the east, recurs with persistent frequency.

it as the nucleus of a ruling caste; according to the
German maps there is a Ukrainian "language-island"
near to Saratov in the Volga district. And at all events
there are the inevitable Swabians who live on the
north coast of the Black Sea and Sea of Azov, the
descendants of the Mennonites brought in by Alexander I. "They developed rapidly, and in the middle
of the last century the German settlements in the
Ukraine became very numerous and stretched along
the Black Sea to the Caucasus." [1] In due course the
rights of these Swabians might become as important
as those of the Swabians of Hungary, Roumania and
Yugoslavia. In 1918 the German officers then in
occupation of the Russian Ukraine rejected the idea of
new colonies of German peasants because the most
fertile land was already over-populated; it was therefore decided at that time that the Russian Ukraine
should be brought into a German customs union so
that Germany should be able to absorb all its surplus
corn and animal produce as the treaty of February
1918 had arranged.[2] The possibility of planting new
German colonies north of the Black Sea has naturally
been considered by the Nazis recently; it would
evidently involve the expropriation and something
like the serfdom of the Ukrainian peasantry if it were
to be attempted on any scale. This would be by no
means inconsistent with the Nazi *Weltanschauung*.
According to a well-informed contributor to the
Neue Zürcher Zeitung last winter,[3] however, the Germans were then concerning themselves, as one might
expect, not with colonization plans but with the

[1] See "Das ukrainische Problem II," in the *Neue Zürcher Zeitung* of Jan.
4th, 1939.   [2] See above, p. 198.   [3] *Ibid.*

application of the Funk System to the Russian Ukraine, i.e. the monopoly of its foodstuffs for Germany, whose representatives were to develop its mineral resources and control and develop its industries. There was a time when the possibility of giving Poland control in the area on the right bank of the Dnieper, where she had had authority in earlier centuries, was considered by Germans, but, as the Poles were quick to appreciate, the Ukrainian projects of last winter had inevitably ruled this out. At the beginning of 1939 the fullest exploitation was intended of the opportunities provided by the new state of affairs in the Carpatho-Ukraine, leading perhaps to "spontaneous" revolt and followed by a campaign of military conquest. It was calculated that the peasants in the Russian Ukraine would be less difficult to manage than in 1918, when they were attracted to the Bolsheviks by their interest in the break-up of the aristocratic estates.

．　　．　　．　　．　　．　　．　　．　　．

The reaction of the Russian Ukrainians to Germany's post-Munich experiment at Chust is particularly difficult to estimate; impartial news from Kiev or Kharkov is virtually impossible to come by. Anti-Soviet sources in Riga announced in December that a separatist plot had been discovered among officers of the garrison of Kiev; they were said to be in touch with people abroad, including Skoropadski's son. Pro-Soviet sources, however, denied the whole story as malicious. The Russian Government, angry with the West and suspicious as ever towards Poland after Munich, had every reason to take care, and the Russian press now paid a good deal of attention to strengthening pro-Soviet sentiment in the Russian Ukraine.

In November 1938 the twenty years' anniversary of the withdrawal of the German Army was loudly celebrated. "The Soviet Ukraine," wrote *Izvestia*, "is neither Manchuria, nor Abyssinia nor Austria nor Czechoslovakia. Never will the fascist boot tread upon Soviet territory. The expulsion of the German Army of Occupation from the Ukraine provides a great lesson in history which no one should forget." In December, after the date when the plot was alleged to have been discovered, there were various military declarations to the effect that no inch of Russian soil would be invaded, for the Red Army would fight beyond its frontiers. And the Polish-Russian communiqué of November 27th was not without its importance.

For in Poland the events of 1938 had brought about a first-rate crisis from the point of view of policy both at home and abroad. Already at the U.N.D.O. Party Congress at Lwów in January the Ukrainians had shown a more intransigeant attitude than that they had adopted since 1935, and had demanded, not only an entirely separate Diet and administration, but also a separate army of their own within the mainly Ukrainian area. The Poles, whose attitude was in any case less liberal than that of the Czechs, were determined to give no encouragement to demands which they felt might develop, like those of Konrad Henlein, into a claim to organic rights and to the control of foreign policy. They had, moreover, a serious practical objection to make. Since 1936 they had been investing money in what they hoped would become a great industrial reservoir around Sandomierz known as the Central District (Okreg Centralny Sandomierz) or the Triangle of Security. This area was chosen for the proximity of the Carpathians, making water-power, petroleum and natural gas available, and for its comparative remoteness from the frontiers of Germany and Russia; great strategic importance was attached to it. But Ukrainian territorial autonomy would cut right across the Central District; this was not to be thought of, least of all in the critical year of 1938.

Relations between the Poles and Ukrainians now deteriorated, and the Polish authorities began once again to make difficulties for members of the Orthodox and Uniate Churches and with regard to the use of Cyrillic script. All through the summer the Ukrainians stood on tiptoe, as it were, watching the Czech-German situation and convinced that Germany's pressure would force the Poles to make concessions to them too. When in October Poland was obviously working for Ruthenia to go to Hungary, her Ukrainians became thoroughly enraged, and the O.U.N. fired Polish farms again and went in for other outrages. But the Belvedere Award of November 2nd, though it chopped down Ruthenia, made possible the autonomous Ukrainian regime at Chust; it constituted a tremendous encouragement to Great Ukrainian hopes, and spelt not only a serious humiliation for Poland, but a breach between Berlin and Warsaw. For in setting up the Ukrainian Piedmont the Germans were, in the Polish view, tacitly repudiating their ten years' guarantee of the frontiers of Poland. The Germans, no doubt, did what they could to persuade the Poles that they need only grant a generous autonomy to their own Ukrainians in order to continue to enjoy Germany's partnership; they tried to suggest that a

triple German-Polish-Ukrainian alliance could then
proceed to reap the fruits of Russia's dismemberment.
But the Poles had watched the First Partition of
Czechoslovakia, and they vowed to prevent the Fourth
Partition of Poland. Meanwhile the Polish-Ukrainian
situation became increasingly tense. In November
there were tremendous anti-Polish demonstrations in
Lwów, Polish students joined in and street fights
developed. The Poles continued to intrigue with
Hungary against Carpatho-Ukraine, while Galician
Ukrainians went off to volunteer at Chust. On
December 9th the Sejm rejected the freshly formulated
autonomy demands from the U.N.D.O.; it was said
that these now conformed more exactly than ever to
the 1938 Sudeten German model, and actually included
the request the Poles had feared to have a say in foreign
affairs; the Poles saw the mark of Germany's hand,
and indignantly repudiated what they denounced as
Ukrainian extravagance. In November Colonel Beck
had made a gesture to Soviet Russia, and on November
27th a Russo-Polish communiqué was issued according
to which the 1932 pact of non-aggression between
Moscow and Warsaw was recalled and underlined.
It had often been supposed that, in concluding her
agreement with Germany in 1934, Poland had im-
plicitly repudiated the 1932 Treaty. But it is probable
that the Polish Foreign Office had had no such thing
in mind, for it was primarily concerned to take advantage of the breach between Russia and Germany
which followed the triumph of the Nazis in the Reich;
after January 1934 the Poles intended, instead of lying
uneasily between the friendly Soviet and Weimar
Republics, to hold a commanding balance between

them. There was nothing sensational about the declaration of November 27th, 1938, but it was said to restore the East European equilibrium; it emphasized a mutual respect for existing frontiers, and in doing so it spelt a joint condemnation of the Ukrainian idea.

When, early in January 1939, Colonel Beck paid a visit to Berlin, the atmosphere was strained. The German Government, well aware of the advantages of a pro-Axis Poland which would be forced to give way step by step with regard to Danzig and the Baltic, made a very great effort to recapture the allegiance of Warsaw. The Polish Foreign Minister was told the Ukrainian agitation would be dropped because the colonial question was to be the order of the day and Poland was to have her share. Colonel Beck, whose interests, it has been seen, inclined him towards National Socialist Germany, belittled his recent negotiations with Russia and invited Herr von Ribbentrop to Warsaw to celebrate the fifth anniversary of the German-Polish Agreement at the end of the month; Herr von Ribbentrop was thus able to announce in the Polish capital that the Ten Years' Agreement had spelt the "final end to the enmity of our two peoples." But since the beginning of January there had been rumours that Germany intended to reincorporate Danzig in the Reich and to build a great extra-territorial motor-road, like the one she was building across mutilated Czechoslovakia, across the "Corridor" to Danzig and East Prussia. It was interesting to see that no amount of propaganda nor all the prestige of Munich nor any sympathy in high Polish places for National Socialism weakened the Polish popular reaction. Herr von Ribbentrop went home without the

smallest concession,[1] and from this time onwards
Colonel Beck was compelled to adapt himself not to
the end, but to a new beginning, of the enmity of the
two peoples. In February, at the time of Count
Ciano's visit to Warsaw, there were demonstrations
not only in the capital, but also in Cracow, Lwów,
Vilna, Poznań and other towns, and the demonstrators demanded that Danzig, and with it East
Prussia, should be Polish. That was the Polish
people's reply.

.   .   .   .

In March 1939 came the sudden elimination of the
Carpatho-Ukraine by the Hungarian Army after an
abortive Czech attempt to restore the authority of
Prague. It had become apparent that Germany's
Ukrainian interest had temporarily subsided in view of
other more immediate objectives, but Chust and the
Sič—with its numerous German officers—were taken
completely by surprise. There was some fairly grim
fighting, and a lot of Sič people were shot by the
Magyars; others were able to retire into Germany as
if they had been an Austrian or a Henleinist Legion in
earlier days. The only public explanation of the
sudden change in German policy was provided in the
Führer's speech to the Reichstag on April 28th, when
he made the strange announcement that only Roumania
had shown an interest in the preservation of the
Belvedere frontiers, and that "we did not dream of
continuing to bear the odium (sic) involved in order
to keep open a German road [2] to Roumania and deny

[1] It is said that at this stage he attempted to bribe the Poles with an offer
of joint partition of the Russian Ukraine.

[2] Actually *eine deutsche Vormarschstrasse*. Herr Hitler declared that
Roumania had begged that this German road should remain open. . . .

the Polish-Hungarian desire for a common frontier."
At first it might indeed have been supposed that
German-Polish relations would now be restored, for
the common frontier between Hungary and Poland,
for which the Poles had clamoured for so long, had
become a reality, and it even appeared that the whole
Ukrainian programme involving the dismemberment of Poland had been dropped. The German
annexation of Memel and the treaty with Roumania,
which both occurred on March 23rd, might be interpreted as intensifying Germany's pressure upon
Russia along the Niemen and the Bessarabian routes.
But actually Lithuania has no common frontier with
the U.S.S.R., and to take Memel from her was more
immediately disagreeable to Poland. Some people
even supposed that Germany's unblushing annexation
of purely Czech territory was not only intended to
intimidate all the smaller nationalities in view of their
hesitations even after Munich but was particularly
designed to bring Poland "to reason." If she would
not take even so broad a hint as this it seemed almost
as if the dismemberment of Russia might now be more
or less admitted to require the preliminary dismemberment of Poland in addition to that of Czechoslovakia;
it almost appeared as if there might be some idea at
Berlin of trying to conciliate Russia. No promise of
help from the West could compensate the Poles for a
Russo-German *rapprochement*. One must destroy one's
enemies one by one; Russia need not be reminded
that her turn was to come next.

For it is improbable that National Socialist
Germany has permanently abandoned the Rohrbach-
Rosenberg principle of Russian dismemberment. Her

increasing control of Hungary may make it possible to force the Magyars to allow Ruthenia to become the Ukrainian Piedmont again; both in Germany proper and the Protectorate of Bohemia and Moravia Ukrainian refugees have been welcomed, and their leaders are said to have gathered at Bratislava recently, on the frontier of Hungary. Meanwhile, at Danzig, signs are said to have appeared of a movement for the liberation of White Russia, a plan which, like the Ukrainian one, endangers the integrity of the stepping-stone, Poland, and of Russia. The break-up of Russia can make available an almost limitless natural wealth which the disintegration of Czechoslovakia, though it unbarred the road to the Balkans, could not supply. The Ukraine is the German road to the oil of Baku, and the "liberation" of the Ukraine leads on to the "liberation" of Georgia, Armenia and Azerbaijan; it is noteworthy that at the height of Ludendorff's *Drang nach Osten* fever in 1918, a German expedition penetrated to Batum and Baku. It has been seen that contemporary German maps mark both Crimea and Kuban as Ukrainian, though even in the latter it is more than questionable as to whether Ukrainians are anything like predominant. It is easy, however, to explain the German geographers by the recent exploitation of iron-ore at Kertch and of petrol on the Sea of Azov and at Maikop in Kuban. As M. Sidobre has written: "une Ukraine de 48 millions d'habitants, qui engloberait le Caucase du Nord et couperait la Transcaucasie de la Russie proprement dite, dominerait nécessairement la Géorgie, l'Azerbaidjan et l'Arménie, c'est-à-dire les manganèses de Tchiatoury, les gisements de cuivre d'Allaverdi et, par-dessus tout, le pétrole de Bakou." The Ukraine is, in the words of M. Lucien Romier, "L'étape la plus fortunée pour qui allait vers le Caucase et la Perse, quand le Turc avait coupé les voies de la mer"; thus, since Turkey has joined her opponents, the Ukraine has become more important to Germany than before. Not only would control of a future great Ukrainia-cum-Caucasus [1] make Germany economically able confidently to defy any coalition in war, not only would Russia be economically emasculated, but it is evident that Germany could threaten the "route to India" perhaps as effectually as Napoleon ever did.

It is still relatively early to judge the Ukrainian reaction to the abandonment of the Carpatho-Ukraine, a reaction upon which Germany's success in pursuing her eastern projects may yet depend. There were Ukrainians who had believed that their liberation, not that of Danzig, would be demanded and put into effect in 1939 in the same way as that of the Austrians and Sudeten Germans in 1938. But there were others, officials in Chust last winter, for instance, who accepted the fact that Italy and Germany would wish to deal with France, and that Germany intended to finish with the question of her former colonies, before she took decisive steps in Eastern Europe.[2] No doubt the agents of Germany have succeeded in emphasizing these necessities—and in showing that the Hungarian occupation of Ruthenia was among them—to some of their Ukrainian friends. Ukrainians had hitherto inclined to the view that "Hitler is like a cold in the head but Stalin is like the leprosy," and the prestige of

---

[1] Cf. Rosenberg, *op. cit.*, p. 93.
[2] See Alexander Henderson, *op. cit.*

Munich, no doubt, still kept the gaze of some Ukrainians upon Germany, the more since, as they say, they had hoped for help from the democracies in vain. And yet the rumours are persistent, and indeed from Poland the news is precise, that March 1939 has caused a revulsion of feeling against Nazi Germany among the Ukrainians as a whole. The backward peasantry of Ruthenia were perhaps the easiest game in Europe for the Nazi propagandists; they had habitually been polite to their masters, whoever these might be, but they had inherited no political tradition whatever to set against the *Gleichschaltung* quickly imposed upon them; the baiting of Jewish shopkeepers and all the rest seemed well enough to them. But the Ukrainians of Eastern Galicia had far more civilized traditions behind them, and their co-operative movement alone was an achievement in practical democracy. Some of them had all along felt uneasy about the patronage of a totalitarian and chauvinist Germany. Early last winter a Polish Ukrainian named Palnski publicly declared that "the Ukrainians know very well Hitler's derogatory opinion of the Slavs, including the Ukrainians; . . . no one of us has any ambitions," he stated, "to become the menu for the German *Herrenvolk*," or to be the food for the "Nordic Beast." [1] After the flagrant destruction in March of the nominal independence of the Czechs, Slavs with whom Ukrainians had often been on good terms, it appears that feeling of this kind had become dominant, and the bitter tension between Poles and Ukrainians, which prevailed and indeed grew in Poland during 1938, has been relaxed; in the

[1] *Manchester Guardian*, Jan. 2nd, 1939.

new stage of all-but-war between Poland and Germany, the Polish Ukrainians have subscribed as enthusiastically as the Poles themselves to the National Defence Fund. It would be incautious to over-estimate the importance of so sudden and so marked a change, and it would be inaccurate to suggest that there is anything like the warm Pan-Slav sympathy which exists between Bulgars and Serbs as yet, but there is certainly a new feeling between the Poles and Ukrainians that they have a common Slav interest to defend against Germany. In the Russian Ukraine the Soviet Government's propaganda has naturally been strengthened by the "fascist betrayal" of the Carpatho-Ukraine, and among the Ukrainians in Roumania it seems that a pro-Russian has succeeded to a pro-German sentiment.

. . . .

That their large Ukrainian population should genuinely stand on their side against Germany now became more important than it had ever been before to the Poles. For the shortening of Germany's frontiers through the seizure of Bohemia and Moravia and Germany's encircling move into Slovakia directly menaced the Poles. Indeed the new position of the German troops in Slovakia more than cancelled out the change in Ruthenia, for the common Polish-Hungarian frontier idea, as envisaged by the Poles, had always included the annexation of Slovakia by Hungary with the cession of small districts in the north to Poland. As for Germany's occupation of Memel-land, while Lithuanian popular feeling has certainly become more anti-German and far less anti-Polish since March, the Lithuanian Republic is actually helpless before Germany, and immediately after the cession of Memel the official *Lietuvos Aïdas* was compelled to refer to psychological difficulties between Lithuania and Poland. From Lithuania Germany can threaten the industries of north-eastern Poland,[1] and it is always possible that Herr Hitler will find it necessary to "liberate" Vilna and restore it to a Lithuania under his control; it would be extraordinarily difficult for the Lithuanians to resist such an appeal to their long-cherished chauvinism about their "rightful capital," a chauvinism the Tautininki Party has carefully cherished.

The Nazis have long been in relation also with the ultra-nationalist groups—the local Iron Guards—in Finland, Esthonia and Latvia, and in the last year or so German pressure in all these countries has been increasingly felt. In April 1938 von der Goltz was sent with his naval colleague and forty veterans of 1918 to impress upon the Finns that they owed twenty years' independence to the Germans. It is interesting that in the elections in Finland in July 1939 the pro-Nazi party lost votes, nevertheless. In Esthonia and Latvia the events of 1938 inevitably stirred up the Baltic German minorities, small though they were. When the old baronial class saw after Munich that the Czechs were forced to undo their agrarian reforms in the interests of Sudeten German landowners like the Schönborns and the Kinskys, they had good reason to hope that the Tallinn and Riga Governments would be coerced in the same way. It was even implied in the *Danziger Vorposten* in July 1939 that the non-aggression pacts of the Baltic States with Germany concealed promises to satisfy Baltic German claims.

---

[1] See L. Tissot in *Politique Étrangère*, April 1939.

These pacts not only endangered the negotiations between Russia and Poland's friends in the West, but also made Poland's relations with Esthonia and Latvia more difficult at least superficially, for they destroyed her idea of the Baltic States as a mainly Polish sphere of influence.

Already in the last week of March 1939 the German press had launched a systematic, an ominous, campaign against the "hate-filled chauvinism" of the Poles and their maltreatment of their *Volksdeutschen*, in exact imitation of the anti-Czech campaign of the previous year. It was noticed that the Germans in Poland at the same time developed a more aggressive aspect, and that, for example, their white stockings multiplied; [1] this, by the way, was like a preliminary hoisting of the swastika flag in Europe after Munich —everyone associated it with the Nazi refrain which had become so popular among Germans in 1938—

> Heute gehört uns Deutschland
> Und morgen die ganze Welt. [2]

The *Essener National Zeitung*, closely associated with General Goering, began to assert at this time that the authorities in Poland were "no longer masters of the situation," an accusation which had constantly warned observers in 1938 that Germany intended to take action against Czechoslovakia. Indeed the *National Zeitung* might have been reproducing word for word the accusations made against the Czechs by the German press in the months before Munich. "Nearly every day," it wrote, "brings fresh attacks on Germans.

---

[1] See *Times*, March 31st, 1939.
[2] Today Germany is ours, tomorrow the whole world will be.

German women and children are threatened on the streets because they use their mother tongue. German farm-houses are assaulted under cover of darkness. In the towns a systematic boycott of German shopkeepers has begun. . . . Wherever the instigators of such attacks on the Germans may have their headquarters, it must be demanded of the Polish authorities that they protect the Germans living in Poland from molestation and outrages and guard their property against attacks." Right-minded Poles, it was also announced, believed French and British agents to be behind the anti-German "outrages."

Within Poland German propagandists were as vigorous along other lines as these attacks of the German press against her. The decadence of the Western Powers since the Munich Agreement was insisted upon in Poland as elsewhere; even after the British guarantee of March 31st and the subsequent introduction of a partial conscription no opportunity was neglected of insisting that the pluto-democracies should in no circumstances be relied upon. The formation of the militia in Great Britain was denounced as nothing but a gesture of feebleness, while the offer of British credit was more and more violently abused as Britain's "Blood-Money" for which Poles and the rest were to die for her.[1] The anti-Semitic trump card was constantly played in this connection and wherever it might be hoped to divide Polish public opinion. The Poles had deliberately kept down their foreign trade with Germany, and even after March 1939 the percentage of their exports to and imports from the Greater Reich was not strikingly

[1] *Völkischer Beobachter*, July 7th, 1939.

high. But the labour shortage in Germany was
beginning to provide her with a new form of pressure
upon smaller and poorer neighbours, since she was in
a position to offer work to their nationals on apparently favourable terms which involved their subjection
to the most direct propaganda; Polish workmen were
forced to take Nazi propaganda back with them into
Poland.

Meanwhile Germany's demand for the reincorpora-
tion of Danzig in the Reich became more and more
loudly insistent. It was true that since the winter of
1936-7 Danzig had been completely Nazified in-
ternally, despite the League of Nations guarantee of
its democratic constitution, but it was not yet part of
the Reich from a military or naval point of view, nor
from that of trade and communications; it was partly
because of this issue that the Poles refused to hear of a
German extra-territorial road across the "Corridor."
Polish public opinion had blamed Beck very bitterly
that things in Danzig had gone as far as they had, and
it was determined that they should not go further,
for it was convinced that Pomorze and Poznán and
Poland's position on the Baltic were at stake. The German Chancellor's speech to the Reichstag on April
28th, in which Germany's demands were repeated, was
necessarily answered in this spirit when Beck replied
for Poland a week later. As for the German offers
which, it was suggested, were meant to give something in exchange, he pointed out that Germany had
offered nothing which Poland had not already got,
except for Hitler's Slovakian guarantee suggestion.
It has been seen that the advance of German troops
into various important positions in Slovakia had pro-

voked indignation in both Hungary and Poland; it
was perhaps with some idea of allaying this that Hitler
on April 28th declared that he would have been willing
to guarantee Slovakia's independence in conjunction
with Poland and Hungary. With regard to any such
proposal Colonel Beck simply replied that he knew
nothing of it.

With the April speech in the Reichstag Hitler
denounced the 1934 German-Polish Agreement; the
full effect of Munich upon the relations of Poland with
Germany became clear, and the Pan-German cultural
and other organizations were once again free to work
against Poland as openly as they liked. The Poles are
nothing like as stolid as the Czechs, and it is probable
that for Germans living in Poland as for the Poles in
Germany life had now become exceedingly disagreeable. The Polish authorities were undoubtedly less
scrupulous than the Czechs had been—they asked
rather pointedly had it helped the Czechs? Graczynski,
the Voivod of Upper Silesia, had always believed that
the Germans only understood strong-man tactics, and
in May and June, at a time when the German authorities in Bohemia and Moravia were breaking all
records of arbitrary administration,[1] the *Völkischer
Beobachter* complained indignantly of *die Graczynski
Willkür* [2] and of the Voivod's dissolution of German
organizations in ex-Czechish Teschen.[3] The Germans
complained, too, that the Polish authorities were
constantly evicting their German citizens and that a
stream of penniless refugees flowed across the frontier

---

[1] This was the period of the Kladno, and other, affairs.
[2] May 5th, 1939, meaning Graczynski's arbitrariness.
[3] *Frankfurter Zeitung*, June 23rd, 1939.

into Germany. It seems, however, that rumours were deliberately circulated by Germans to the effect that the frontier would soon be closed and that those who were for Hitler had better safeguard themselves as against both the Germans and the Poles by getting on to the German side. It is worth while for one moment to compare the position of the German minority in Poland with that in Hungary, Roumania and Yugoslavia at the time. Whereas in the three former countries the Germans were seizing all the privileges of a *Herrenvolk* and being used as a powerful economic lever, in Poland they were not only losing riches and rights at least as fast as in immediately post-war days elsewhere, but they were being evicted on the one hand and on the other prevented from making the type of Pan-German journey in which other German minorities now so frequently indulged; difficulties, for instance, were placed in the way of German singers from Poland who wished to attend the *Weichselland Sängerfest* at Danzig in June.[1] Poland with her population of 35 millions was, of course, more able to stand up to the Reich, and while she had avoided too high a proportion of foreign trade with Germany, she was not a Danubian country and the fall of Austria and Czechoslovakia did not affect her in the same way; only in Galicia a few economic ties with pre-war Austria remained. It was also of inestimable value to Poland that the Ukrainians, unlike, for example, the Magyars in Roumania, were no longer willing to make common cause with the Germans in Poland.

During the summer a series of Danzig frontier incidents, which were particularly easy to provoke in

---

[1] *Frankfurter Zeitung*, June 23rd, 1939.

view of the Polish customs control in the "Free City," kept up the tension; the German and Polish accounts of them were, it goes without saying, always diametrically opposed. Both sides now organized nationalistic demonstrations with an almost comic frequency. Late in June occurred Poland's "Sea Week"; the President of the Republic made a speech in which he emphasized the importance of both Danzig and Gdynia to Poland, and there was a great festival at Gdynia itself. The Poles had already borrowed the *Lebensraum* phrase from the Germans in order to apply it to their own claims in Danzig. This led both Sir Arnold Wilson [1] (in a letter to *The Times*) and Dr. Goebbels to discover a parallel German claim to Rotterdam, as if Holland menaced Germany in the manner in which Germany menaced Poland. The Germans all this time were finding it necessary to insist upon the particular qualities of German *Kultur* precisely in Danzig; German singers, sailors and the rest were compelled to foregather there, week-end after week-end. About the time of Poland's "Sea Week" it became evident that the Germans were organizing a *Free Corps* in Danzig, on the model of the Henleinist "Black and Tans," who had harried the Czech frontiers less than a year before, and guns were brought from East Prussia into Danzig. The danger of a "spontaneous" rising of the Danzigers in favour of the slogan *Zurück zum Reich*, which had always headed newspapers like the *Danziger Vorposten*, seemed acute.

Up to the time of writing the Poles had kept up a remarkable spirit. Not only had the German technique of inducing "race-consciousness" among certain leaders

[1] June 7th, 1939.

of the minorities had the opposite effect from the one desired, so that the Ukrainians of all people were now in favour of Warsaw, but political unity had been tremendously strengthened in other ways. Anti-Semitism, for instance, seemed to disappear. In Czechoslovakia there had been political leaders opposed to Dr. Beneš who had coquetted with Berlin until, as they now would readily admit, far too late a date. In Poland the nation and the oppositional political leaders had been more awake to the Nazi menace than the actual regime. When the Government admitted the gravity of the danger there was no one left who doubted it, and the old Peasant Party leader, M. Witos, and the strongly anti-German Catholic Democrat, M. Korfanty, who had once represented the Prussian Poles in the Reichstag in Berlin, returned from exile to rally their followers in favour of resistance to Germany— the authorities, with questionable wisdom, imprisoned M. Korfanty for a time.[1] The Poles now lived in a state of mobilization which involved a tremendous economic strain. They were short of material and they had no fortifications. They were still obstinately —perhaps foolishly—determined, like the Latvians, the Esthonians and the Finns, that no Russian soldier should cross their eastern frontier, and, even independently of German propaganda, they regarded Mr. Chamberlain as still quite capable of another Munich at their expense. But they were determined to fight the moment the Germans should move, and were full of plans, not only for shooting Danzig to pieces if necessary, but also for the occupation of East Prussia and the liberation of the Slovaks and the Czechs.

[1] He has since died.

PART TWO
WEST OF THE AXIS POWERS

CHAPTER V

ONE advantage which contributes, among others, to the success with which Nazi Germany wages her undeclared war is the insignificant fact that its strategy and tactics are peculiarly monotonous to describe; to read propaganda may be made tolerable, but to read *about* it is almost certainly dull. There can, at all events, be no object in making list after list of similar Nazi devices employed in different countries except to the extent to which they have different results. The impact of the German totalitarian machine upon Eastern Europe can, however, be clearly and perhaps profitably distinguished from its impact upon Western Europe. To the East, Germany can exploit her technical achievements, her intellectual distinction in the past, as against small, economically backward countries whose history has been far too much interrupted for them to have developed a convincing political coherence; here, too, because of the more primitive social structure, Germans have been able to assume a superior social status and something of the pose of the *Herrenvolk* or ruling race which the National Socialists declare them to be. To the West lie communities which have perhaps enjoyed a less interrupted evolution than Germany herself, and from which she has, in the past at any rate, been willing to learn; here lie countries, some of them small, but most

253

of them about as thickly populated and as highly industrialized as the Reich itself, countries whose social evolution may be regarded as more highly advanced.

Even if space and time should allow, it would scarcely be· profitable to examine Nazi Germany's campaign against the West in every case. France is too large, and in some ways too familiar, a subject to be treated here; Spain, on the other hand, is perhaps rather Southern than Western. About the Scandinavian countries, which geography may hesitate to call Western yet history will not, a word or two must be spoken. Denmark, Sweden and Norway enjoy a particular prestige in the eyes of the present rulers of Germany, who obviously enjoy such circumstances as occasionally justify the theories in which they force others to believe and by which they are glad themselves to feel convinced when opportunity offers. The Scandinavians are mostly as fair and tall as Alfred Rosenberg would like every German and every Ukrainian to be, and ethnically they are probably of less confused descent than the German and other inhabitants of Central Europe. The Nazi regime has exerted itself to draw respecting glances from the North for the great German Reich as a Nordic headquarters. There have been festivals in Germany like the Nordic Days in Lübeck in June 1935, and Germans of all kinds have constantly been sent to the Scandinavian countries since 1933, with the object, particularly, of explaining away the patently disagreeable features of National Socialism from the point of view of these highly developed democracies.

Perhaps the most successful message brought from

the Reich to the Scandinavian countries was, as in France and Great Britain, that Adolf Hitler meant peace. In pre-war days, when the Danes in Germany were treated with little consideration, Denmark had felt bitterly hostile to German imperialism, and Danish professors had exchanged notes with Czech colleagues on germanization. But after the war Denmark had disarmed completely, and if, as she naturally tried not to believe, Hitler meant war, she lay at his mercy. The Treaty of Versailles had brought about the transference to Denmark of the Schleswig territory annexed by Germany in 1864, and this had brought with it a small German minority of 3000 [1] which was perfectly well treated; after 1933, however, its members began gradually to demand the usual imperialistic privilege involving the loss of the individual rights guaranteed to them by the laws and habits of Denmark. To Denmark, further, the German market for her farm produce was exceedingly important, while Sweden was accustomed to send a large proportion of her iron ore to Germany, so that their degree of economic dependence upon the Reich was considerable. These facts accounted for the timid foreign policy and generally helpless attitude especially of Denmark; from about the turning-point year of 1936, one heard that Danish and Swedish firms were dismissing Jews solely because German firms otherwise refused to have dealings with them. In this way Nazi Germany, in nominal peace-time, not only added to the already arbitrary characteristics of East European administra-

---

[1] According to the Danish census of 1930, out of a total population of 3,550,656, Denmark had 9373 German-speaking citizens, of whom 3106 lived in Schleswig.

tion, but perverted the old-established constitutionalism of neighbouring Denmark and Sweden. It did
not matter so much, perhaps, that Germany should
affect the tone of the news service, where the press, as
in the Eastern countries, was in any case not free, but
after Munich she successfully asserted a claim to
destroy the freedom of the Scandinavian press. On
December 3rd, 1938, the *Völkischer Beobachter* declared,
à propos the Northern countries, that if the press in the
small democratic States continued to write as it had,
they were running the risk that in spite of their neutral
attitude they would be considered as enemies just as
much as those who were organizing war against
Germany; already in October one of the editors of
the leading Copenhagen newspaper, the *Berlingske
Tidende*, had been dismissed for his anti-Nazi views.
The importance to Germany of muzzling Scandinavian
opinion was clear—the Northern countries controlled
the way into the Baltic, and the loss of Swedish iron,
which was of finer quality than that of Yugoslavia,
and was produced on a far greater scale, would be
crippling. There was yet another consideration.
Denmark, Sweden and Norway together have only
about sixteen million inhabitants, and Paul Haushofer
has written a book about them called *Raum ohne Volk*.

Holland and Belgium, with Luxembourg, share
some of Denmark's dangers, and in Eupen-Malmédy
Belgium has her Schleswig question, though there
was a better case for the transfer of territory to Denmark in 1919. The Dutch have a relatively long
common frontier with Germany, a frontier which
incidentally has no natural defence save that of rever-
sion to the historic device of cutting the dykes; more-

over, in the National Socialist Pan-German view [1] the Dutch, whose independence of the Holy Roman Empire was only recognized by the humiliating Treaty of Westphalia, are Low Germans who will have to be reclaimed; so far back as 1802 the Pan-German prophet, Ernst Moritz Arndt, had written: "Bis heute ist Holland die schreienste Verletzung von Deutschland's Naturgrenze." [2]   Pre-war Germany made the impression [3] of taking a very great interest in Holland, both on account of the mouths of the Rhine and on account of the qualities of Dutch seamanship; the Nazi successors of William II, whatever they may say, may be relied upon not to have discarded any useful Wilhelminian ambition, least of all one capable of racial justification.   Belgium, and for that matter Luxembourg too, is regarded as inconsistent with the *Zeitgeist* of the twentieth century and the future on account of its bilingual character, and the Flemings, like the Dutch, can always be regarded as Germans to be reclaimed in due course.   It is interesting that elections in both Holland and Belgium, as in Finland, after the German march into Prague, showed a reaction against National Socialist influences, and the Walloon-Fleming situation in Belgium seems to have improved.

Although Switzerland, unlike the Netherland countries, is innocent of a colonial empire, the problem of

---

[1] See for pre-war Pan-German claims to Holland the dispatch from the British Consul-General in Munich to Sir E. Grey referred to above, Chapter II, p. 89, note 1.

[2] Ernst Moritz Arndt, *Germanien und Europa*, 1802, p. 337.

[3] See Sir F. Bertie's Memorandum of Nov. 9th, 1901 ; in Great Britain: Foreign Office, *British Documents on the Origins of the War*, edited by G. P. Gooch and H. W. V. Temperley.   Vol. ii.

Switzerland in relation to Hitlerist Germany embraces the problems both of Holland and Belgium; Switzerland, too, has a vulnerable frontier, and above all, she is multi-racial and multi-lingual. She has, moreover, a remarkable federal constitution, and presents from every point of view the complete antithesis to the German Reich to-day. And since, as Bryce wrote,[1] the virtues of the Swiss constitution have not attracted the attention of the world, there seems every reason to examine the impact of the New Germany upon the West by examining her relations with Switzerland.

The Swiss look back upon a continuous history since 1291, when the men of the Forest States of Uri, Schwyz and Unterwalden entered into the now celebrated pact which bound them "in view of the bad times and for their better protection and defence, to stand by one another, with counsel and with action, with life and with property, with united force and strength, against any and all who threaten oppression and injustice." These mountain people were, like the people of Alsace and Baden, of Alemannic descent and spoke purely German dialects; they lived within the Holy Roman Empire as subjects of the Habsburg Dukes of Austria. It was against the administrative interference of the Habsburgs' bailiffs and nobles that the pact of 1291 was mainly directed, and the legendary national hero, William Tell, is supposed to have been a man of this time whose action typified the independent spirit of the Swiss. Owing to the mountainous character of their homes, but also to a remarkable combination of independent spirit with competence, the Switzer people were able to win astonishing

---

[1] *Modern Democracies*, vol. i., p. 505.

victories over the armies sent by the Habsburgs against them in the fourteenth century; in 1332 Lucerne had joined in association with the three original cantons, and just after the middle of the century she was followed by Zürich, Berne, Zug and Glarus. The union, however, was nothing but an *ad hoc* alliance; as in the case of Magna Carta, a modern significance has often been read into its mediaeval words. It is true that the inhabitants of the allied cantons lived a life relatively free of the more feudal circumstances which prevailed elsewhere, and while the early Swiss victories were won by free fighting peasants, not by an unsteady combination of knights and unwilling serfs, the Switzer townsmen and peasants soon learnt to co-operate. But the alliance was such that the allies were sometimes at war with one another, for instance in the fifteenth century.

The Reformation, which was in a sense a widespread German revolt against the international authority of the Habsburgs, linked with that of the Papacy as it was, provided a fresh opportunity for the expansion of Swiss liberties. Although he came from St. Gallen, the great Swiss reformer, Ulrich Zwingli, is always associated with the city of Zürich, which became his home and headquarters. The west of Switzerland gradually accepted the teaching of the Frenchman, Calvin, who later established himself at Geneva, but in so far as the German Swiss became Protestant they became Zwinglian. To-day perhaps about half of them are Protestant, but it is characteristic that they belong to differing local Zwinglian churches without a centralized uniformity. The contrast between the rougher, more obscure, less independent Luther with the extremely civilized rational humanist, Zwingli, a man representing the life of the Renaissance city-state, is remarkable. Luther, with all his intense German feeling against the foreigner, was willing to subject his church to the absolute authority of the secular State, while Zwingli, truly Swiss, wished each congregation to have its religious independence. In 1529 the two were brought together at Marburg in Hesse by Duke Philip, who hoped they would be able to work together, but they were hopelessly alien to one another. *"Ihr habt einen anderen Geist als wir,"* [1] Luther said to Zwingli, after hours of dispute, and they parted for ever.

During the Thirty Years' War the Swiss attitude was already one of neutrality, and at the end of the war, when the Peace of Westphalia in 1648 reduced the Holy Roman Empire to nothing but a confederation, the complete independence of the Swiss cantons was recognized. Although since the early sixteenth, and especially in the seventeenth century, French influence had gained ground in Berne, and particularly in Fribourg, the Swiss Confederation was on the surface wholly Germanic until the end of the eighteenth century, for Neuchâtel (which belonged to the Hohenzollerns until 1857) and Geneva were still outside it, while Vaud and Ticino, like Aargau, Thurgau and St. Gallen, were territories subject to the Confederate cantons. Within the cantons authority was now mostly concentrated in the hands of a few patrician families, so that more popular elements were eager to welcome the French invasion of 1798 bringing with it the notions of 1789

---

[1] " You have a different spirit from ours." The greatest difficulty between Luther and Zwingli was presented by the question of the Sacrament which Zwingli regarded as only commemorative.

in France. But an attempt at a unitary Swiss regime broke down badly, and Bonaparte himself, the man who perfected the centralization of France, came to the rescue. The Swiss have recorded, not without pride, that Napoleon frankly admitted in 1802 that though he had won the confidence of the French people he would regard himself as unfitted to rule over the Swiss. "Plus j'ai réfléchi sur la nature de votre pays et sur la diversité de ses éléments con-stitutifs," he said at this time, "plus j'ai été convaincu de l'impossibilité de la soumettre à un régime uniforme; tout vous conduit au fédéralisme. . . . La nature a fait votre État fédératif, vouloir la vaincre n'est pas d'un homme sage." It was to Napoleon that the Swiss owed, not only a return to the federalism whose importance to them he so fully appreciated, but also, by the Act of Mediation of 1803, the extension of cantonal rights to the subject territories, and in fact the establishment of the tri-lingual federation at the beginning of the very century which was to be domin-ated by hostile notions of uni-lingual nationalism. In 1815, while Swiss neutrality was internationally guaranteed, a Federal Pact was concluded between the now sovereign cantons which, with Neuchâtel and Geneva, became twenty-two. It was not until 1848, after dangerous quarrels between the Catholic and the Protestant cantons, that they gave up their sovereign veto right and, borrowing certain principles from the constitution of the United States, established the democratic federal Swiss State of to-day; certain important changes were introduced in 1874, but the essential character of the Swiss Confederation emerged ninety-one years ago.

The Swiss Constitution, as it stands to-day, probably provides the least imperfect democracy in the
world; without indicating its main features, it is
impossible to appreciate the meaning of Switzerland
in a world over-shadowed by the menace of totalitarianism.   There are two legislative chambers, the
National Council, consisting at present of 187 members
elected by universal suffrage by all men over 20 and
since 1918 by proportional representation, and the
Council of Estates, in which each canton is represented
by two people chosen as the canton may decide.   The
two houses sitting together form the Federal Assembly,
which elects the seven members of the Federal executive
body, the Federal Council.   Neither legislature nor
executive can get rid of one another—they are both
elected for a period of four years.   There is no one in
the pre-eminent position of the President of the
United States; the Federal Councillors elect one of
themselves to preside each year; though Federal
Councillors can be re-elected indefinitely no one of
them remains President for more than a year.   Each
canton, according to its own law, elects a democratic
cantonal assembly and executive body with wide
administrative powers, and within each canton the
towns or villages, again, enjoy democratic autonomy.
There are still three cantons, Appenzell, Unterwalden
and Glarus, where the ancient custom of direct
democracy has survived and the whole adult male
population forms the cantonal assembly or *Lands-
gemeinde*; the men of Appenzell attend, each armed
with a sword, the mark of the freeman.   The still more
remarkable characteristics of Swiss democracy are the
election of judges and generals, and the use of the

initiative and of the referendum. These things all make legislation and its execution the direct affair of the people. On the whole, it should be added, the proportion of voters is high on the many occasions when voting occurs, and the initiative and referendum are constantly used. In Switzerland one hears no charges of corruption, and it is evident that voting is carried through in the spirit of the laws without propagandist distortions of the will of the people. The small scale of Swiss life is undoubtedly an advantage in making democracy work. On the other hand, there are certain flies in the ointment. Apart from the inevitable complaint that democratic machinery moves too slowly, it is very generally held that too many old people are in command. The tendency for Federal Councillors to be re-elected has developed into a habit, and young men feel that all the interesting positions will be blocked until they themselves have lost their best vigour. The case of M. Motta, whose foreign policy certainly fails to inspire general confidence, is often cited, for he has been continuously elected as a Federal Councillor since 1911 and has been responsible for Swiss Foreign Affairs since 1920 without interruption. M. Motta belongs to the Catholic Conservative Party, whose influence is held by progressives to be artificially exaggerated by the Constitution as it stands. Each canton, regardless of its population figures, is equally represented in the Council of Estates; since the predominantly Catholic cantons are small, the Council of Estates, and therefore also the Federal Assembly, overweight the Conservative Party. This question and several others related to it were raised in December 1938 in an interesting

test case. The resignation of M. Mayer, the Minister
of Finance, induced, it was whispered on the Left, by
the fact that he was progressively inclined with regard
to the introduction of new fiscal methods, led to
the nomination of two candidates for his post.
According to the tradition that the canton of Zürich
shall always be represented in the Federal Council, they
had to be Zürich men. One was, in fact, Dr. Ernst
Wetter, a member of the Freethinking Party, a director
of the *Crédit Suisse* and a man prominent in the Swiss
Trade and Industry Federation and in the aluminium
industry—in other words, a man of importance in
industry and finance. As against him, the much-
respected Social Democrat Mayor of Zürich, Dr.
Klöti, was put forward. Now the Federal Council, as
it stood before this contest was decided, consisted of
3 members of the Freethinking Party, 2 Catholics
and 1 member of the old Conservative Peasant
Party, although the Social Democrats with 50 members were the biggest party in the directly elected
National Council and were backed by various small
progressive groups of Young Peasants, Young Catholics, etc. The Catholics had 42 members in the
National Council and the Freethinking Party 48, with
18 and 15 members respectively of the Council of
Estates, where only 3 Social Democrats had a place;
the old Peasant Party had only 24 representatives in
both houses together. While the aims of other parties
are what one might expect, a word requires to be said
about the history of the Freethinking Party (*Freisinnige Partei*), or Radicals, as they are called in the
French-speaking districts. This party represents the
continental anti-clerical liberalism of the nineteenth

century which brought about the constitutions of 1848 and 1874. Since then its individualistic doctrines have been made by economic developments to appear as the callousness of those who possess, since the leading bankers and industrialists belonged to the *Freisinn* Party and for many years doggedly resisted legislation to protect labour. This led to a particularly violent feud between the Freethinking Party and the Social Democrats, who became very strong immediately after the World War, and the *Freisinn* people found themselves pushed back into an alliance with the enemy they had once existed to destroy, the conservative Catholic Party. This curious *mariage de convenance* in the Federal Council, where the Catholics have made up for the Freethinking majority by the tenacious character of M. Motta, has therefore dominated Swiss political life since the war. People who admired the British constitution were content that the Socialists should be a strong opposition out of office, the more since they had taken up an extreme pacifist position and objected to all military expenditure until 1936. In that year, however, the Socialists, realizing that pacifism was a language incomprehensible to National Socialists, completely revised their attitude, and since the Swiss was not the British constitution, and as the menace from Germany to small neighbour countries grew, it was more and more felt that in the interests of national unity the Socialists should be brought into the Federal Council.

The election in December 1938 provided an opportunity to bring this about. There was still, however, a profound distrust for Socialist finance on account of the free-handed behaviour of the Socialist municipal councils of Zürich and Basle, and it was, after all, the Minister of Finance who had to be chosen with a view to the need for a big increase of revenue; according to Socialist opinion big vested interests were afraid of unwelcome reforms. In the event, 117 votes were given for Dr. Wetter and 98 for Herr Klöti. Soon after this the Social Democrats began to work for an initiative in favour of the direct election of the Federal Council, like the American President, by the whole people, and for an increase in its membership from seven to nine. This latter proposal was taken up and supported by many members of the Freethinking Party though it was clearly intended to bring the Socialists on to the Federal Council. In the autumn of 1939 both Chambers and the whole Federal Council are due for re-election, and these controversies will have to be settled one way or the other. They give rise, of course, to inevitable grumbling that there is altogether too much voting and too much party strife. But Swiss opinion on the whole probably shares the feelings of relief enjoyed by the foreign observer, who may, for a moment, feel anxiety at the bitter enmity hostile politicians express towards one another, but quickly reminds himself that this is a mark of real political vitality, and that outspoken criticism is a thousand times better than the sycophantic obedience and pernicious whispering which prevail in totalitarian States.

Perhaps the main political controversy in Switzerland, an issue to which most others relate, is that between those who cherish the extremer aspects of federalism and those who advocate greater centralization. Since the smaller cantons are conservative and

Catholic, and since the Catholics are in the minority—
if a large one—in relation to the Protestants in Switzerland, the Conservative Party is strongly anti-centralist,
with the Catholic University of Fribourg as the
federalists' intellectual headquarters; for the same
reason the Social Democrats, and some of the smaller
groups who sympathize with them, are centralist.
The Socialists' interest in economic life, where federal
interference often facilitates rapid action, also inclines
them to favour the expansion of the powers of the
Federal authorities; many of them believe that only
educational and some hygienic matters should ultimately be left to the cantons. The whole tendency since
1848 has been in the direction of a slow and cautious
centralization. A federal coinage and a federal postal
system were early established, and the Franco-Prussian
War and its effects, just as they helped to bring about
the slightly more centralized constitution of 1874, led
to a Swiss Federal army instead of separate cantonal
contingents. Until recently each kind of law varied
from canton to canton, and there was no Federal police
force, only the police of each canton. The civil and
commercial codes have now become federal and even
the criminal code is being co-ordinated, so that the
death penalty which existed in some cantons and not
in others is about to be abolished throughout the
Confederation. Until after the war direct taxation
was a cantonal and communal affair, and the Federal
authorities relied solely upon indirect taxes—mainly
the income from customs duties which had long been
co-ordinated. But as the economic responsibility of
the Federal authorities has admittedly increased, and
especially since the world depression has presented

the problem of unemployment—a particularly serious problem in Switzerland, and one which cannot be left to the local authorities—it has become necessary for the Federal Government to levy direct taxes and work out a new fiscal plan. Thus natural evolution has strengthened the central power, arousing *en route* those meaner resentments which new taxes are certain to provoke. This is the uglier side of the federalist opposition to the extension of the central authority, an extension which has also been emphasized by the increase and development of military preparations and by the establishment of the *Bundespolizei* [1] or *Bupo*; since the events of 1933 have led to an ever-augmenting disturbance of Europe's tranquillity, these changes have become inevitable.

The extraordinary variety of Swiss life from canton to canton, from city to city, even from valley to valley among the mountains, is a quality only too precious in a growingly standardized world. For a moment one might think of Transylvania [2] with all its individualisms as a rival to Switzerland, but this it cannot be since the Helvetic Confederation keeps alive something which Transylvania never really had, the tradition of the city-state. "Ainsi, notre originalité dans le monde," writes M. Gonzague de Reynold, in his recent book, *Conscience de la Suisse*, "c'est de maintenir et de représenter une forme de civilisation que les grandes concentrations nationales des temps modernes ont peu à peu absorbée, détruite: celle de la cité. Ce fut la civilisation de la Grèce. Ce fut la civilisation de second moyen âge. Ce fut, à la Renaissance, la civilisation de l'Italie. Songez que nous

---

[1] =Federal Police Force.   [2] See above, p. 85.

sommes seuls à continuer la lignée d'Athènes, de
Cologne, de Nuremberg, de Bruges, de Florence.
Nous devrions en être fiers." [1] The educational life
of each canton, as of the city, such as Berne or Zürich
or Fribourg which often gives it its name, is something
quite independent. Though Federal Polytechnics and
other Federal institutions are gradually appearing, the
universities of Switzerland are autonomous cantonal
institutions. Each canton uses it own school text-
books, and the school-child grows up to regard himself first as a citizen of the canton of Vaud or of Lucerne
or of the Ticino; it is only later that he becomes
consciously Swiss. And while the many units of
government mean that administration goes slowly,
they also, by keeping down the scale of things, give
self-government a practical, not merely an academic,
meaning. If contemporary economic and military
requirements have brought about an approach to
uniformity in some directions, the very defence of the
country has something to gain from the self-depend-
ence bred by decentralization; much can be destroyed
and yet, where there are many centres of control, much
can continue to function. Above all, the individualism
bred by the federal life of Switzerland, through that
quality which makes it an end in itself, is also stronger
to resist the propaganda and even the economic
pressure of undeclared war.

The most remarkable diversity in Swiss life derives
from the multi-lingual character of this State. To
those familiar with Eastern Europe, or with Canada,
or Belgium, this quality is by no means unique, but it

---

[1] Gonzague de Reynold, *Conscience de la Suisse*. Éditions de la Baconnière,
Neuchâtel, 1938, p. 241.

is generally agreed that the problems arising out of it are more happily solved in Switzerland than anywhere else in the world. This again provides the federalists with an argument against centralization, for they claim that the various racial groups of the Confederation live harmoniously together because the small autonomous units of administration give each of them ample self-expression. A further extension of the central authority over the cantons would, on the other hand, in their view, create the aggrieved feelings entertained by powerless minorities, would, that is to say, create minority problems where none have existed hitherto.

It has been seen that the mainly French- and Italian-speaking cantons were put upon an equal footing with the mainly German-speaking ones through the mediation of Napoleon at the beginning of the nineteenth century. Thus the Cadmus, who did so much to sow nationalistic dragons' teeth to breed men to bring down political structures elsewhere, here created the basis of a common political life for three different national groups, which then provided themselves with the equally necessary individual democratic rights contained in the constitution of 1848. This was at a time when German Liberalism was already about to be seduced by nationalistic greed into the attempt to force the Slavs of Bohemia and Moravia into a German State which they utterly rejected.[1] By the time that German and Italian nationalism had been able to establish themselves politically in the 'seventies, the Swiss Federation had had time to grow secure; helped by its mountainous

[1] See my *Czechs and Germans*, Oxford University Press. Chapter iii.

remoteness, it could ignore the claims of those who wished to unite all those speaking one language in the same State; it was able, in fact, to achieve stability and prosperity on the basis of the absolute negation of that nineteenth-century nationalism whose triumph had been celebrated in Germany and Italy.

To-day there live in Switzerland some three million German-speaking Swiss citizens, some 850,000 French-Swiss, about 250,000 Italian-Swiss and about 45,000 who speak another Latin language, *romanche* or *romantsch*, as a few thousand inhabitants of the Italian South Tyrol also do. It is entirely misleading to suggest, as ignorant propagandists constantly have, that these groups live compactly with neat linguistic boundaries clearly marked between them, nor are Swiss cantonal frontiers intended to be of such a kind. It is true that these frontiers are old historic ones and no one therefore feels aggrieved about them; they might if they believed that they had been drawn with the purpose of cutting up natural unities, as the Croats felt about the boundaries of King Alexander's Banovinas in Yugoslavia.[1] Out of the twenty-two cantons,[2] only seven are not well over 90 per cent. German-speaking. Of these, Vaud, Neuchâtel and Geneva are predominantly French and Ticino predominantly Italian, although only about three-fifths of the Italian-Swiss live in the Ticino, the rest being scattered about the Confederation mostly in the cantons of Zürich, Geneva and Graubünden (Grisons). Fribourg, Valais

---

[1] See above, p. 111.
[2] Three of the twenty-two are divided into half cantons for administrative purposes.

and Graubünden (Grisons) are fairly thoroughly
divided, for according to the 1930 census figures,

> Fribourg was 32·1 per cent. German-speaking and
> 66·7 per cent. French-speaking.
> Valais was 32·5 per cent. German-speaking and
> 64·9 per cent. French-speaking.
> Graubünden was 53·7 per cent. German-speaking
> and 30·9 per cent. Romanche-speaking.

Religious differences coincide even less with cantonal
boundaries, for in Glarus, Solothurn. Graubünden,
St. Gallen, Aargau and Thurgau, Protestants and
Catholics are completely mixed; the proportion of
Protestants to Catholics in the whole Confederation is
57·3 per cent. to 41 per cent, ·4 per cent. of the population being Jews and 1·3 per cent. without any confession (1930 figures).

How do the different linguistic groups in Switzerland live together? It would be absurd to suggest, as
some sentimentalists have, that they dote upon one
another. At first one is struck with how separately
they live until one realizes that each Swiss village,
perhaps each family, lives in a sense apart from the
rest. While a great many German-Swiss speak some
French or Italian, it is rare that the others speak
German beyond a few words; the French accent
of the French-Swiss, even when they speak fluent
German, is usually strong, and in other words the
Swiss as a whole are not even bi-lingual in the sense
of speaking two languages equally well. They cannot
compare at all with the young men one often meets in
the Banat, perhaps, who can rattle off Hungarian,
German and Serb or Roumanian, one after the other.

On the other hand, among the Swiss who read—and there is a high proportion of these—most people do so in their three languages and know something of the three literatures first-hand. The German-Swiss are inclined to consider the French-Swiss to be rather mean and incompetent in business matters, while the French-Swiss resent the control of many affairs which tends to be acquired by the bankers of Zürich and Basle. In general, one has the impression that a gentle contempt for one another exists between the racial groups of Switzerland, a gentle contempt which is extremely satisfactory since it is a sentiment which most men thoroughly enjoy.

There was a time when a good deal was heard of the claims of fascist Italy to annex the Ticino, and Italian agents there were not without success. To-day, however, the Ticinese are increasingly aware of the economic privation supported by the Italians beyond the Swiss-Italian frontier, and it is sometimes said that the peasants of the Ticino are the best Swiss democrats of all. Apart from pretensions to this Italian-speaking canton, Italian propaganda was busy not long ago with complaining of the "oppression" of the 45,000 *Romanche*-speaking Swiss whose homes are mostly in the Graubünden canton. At the suggestion of certain academic circles in Zürich it was constitutionally decided early in 1938 to recognize *Romanche* as a fourth national language. This, on the one hand, means that villagers who speak nothing but *Romanche* are qualified to hold small official jobs locally, say as postmen; on the other, it is a very generous gesture, and may be said to have solved any *Romanche* minority problem that had previously existed. The fourth language did not become "official," so that the routine of the translation of official declarations and transactions was not further complicated by its recognition.

At the time when the Sudeten German question was the topic of the day, one constantly heard the Czechs blamed because they had not introduced a Swiss system of language laws. The fact is that there are, to all intents and purposes, no laws of the kind in Switzerland. Two articles of the constitution refer to linguistic differences. Since February 20th, 1938, Article 116 runs as follows: "German, French, Italian and *Romanche* are the national languages of Switzerland. German, French and Italian are declared to be the official languages of the Confederation." And according to Article 107, "The members and deputy members of the Federal Tribunal are nominated by the Federal Assembly which will consider that the three official languages of the Confederation should each be represented." In fact the relations between the various language groups of Switzerland are governed, not by law, but by convenience and habit. It goes without saying that at least one Federal Councillor shall represent *la Suisse romande* and one the Ticino. For official business the language which suits most people concerned is employed, with arrangements for translation if there are sufficient people present who do not understand. On the railways, in the post offices and so on, it is the same; there is no law to say where two languages must be used, or where one shall begin and the other leave off, but it is all unofficially arranged without friction.

On returning from Central or Eastern Europe to-day one asks oneself how it is possible for human beings to behave in so sensible, so civilized a way. The first reason, perhaps, is that the Swiss have had time to acquire the necessary conventions and habits; the second reason is that, whereas the French-Swiss speak French and the Italian-Swiss Italian, the members of the big German-speaking majority writes German but speaks an array of different, sometimes very different, German dialects, so that they cannot always understand one another—the German dialect spoken in the Valais is notoriously incomprehensible. This diversity of speech among the German-Swiss would in itself be a check upon any impulse to insist that the Latin-Swiss should speak German, but indeed no such impulse seems to exist; it was the German-speaking professors of Zürich who pressed for the recent recognition of *Romanche*. The thing which strikes one most forcibly on coming from the East is the complete absence of social stigma in relation to difference of language, the complete absence, that is, of even the shadow of the *Herrenvolk* idea. This is partly due to the complete abolition of what little feudalism Switzerland ever knew and the early prevalence of democratic standards, partly to her neutrality perhaps, and to her geographical isolation, which have excluded all traces of any kind of imperialism. It is also undoubtedly an important thing that the German-Swiss, the French-Swiss and the Italian-Swiss each have behind them a great national civilization, so undoubtedly great that no one of them can ever seriously despise the others as being less civilized. And since Germany, France and Italy are all Great Powers, no one of the three has exerted an overwhelming influence such as to inflate the prestige of the racial group speaking their language. This fact alone would distinguish Switzerland from pre-Munich Czecho-slovakia, where the Czechs, with no great nation behind them, were always bound to identify (and were justified in doing so) their Germans and Hungarians with the unfriendly Germany and Hungary across the frontiers.

Undoubtedly the federalists are largely right when they insist that it is the decentralization of Swiss administration which prevents the development of a minority mentality among the French- or Italian- or *Romanche*-speaking Swiss. In the cantons and the communes the smaller groups have plenty of scope to develop their own way of life; they are aware that in France or in Italy they would be far more restricted. Yet it is misleading to put too much emphasis on the cantons whose boundaries do not coincide with linguistic difference so that a canton like Fribourg might, if its French majority chose, become the scene of coercion of the German-speaking minority; or, again, the *bâlois* might object when one speaks to them in French, though in fact they never do. Fundament-ally there is no oppression in Switzerland, not so much because the country is decentralized, but rather because it is really democratic, because it is politically con-structed upon the basic idea of respect for the indi-vidual, which includes respect for his language, religion and way of living in general. No minority problem can arise where this is so; on the other hand, the Nazi conception of a "nationalities-state"—as expounded by Konrad Henlein and never intended for any use other than propagandistic disruption—as a committee of *Führer* each dictating to a language group would mean only that the strongest of these

Führer would dictate to the others, while these, if they were able to defend the linguistic freedom of their followers, would have denied them any personal freedom. It is difficult to see why minorities should have rights as organic groups, if the rights of their individual members perish *en route*. And if it were to be organized in such groups, so that the French-speaking population of Berne or the Italian-speaking population of Zürich ceased to regard themselves as fellow-citizens of the canton with the German-speaking majority, Switzerland would inevitably be destroyed.

The relationship between Germans and German-speaking Swiss has long been complicated and perplexing; and since the German-speaking Swiss made, and even to-day make Switzerland, this relationship has meant nearly the same thing as that between Germany, whatever its form at the time, and Switzerland. Inevitably the German nationalism aroused by Napoleon at the beginning of the nineteenth century claimed to embrace Switzerland, too, in the Greater Germany of the future; at that time, after all, Arndt had put all the emphasis of nationalism not upon race but upon language, and a Prussian diplomat in Berne in 1819 referred to the mountains of Switzerland as the eternal walls of Germany. In 1841 an article called "Germany and Switzerland" appeared in the eminent review, the *Deutsche Vierteljahrsschrift*; it expressed the views of enthusiastic German patriots at the time and was generously reprinted and quoted. According to its author, Switzerland must return to its parent Germany, for it could not develop a nationality of its own from its clashing German and Latin elements.

German professors at Swiss universities should bring about a silent conquest of Switzerland during Germany's imminent regeneration; meanwhile Prussia's Customs Union policy would force the Swiss to throw in their lot with the Customs Union States.

For the German-Swiss of the first half of the nineteenth century a tremendous conflict of allegiances was involved. The educated classes were accustomed to look to Germany as their spiritual home, as the land, after all, of Goethe and Schiller—whose pen had done so much honour to William Tell—and of all the poetic inspiration expressed in the language they knew best. In their own schools and universities they were accustomed to study German language and literature from German professors whose *hochdeutsch* was impeccable ; or on the other hand, they studied in Germany itself. Many German-Swiss at this time undoubtedly responded to the German call, and only waited for the day when, as their German Liberal friends readily promised them, the German Nation should achieve unity and democratic liberty at one blow. Opinions might differ as to whether the French- and Italian-Swiss should join France and Italy, or be absorbed, as the Great-Germans wished for the Czechs of Bohemia, into the German Reich of the future; after all, Italy was not yet in existence either. The attitude of a great Swiss figure of the time, the Zürich poet, Gottfried Keller (1819-1890), to the German question has recently been examined afresh by an eminent professor, Jonas Fränkel of Berne University;[1] it is illuminating both with regard to

[1] See Jonas Fränkel, *Gottfried Keller's politische Sendung*, Verlag Oprecht, Zürich, 1938.

Swiss feelings nearly a hundred years ago and with regard to the conflict facing the German-Swiss to-day. When the young Gottfried Keller, for instance, set out in 1840 to discover the Germany of the poets for himself, a Bavarian official, as soon as he had crossed into Germany, roughly snatched his cap off his head and threw it on the ground because he had put it on sooner than one should in the Kingdom of Bavaria— after Baden probably the most liberal of the German States at that time.   As Professor Fränkel writes, Keller could not escape the consciousness of a very different conception of *Menschenwürde* [1] from the one to which he was accustomed at home.   Incidents of the kind constantly startled the visiting Swiss, though some of them were content to suppose that in the future all this would be different.   There were at this time, too, German democrats who lived in exile in Switzerland and believed that the spirit of Switzerland would achieve the emancipation of Germany, not as foreign inspiration but because Switzerland was the truest part of Germany itself.   To all these pre-1848 hopes Keller's response, both while he lived in Munich and Berlin and after his return, may probably be accepted as typical of the German-Swiss of the time. Already at Munich he had insisted that to be descended from the same tribes had nothing to do with national feeling, because the spirit of succeeding generations can so profoundly change.   Later, when he was back in Switzerland in 1844, he expressed the Swiss idea in a series of sonnets which he called *Swiss nationality* and in which his main theme was that, strong though the

---

[1] = human dignity.   Keller described much of his experience in Germany in his novel, *Der Grüne Heinrich*, written later (1850-55).

bonds of language may be, one link is stronger still, political belief. Thus, as Professor Fränkel shows, Keller's conclusion was that, not blood and language make a nation, but rather a common conception and the wish to be united in accordance with it. Above all, the common conception must carry with it, not merely unity, but freedom within that unity. Then as now it seems that the German-Swiss were puzzled and amazed that the Germans should be able to mistake unity for freedom.

> Was scheret uns ein *freies* Land,
> Wenn, die drin wohnen, Knechte sind?[1]

wrote Gottfried Keller. It was this feeling which perhaps contributed as much as anything else to the Swiss federal union of 1848; and when the Swiss saw what German unity in fact meant in 1866 and 1870, they rejected it more definitely in the slightly closer union created by the constitution of 1874.

If, politically, Germany was drifting further and further from the Germany of Goethe, it was never from that Germany that men like Keller asked to live apart. While he insisted upon the separate national existence of Switzerland, Keller insisted also that the German-Swiss should never think in terms of a literature separate from Germany's; he believed that one should belong to as large a cultural area as one could, and that the common *hochdeutsch* language was a link so precious that it should never be ignored. Despite the advancing prussianization of Germany which was so repulsive to the Swiss, a powerful emotion was fostered by this feeling of partnership in

[1] = " What do we care about a ' free ' country if those who live in it are slaves ? "

a common literary civilization, an emotion which occasionally mastered the more rational conclusions of the educated Swiss so that Pan-Germans exult over haphazard utterances about coming together in the end; in the Swiss mind, of course, this reunion was always represented as a German return to the common humanistic heritage which the Renaissance buildings of the Swiss cities, and most of all, of Erasmus' Basle, still so genuinely cherish. Meanwhile it was absolutely inevitable that the academic life of Germany, Austria and Switzerland should be intimately connected, and that professors should be exchanged between Zürich and Heidelberg and Vienna. In spite of the Zwinglianism of the German-Swiss, the links between the German-Swiss and the German, Protestants were close; between Switzerland and Austria there was actually less interchange. And yet all the time that international wisdom which was most easily accessible to citizens of multi-lingual Switzerland and which was gloriously represented by men like the great *bâlois* scholar, Jakob Burckhardt (1818-1897), was, as Burckhardt himself knew only too well, losing ground to the pagan destructiveness of chauvinist Pan-Germanism.

During the World War opinion in Switzerland was divided. Swiss sympathy with Germany has on the whole been over-emphasized, though it is true that it was strengthened by the links which bound the Swiss Army to Germany and by the strategical fact that France had more to gain than Germany by entering Swiss territory—perhaps also by a traditional anxiety engendered by the long-vanished ambitions of both the Napoleons. With the establishment of the democratic Weimar Republic, the possibility of actual co-operation between the Swiss and the German Republic arose, for the latter now flew the black-red-gold colours of the 1848 Liberals, while Swiss opinion felt very great sympathy for the hardships suffered by Germany in the post-war years. And then came 1933 and the end of tolerance and clemency in Germany. Humane and Christian conceptions were taboo; German federalism, weakened as it had been by the Weimar constitution, was destroyed, in spite of the boasts of the Bavarian Government that it would resist the Nazis; an uncompromising centralism was established which simultaneously rejected the whole idea of *Menschenwürde*. Only a race had rights, so that race became the ruling criterion, by the side of which less tribal political conceptions were utterly discounted. And in the shadow of racialism lurked the figure of naked imperialism ready to spring into action when the racialist disguise should have served its purpose. In the National Socialist view a multi-national state like that of the Czechs or the Swiss had become an anachronism, indeed a contradiction in terms; it has been seen that the very use of the word *Nationalitätenstaat* became ominous, for it seemed to foretell destruction by the Nazis. The *völkisch* maps now brought out by the *Volksbund für das Deutschtum im Auslande* [1] marked most of Switzerland as racially German, and the implication here, as in the Hitler Youth Primer [2] or wherever one looked in Germany, was clear—that National Socialist Germany would see to it that

---

[1] See *Grosse Sprachenkarte von Mitteleuropa von Triest bis Trollhättan, von Dünkirchen bis Dünaburg und Konstanza, bearbeitet von Dr. Friedrich Lange.*

[2] See *Handbuch für die Schulungsarbeit in der H. J.* (The Nazi Primer).

political and racial frontiers be made to coincide, provided, of course, that she profited by the change. Switzerland had withstood the more literary forms of nineteenth-century chauvinism and had even gained in federal coherence, although the basis of the Helvetic Confederation ran counter to the spirit of the age. But could she survive this twentieth-century tornado whose emphasis on the *Zusammengehörigkeit*[1] of all those of Germanic descent was a still more direct challenge to her very existence, at a time when not only the notion of racial self-determination, but also economic development, seemed utterly to condemn it?

At first sight Switzerland appeared extraordinarily vulnerable. Decentralized democracy is a delicate machine, all the more if it has to be worked in several languages. M. Gonzague de Reynold, who, like Keller, insists that "Les sources premières de nos littératures, de nos arts, de notre pensée jaillissent bien au dehors de nos frontières politiques," very frankly refers to the fragility of Switzerland:—"un peuple à civilisation composite et qui, loin d'avoir une langue nationale, parle celle de ses voisins, renferme dans son organisme des forces centrifuges qu'il doit compenser par beaucoup d'intelligence et par une volonte créatrice."[2]

The German National Socialists were convinced that *Gau Schweiz*, as it was designated by them, would, like Austria, be easy game. They had intrigued in Switzerland before 1933 and aired their *Weltanschauung* as completely as they could, but in 1933 they set seriously about the undermining of Swiss resistance.

[1] Meaning, literally, " belonging-togetherness."
[2] *Op. cit.*, p. 248.

The usual methods were employed. A particularly large number of Reich Germans lived in Switzerland and the Nazis organized them in Nazi party groups, using cajolery and all the forms of intimidation in which they excelled if direct persuasion failed. These Nazi groups were trained to circulate Nazi ideas among the Swiss; they published an exceedingly aggressive paper called *Der Reichsdeutsche* which the Swiss Federal Government forbade later on. Whenever their activities were criticized as unwarrantable interference, their leaders were up in arms against the intolerance shown towards harmless cultural organizations. Meanwhile a number of German-Swiss were induced to form a National Front with its headquarters at Zürich and with groups in Schaffhausen and elsewhere. The National Front, which received support in Swiss officer circles, did not dare declare openly for union with Germany, not even for an autonomous attachment such as that of which moderate Nazis in Austria spoke; the *Frontisten* contented themselves with Swiss national regeneration as their programme; indeed they posed as more Swiss than the Swiss. They busily agitated against the evils of democracy, the delays, the senility; they cried for discipline and lamented the fall in the birth-rate, they were cautiously anti-Semitic and violently anti-Communist. Above all, they set out to praise everything in Germany under Hitler, and seemed frivolously indifferent to the fact that the theories of Hitler were intended to wipe their regenerated Switzerland right off the map. They devoted a great deal of energy to explaining that Hitler was the greatest champion of peace, nursing no aggressive designs at all, and they eloquently maintained that he was no enemy to religion but perhaps its true friend since he wished to free it from the usurpations of corrupt priests. And the Frontists early developed the valuable thesis that public criticism of Nazi Germany was provocative to Berlin, in other words that the press in foreign countries should come under German censorship. The National Front, incidentally, was soon equipped with Storm Troopers of its own—known as the Grey Guard—who were the usual "tough" type, trained to silence or remove any hostile critics who should venture to express their disapproval at Frontist meetings. In the Zürich municipal elections in the spring of 1934 the National Front won 10 seats, and in the Zürich cantonal elections a year later it won 6; later in 1935 it was able to send one deputy, Richard Tobler, to sit on the National Council.

For in the years immediately following the Nazi Revolution in Germany pro-Nazi influences were not without effect in German Switzerland. There was a good deal of sympathy for the anti-Versailles notes in the Hitlerist cry and a good deal of readiness to make allowance for temporary revolutionary excess. There was a certain irresistible appeal to young people about the excitements across the frontier; the small scale upon which Swiss life was lived, as well as its diversity, the isolation of each small community from the next, left many young people very much alone, unless they were able to indulge in higher education, between the end of their elementary schooling at the age of 15 and their military service at 20. It was often impossible even to find work, and it was only too natural, therefore, to feel attracted by the large-scale organization, with all its enticements and sidelines, offered to their contemporaries in Germany, and by the whole Nazi emphasis on "We are young—come to us."

While large numbers of Swiss people had relatives in Germany and most University professors and business men had many connections with the Reich, the professional Swiss officers had mostly received a good part of their training from Germans and felt great admiration for the professional prowess of their German colleagues; their attitude was often slightly anti-French. Colonel Wille himself, who had been at the head of the Swiss Army during the World War, was constantly in Germany and had many close German friends, including the Nazi leader, Rudolf Hess, the Führer's deputy. Many Swiss officers approved warmly of all the anti-Marxist Nazi talk because they hated their own Socialists at home who opposed all military expenditure and wished to dissolve the Army. It was perhaps Hitler's claim to have saved Europe from Communism which was most successful in Switzerland in those days. Both Conservatives, Peasants, and *Freisinnige* were frightened of the power of the Trades Unions at home and terrified of the influence of the U.S.S.R.; indeed Berne, like Belgrade, refused to have diplomatic relations with Moscow, and the Swiss authorities very much disliked the appearance of Russia at Geneva in September 1934. One constantly heard in Switzerland, as elsewhere, that Hitler's ways might be temporarily rough but that they were vastly preferable to Bolshevism—the similarity between National Socialism and Communism was not observed.

Perhaps the weakest spot in Switzerland's defensive armour was the conflict created in the Freethinking

Party by her economic position. These Swiss liberals had been the creators of the democratic Swiss constitution, including the grant of full civic rights to the Jews; theoretically they should have been diametrically opposed to National Socialism, the more since the Nazis were bitterly anti-capitalist in spite of their skill in posing as the friends of employers when they needed to replenish their funds. But the Swiss Freethinking Party was largely dominated by industrialists who depended upon the German market and financiers who looked for returns upon their substantial investments in the Reich; there were also the *hôteliers* who had long counted on the tremendous influx of tourists from Germany. Switzerland, contrary to the ordinary visitor's impression, is a predominantly industrial country, and its industry is old. Its Renaissance towns already had their industrial activities, which were greatly stimulated by the expulsion of the Huguenots from France in 1685. And then in the eighteenth and nineteenth centuries came big mechanical developments which kept pace with England and were mostly ahead of Germany and France. To-day, therefore, in addition to the ancient watch industry in the west, there is first and foremost the big machine industry with its largest centres at Zürich and Winterthur, but also a large cotton industry mostly in the east around St. Gallen and elsewhere, a chemical industry, with its headquarters at Basle, and a furniture-making industry centred at Basle and Zürich; this is only to mention the most outstanding industrial activity. But it all depends upon imported raw materials and markets abroad, and was built up in the nineteenth century on Manchester assumptions about international trade. In those days it had worked out excellently; the Swiss had accumulated capital and invested it abroad, particularly in Germany, and, like the British, they had relied upon dividends to come in from other countries as against the fact that they imported more than they exported. The Nazi idea of economic self-sufficiency—recklessly preached in conjunction with contradictory plans for the economic domination of Germany's neighbours—spelt economic death to Switzerland, whose lack of outlet to the sea left even her trade routes in other countries' control. The world depression dealt Switzerland a more severe blow than it could to those countries, which, while shaken by the collapse of the grain market, yet remained in a position to find food for their people. Swiss Labour had built up for itself perhaps the best living conditions to be found in all Europe, but the slump brought large-scale unemployment, and a struggle all the more bitter, on account of the prosperity both had known, between Capital and Labour as to who should pay for adversity. Germany was far and away Switzerland's best customer, and the industrialists were alarmed at the thought of the consequence of a quarrel with Berlin, nor could the Trades Unions contemplate the possibility with light hearts. Swiss financiers who found their capital frozen in Germany were eager to propitiate the Nazis in order to recover what they could. And, until the depreciation of the Swiss currency in the autumn of 1936, Swiss prices were so high that British, American and other tourists preferred to go ski-ing in Austria—sometimes to help the Austrians against Germany. This meant that Germany with its large population was all-important to the Swiss *hôteliers*. The German mark was still nominally high, and in any case the German Government with its closed economy only allowed German tourists out of Germany in whatever direction was politically expedient. At this time it was out to prevent Reich Germans from visiting Austria, and it bargained grimly with the Swiss, using the exceptionally large number of tourists at its disposal as a political lever. As compared with 104,800 people employed in 1929 in Switzerland's biggest industry, machine-making, it was reckoned that the hotels had employed 63,300;[1] all other industries came far behind. In these circumstances the industrialists in Switzerland, in spite of their liberal political principles and ignoring, of course, the Nazis' short ways with the German employing class, discovered that Hitlerism was not so bad as it sounded and perhaps secretly longed to treat the Swiss Trades Unions in the same way; some of them consequently showed sympathy, and even generosity, to the Frontists.

Though some of its effects only emerged in 1938 and 1939, the year 1936 was a great turning-point all over Europe and in Switzerland too. In February Gustloff, the *Gauleiter* of the Reich Germans in Switzerland, was shot dead at Davos by the Jewish youth, Frankfurter. There was a tremendous uproar in Germany, but, owing to more important preoccupations, nothing much else beyond the naming of a *Kraft durch Freude* ship after the victim. On the whole, Swiss feeling had no sympathy for Gustloff, who had made himself thoroughly unpopular. There were, however, some disquieting incidents in relation to the Gustloff affair,

[1] Figures published by the Federal Statistical Office, Berne.

the case, for instance, of Captain Hausammann of St. Gallen. This man was the publicity organizer for the Swiss Officers' Society; he now circulated letters in which he complained that the Left press was responsible for Gustloff's death and was storing up justification for a German attack upon Switzerland; Hausammann, in other words, offered the liberty of the Swiss press to the Nazis on a plate. The Officers' Society declared that it did not share his opinions, but he was not required to resign, and it was felt that military opinion did not sufficiently condemn his views.

In March the Germans remilitarized the Rhineland and the Swiss National Assembly agreed to devote credits to the tune of 235 million Swiss francs to rearmament; all parties agreed to this, and the Social Democrats now became Switzerland's most enthusiastic patriots. On the whole, opinion was hardening against Hitler. The National Front gradually crumbled into various pieces, but while the central core remained with Tobler as its chief, several other more pugnacious groups were formed by ex-Frontists. The chief of these was the *Eidgenössisch-Sozialistische Arbeiter Partei*, usually known as the E.S.A.P. and led by an ex-Grey Guardsman, Ernst Hofmann of Zürich; another group directed by Herren Oehler and Zander emerged rather later and called itself the *Bund treuer Eidgenossen nationalsozialistischer Weltanschauung*; the former started a newspaper called the *Schweizervolk*,[1] the latter another called the *Schweizerdegen*. Hofmann, whose activities attracted more attention for a time, seems, according to his neighbours' accounts, to have been a quarrel-

---

[1] This name was only adopted after two others had been discarded.

some young man who knocked his mother about when it pleased him and who was often out of work. He had S.S. and S.A. connections and often crossed into Germany; he required his followers to be purely Aryan; his printers and other collaborators were often Germans or partly so. He appears to have been partially financed by one or two Swiss banking people, one of them very well known, with a son who had brought home Nazi opinions from his studies in the Reich. Hofmann published a programme (with twenty-seven points) full of comic attempts to adopt Nazi language to Switzerland; he spoke, of course, of the gigantic struggle (*Riesenkampf*) in which he and his comrades would be victorious or go under. His twenty-sixth point was a synthetic masterpiece, demanding a totalitarian state with cultural individualism for the cantons.[1] He hoped, of course, to enlist the unemployed and concluded with a special appeal to the working-man, and a final assurance that the E.S.A.P. was absolutely uninfluenced from abroad.

After Gustloff's death, the German National Socialists, here as elsewhere, finally captured their own diplomatic service, and the German Legation at Berne became the centre of Nazi activity in Switzerland. The Reich Germans in the country were nearly all compelled to submit to superficial Nazification; Nazi agents went about more confidently declaring that Hitler would soon take over *Gau Schweiz*, and, there seems no doubt whatever, black lists of strongly anti-Nazi

---

[1] " Die Esap vertritt den Standpunkt der politischen Totalität des Staates und der Kulturellen Eigenart der Kantone." See *Das Programm der Eidgenössischen Sozialen Arbeiter Partei*, 1936.

Swiss people were prepared; at any rate, they were made to feel that they would not be spared when the day of reckoning came. Nazi German students were active at Swiss Universities, especially, as it happened, at Geneva, where ridicule of the collapsing League of Nations was not unwelcome. At this time German propaganda had its best Swiss successes in French Switzerland. The most articulate circles there, those represented by the very conservative *Journal de Genève* and *Gazette de Lausanne*, were ready to take the German view that the Franco-Soviet Treaty of 1935 supplied the justification for the German action in the Rhineland. These people, moreover, had long expressed great apprehension with regard to the intentions of the Socialist Mayor of Geneva at that time, M. Nicole, and of the French-Swiss Popular Front. Although the German-Swiss Socialists refused to work with the Communists, the French-Swiss Conservatives attributed German-Swiss anti-Nazi feeling to the strength of the Socialists in Zürich and Basle. When M. Blum became Premier of France they seemed to be far more afraid of France than of Germany. The Radicals of Geneva, the French-Swiss version of the Freethinking Party, led by MM. Picot and Lachenal, was actually larger than the Conservative group, but while talking less nervously it was not uninfluenced by the anti-Red cries; French Switzerland, too, was industrial and the slump had embittered the conflict between Capital and Labour.

Among the German-Swiss it is easy to see that the Nazification of Germany had revived some of the most perplexing emotions of the nineteenth century, while economic circumstances had inclined the possessing classes, at any rate, towards compromise with Hitler. The devaluation of the Swiss franc, following that of the French franc in the autumn of 1936, markedly eased Switzerland's commercial situation, and Germany's economic policy increasingly shook the confidence of Swiss bankers. It may be said that Switzerland now gradually rallied against the Nazi challenge to her existence although the effects were only conspicuous so late as the autumn after the Munich Agreement. It was perhaps in the Ticino, a canton of peasant-farmers and wine-growers where no real Capital-Labour conflict existed, that a clear democratic reply to the Axis Powers was first heard. But all along the resistance in German Switzerland was solid, even, it was said, among the peasants of the more remote cantons. In the early Nazi days certain frontier kidnappings had brought home to the Swiss what Nazi methods were like; indeed, thanks to their proximity, the German-Swiss were much better informed than, say, the British as to what was happening in Germany; the horrors of June 30th, 1934, profoundly shocked Swiss opinion. Swiss Protestants knew very exactly about the persecution of the Christian churches in Nazi Germany; it was not for nothing that the Nazis expelled the great Calvinist Swiss theologian, Karl Barth, from his post at Bonn University and sent him back to his native Basle. As for the Jews, the German-Swiss had always preferred them to keep a little in the background, but there were only some 17,000 in the whole country. Moreover, Switzerland had so long ago discarded the last traces of a feudal social structure that the Swiss themselves had thronged into academic life, the professions, industry and finance, and Jews were no more prominent than in England—in other words there was nothing like the Jewish problem of Central and Eastern Europe where the Jews had often taken the place of a non-existent middle class. That they should be odiously maltreated the Swiss altogether condemned. Even at the Universities there was little strong anti-Semitism except among the medical students. The younger generation in Switzerland—and here it should not be forgotten that Swiss social distinctions are nothing like so marked as those in England, so that the University student is not far from the "proletarian" youth [1]—has shown itself to be unattracted by "ideologies." In the big political parties, rebellious groups of Young Catholics, Young Peasants and Young Freethinkers have emerged and have taken up their stand on the Left; the Young Catholics, whose centre is Lucerne, are bitter opponents of M. Motta and great fighters against National Socialist influences. There is, on the whole, an anti-Marxist inclination and a demand for discipline, but only perhaps 5 per cent. of the students are attracted by racial talk and the idea of a union with Germany to which it must lead, and it is significant that this 5 per cent., like the National Front (to which it has probably belonged), or the E.S.A.P., would never dare to admit that they would welcome an *Anschluss*. Though the younger generation shows no particular enthusiasm for any of the churches, it has consciously inherited a really Christian tradition with the individualism which Christianity implies. On the whole, these young Swiss make an unenterprising and stolid impression, but their indifference to violent Nordic

---

[1] All Swiss children go to the same *Volksschulen* till they are 15.

romanticisms and their contempt for brutal methods give them strength. Their major enthusiasm often centres round their military service where all social strata mix together; they regard the Swiss Army as an expression of democratic vigour.

Switzerland was already profoundly disturbed by National Socialist Germany, but the events of 1938 may be said without exaggeration to have shaken her to her foundations. In February the German annexation of the sovereign state of Austria, with two million more inhabitants than Switzerland, came as a very real shock, and the Munich Agreement made an even more devastating impression. It was now no longer possible to suppose that the conscience of the world or the opposed interests of other Powers would protect a small, even a neutral, State, if Germany or Italy decided to annex or partition it. If Germany took the mainly German-speaking districts of Czechoslovakia, drawing their boundaries exactly where she chose, why should she not take German-speaking Switzerland—she could easily enough use Holy Roman Empire claims to take the rest of the country too. With the acquisition of the Austrian Vorarlberg the Swiss-German frontier was greatly prolonged, and, if the Axis decided for war in the West, it might wish to control the St. Gotthard and Simplon passes to add to the Brenner line of communication between Italy and the Reich. Further, Germany's economic difficulties had obviously impelled her to exert arbitrary pressure upon the Czechoslovak National Bank in the matter of its gold reserves, and Swiss gold reserves might at any moment seem equally desirable.

After Munich, naturally, German pressure of all

kinds increased and the voice of defeatism could be heard in Switzerland. The worst weakness was unemployment, the one thing, apparently, which made Swiss working-people ready to listen to German agents or the E.S.A.P. The lace-makers in the Rheintal near the old Austrian frontier (like lace-makers all the world over since the war) were in very great distress, and in the spring of 1938 they responded to the stories that there was work for everyone since the Nazis had Austria. The Federal Council, and especially M. Motta, made a timid impression; M. Motta was among those who argued against Dr. Klöti's candidature in December [1] that a Socialist Federal Councillor would be regarded as provocative by Germany, an argument only too effectual all over Europe in keeping opponents of National Socialism out of office.[2] The Nazis had long shown an ingenious eloquence in demonstrating that National Socialism was not incompatible with the existence of Switzerland, and at this time they were busily pointing out that the voting in Austria and the Sudeten German districts on the annexations which had *already* taken place had shown a spirit akin to that of Swiss political life. The German *Nationalsozialistische Monatshefte* now voiced the same demand as that made in Scandinavia [3] and elsewhere that Swiss neutrality should be re-defined, and that by suppressing all public criticism of Germany and Italy the Swiss press should become part of the Axis propaganda machine. At about the same time the Germans began to issue orders to the

[1] See above, p. 264.
[2] Cf. the arguments against Dr. Maček as a Yugoslav Minister. See above, p. 132.
[3] See above, p. 256.

Swiss with regard to Balkan trade and investment, for
Switzerland had steadily increased her commerce with
South-Eastern Europe from 1935 and the Swiss had
large investments in the Balkans, especially in Bul-
garia, where they were second only to those of the
Belgians. "The time is not far distant," wrote the
Deutsche Volkswirt on October 21st, 1938, "when the
question will arise whether, and in what way, Switzer-
land should place her investment policy in Central and
South-Eastern Europe upon a new basis."

It was the Swiss people's determination which
caused the Swiss Government and perhaps even the
Swiss bankers to ignore Nazi Germany's requests.
The German-Swiss press, led by such admirable papers
as the *Neue Zürcher Zeitung*, the *Basler Nachrichten* and
the *Basler National Zeitung*, now provided the only
important non-Nazi papers appearing in German in
Europe, and it mattered to the Nazis to silence them.
Swiss public opinion was alive to the implications of
the German "moral neutrality" claim—the Swiss
reminded one another that Austria had made a press
truce with Germany in July 1936 only to be devoured
eighteen months later. So the Federal Government
ignored the orders from Berlin and left the surveillance
of the press to a journalists' commission; the papers
were simply requested to avoid violent and abusive
terms. The French-Swiss conservatives, no longer
afraid of the Popular Front and of MM. Blum and
Nicole who had fallen from office, were startled by the
Austrian and Czech affairs into a tardy realization of
what was at stake, and their newspapers, too, gradually
turned against Hitler.

Already intellectual society had arisen to defend

the whole individualistic, humanistic attitude to life, in fact to organize, as it was called, Switzerland's "Spiritual Defence." Professor Max Huber had already made a contribution in 1934,[1] and a little later Professor Rappard's "L'individu et l'État" was something of a landmark.[2] In 1938 and 1939 anti-totalitarian books poured out from the publishers, books such as M. Gonzague de Reynold's *Conscience de la Suisse* or Herr Arnold Jaggi's *Von Kampf und Opfer für die Freiheit*, which insisted that the Swiss knew how to face material deprivation for the sake of their beliefs. On September 23rd and October 20th the *Neue Zürcher Zeitung*, by no means incautious hitherto, printed in the place of its leading article lectures just pronounced by the ardently anti-Nazi Professor Karl Meyer of Zürich. Dr. E. Fueter's letter, *Zur Geistigen Lage der Erzieher*, published in the Swiss University Review in December 1938 was also a sign of the times. "Perhaps you feel," he wrote, "how our forefathers begin to speak to us more impressively, how we begin to understand them, how their words and their deeds acquire an ever greater and braver meaning—in short, how literature is turning into life." [3] Many people were incensed by the news that German students were being asked to enrol for Swiss Universities under the heading of *Einsatzbereit*,[4] i.e. to make the sacrifice of doing propaganda among their Swiss comrades. Swiss students were forming anti-totalitarian groups, and

[1] *Grundlagen Nationaler Erneuerung.* Schulthess & Co., Zürich, 1934.
[2] Zürich, 1936.
[3] See *Schweizerische Hochschulzeitung* (*Revue Universitaire Suisse*), Dec. 1938, p. 344.
[4] This word is almost untranslatable—it means, approximately, a condition of being ready to be disposed of.

the Federal Polytechnic at Zürich organized a series of lectures entitled "Switzerland in the Europe of today" for the winter of 1938-39.   The first of these lectures, on the Swiss Idea of the State (*Der Schweizerische Staatsgedanke*) was delivered by Dr. Strebel, the President of the Federal Tribunal.   "Why," asked Dr. Strebel, "should diversity of language be an obstacle, if we feel and think and behave in the same way over the essential things?" [1]   And in the *Neue Schweizer Rundschau* of January 1939 the legal expert, Professor Schindler, laid down that Swiss neutrality comes into operation only in time of open war, and further that as it was defined by the Hague Convention of 1907 it cannot affect the liberty of the press or any civil rights of the citizens of Switzerland.   The meetings of the eminent New Helvetic Society placed more and more emphasis upon the meaning of Switzerland as the country where human rights (*Menschenrechte*) were most fully respected, and upon William Tell as their symbolic defender.[2]   Meanwhile the Swiss publishers, who for some years after 1933 had suffered from the loss of the Reich German demand for non-Nazi books, found the sale of such books increasing so satisfactorily at home as to make up for their losses; the progressive *Europa Verlag* in Zürich had a great success with the publication of Dr. Rauschning's admirable attack upon National Socialism towards the end of 1938.   The Swiss theatres were proud to put on plays now forbidden in Germany, like Lessing's great plea for toleration, *Nathan der Weise*, and later

[1] *Der Schweizerische Staatsgedanke*, Polygraphischer Verlag A-G, Zürich, 1938, p. 32.
[2] See their meeting on March 23rd, 1939, reported in the *Neue Zurcher Zeitung*, March 26th, 1939.

the Zürich Music Festival in 1939 did honour to Hindemith. The Nazis had boasted that they could force the *Gleichschaltung* of German-Swiss cultural life, the extinction of the last independent thinking in German in Europe.

As for the more popular reply to the Munich Agreement, the German-Swiss had long taken pride in talking their *Schwyzerdütsch* dialects, but they put a tremendous emphasis upon doing so now and it became positively embarrassing to speak *hochdeutsch* among them. There were dozens of small indications of anti-German feeling and an unofficial boycott of German goods, though the Government tried to discourage it; and the German *Mitropa* restaurant-car waiters took very good care to get out of their uniforms before walking around Zürich or Basle. Anti-Nazi feeling was particularly strong in these great industrial centres with their Socialist municipal majorities, though Basle lies at the frontier and could not be defended in the case of war. Schaffhausen, where the woollen and metal industries flourish and the manufacture of aluminium has been becoming important, forms a peninsula jutting right out into Reich German territory, but the feeling there is just the same. Here, as in Bohemia before Munich, Germany sees to it that all the German railwaymen who cross the frontier are reliable Nazis, but the mayor of Schaffhausen keeps a careful watch upon their activities, and if he regards them as dangerous he sends these railwaymen home without permission to return. The Federal police, popularly known as the *Bupo*, also keeps an efficient eye on visitors from the Third Reich. It was interesting to observe that in the Zürich municipal elections shortly after Germany

seized Austria the Frontists lost all their ten seats.
After Munich the pressure of public opinion brought
about the suppression both of the *Schweizervolk* and
the *Schweizerdegen* and an enquiry into the sources of
their funds. Before the Zürich cantonal elections on
March 19th, 1939, the National Front made renewed
efforts to persuade the public that it had nothing to do
with Germany. It abandoned the abuse of democracy
and indulged in a feverish patriotism and cries of
"Switzerland for the Swiss." [1] This slogan, one discovered, on reading Frontist literature, was part of an
anti-Semitic campaign, for it was thought to be the
only expedient thing to try to play upon the feelings
aroused against refugees. But the Swiss had known
only too much about the pogroms of November 1938,
and they still preferred to blame the friends of the
Frontists in Germany for the increased number of
immigrants. When, four days before the Zürich cantonal elections, the Germans occupied Prague, it was
a foregone conclusion that the National Front would
disappear from the Cantonal Council; it lost all six
seats, its voters apparently going over to the independent and certainly not pro-German group led by
Herr Duttweiler; [2] the Social Democrats also gained
some seats. German agents had long complained that
their propaganda made less progress in Switzerland
than anywhere else. The Pan-German Swiss writer,
Jakob Schaffner, who declared at a lecture in Berlin [3]
before the *Einsatzbereit* German students preparing to
conquer the Swiss that he considered that he could

---

[1] e.g. in their election appeal headed " National Regeneration."

[2] Herr Duttweiler is a successful business man believing in efficiency
à l'américaine. He appears to wish to apply similar methods to democracy.

[3] Late in February 1939.

only be a Swiss patriot if he were a good German *in politisch-kulturellem Sinn*,[1] confessed at the same time that the Swiss lacked all understanding for the great developments of our days—they did not know how to respond to National Socialism. The Zürich Frontists themselves admitted in private that there was such an obsession of hatred against Germany that for the time being there was nothing they could do; in other words, the Swiss refused to be deceived.

Another interesting development during the winter of 1938-39 was the *rapprochement* between the Social Democrats and a number of Swiss officers who appreciated the importance of the anti-Nazi enthusiasm of the Trades Unions; it was observed that Colonel Wille, for instance, was willing to make public gestures towards his old Socialist adversaries. To judge by the bookstalls and kiosks, *Unsere Wehrmacht* [2] now became the most popular paper in the country. Military service was prolonged from twelve weeks to sixteen, and frontier defence companies were newly organized. It was the pride of the Swiss free man that he kept his equipment and gun at home, and each man also knew exactly where to find the machine-guns of his company; indeed in September 1938 the villagers here and there began to mobilize on their own. It was whispered that the *Bundesrat* and one or two higher officers might be afraid of Germany—after all, the Swiss forces were not motorized and there was virtually no defence against air attack, and there was no hope of holding up the Germans for more than three to six weeks if the Swiss fought alone. But the ordinary people vowed that if Germany touched

[1] In a political-cum-cultural sense.   [2] Our Army or Militia.

Switzerland the frontier barriers should spring up and the guns be fired whatever *mot d'ordre* they received. They feared some Nazi trickery, of course, but, when the Federal Councillor Dr. Obrecht addressed the New Helvetic Society at Basle on the day after the German occupation of Prague, he declared that no Swiss envoy would be making pilgrimages abroad, and this statement was generally applauded.

Unemployment was still the only really demoralizing thing, and Germany's new demand for labour was a powerful new weapon in her armoury. Swiss skilled labour was something which she was particularly anxious to attract, and much apprehension was felt about the plan according to which about 700 Swiss watchmakers had been invited to establish themselves at Pforzheim in Baden and were of course royally *fêted*; a rival watch-making industry in Germany might do very serious harm to the specialized and fluctuating watch-making industry of the Swiss. In Switzerland, however, great efforts were being made to use the victims of unemployment for various military purposes, and on June 4th, 1939, the Swiss people were asked by their Government to approve a new credit of 327,700,000 Swiss francs to be spent on defence and the creation of work. The result was that 443,960 people voted in favour of the new expenditure and 198,598 against, with a majority in favour in each of 19 cantons, the 3 French-speaking cantons alone showing majorities against. Already, however, the unemployment situation had improved almost out of recognition, for at the end of June only 24,000 wholly unemployed people were counted in Switzerland, the

most favourable figure since the same month in 1931.
This was due partly to internal Swiss activity but
also to increased foreign trade. In spite of commercial difficulties with Germany, the loss of trade
with the Czechs and the difficulty of competing with
the Germans in South-Eastern Europe,[1] the financial
recovery of France was beneficial to Switzerland, and
her exports to Great Britain, Holland and the United
States increased considerably. During the first half
of 1939 her imports were valued at 862,600,000 Swiss
francs and her exports at 670,600,000 Swiss francs,
compared with 781,300,000 and 618,400,000 francs
respectively in the first six months of the previous
year. Though everyone welcomed the increase of
trade with the free-exchange democratic countries in
order to be less economically dependent upon
Germany in spite of the increase of her territory,
commercial difficulties with the Reich became an
anxiety. The unofficial boycott of German goods
had apparently made itself felt: imports from Germany
certainly diminished, and the Germans threatened to
cut down their tourists even further until on July 6th
an agreement was reached, an agreement which
accepted a reduction in German-Swiss trade.[2]

Though foreign trade had increased, the relative
excess of imports over exports had increased too, and
gave some cause for concern. One of Switzerland's
gravest problems to-day is the necessity, created by
the partial breakdown of international trade, to reduce

[1] According to a correspondent writing in the *Neue Zürcher Zeitung* of
July 20th, 1939, the Swiss are getting 8 Swiss francs for 100 dinari worth
of goods sold in Yugoslavia, where Germany, owing to pressure upon the
Yugoslavs, is getting 53 per cent. more.

[2] *Neue Zürcher Zeitung*, July 7th, 1939.

her standard of living. But yet one of the pavilions of the Swiss National Exhibition at Zürich in the summer of 1939 bore a courageous retort to the cries from next door; "Switzerland," it read, "a country without colonies and without raw materials, owes its prosperity to the industry and concord of its people." The Swiss themselves flocked to the Zürich Exhibition, but the hopes that it would attract foreign tourists on a large scale were doomed to disappointment. German tourists to Switzerland had long ago fallen off on account of currency difficulties now, but after the depreciation of the Swiss franc, British, Dutch and other visitors had made up for them. The international tension in 1939, however, kept many people at home, and the Swiss had to resign themselves to the losses involved.

On the whole, Swiss self-confidence was undoubtedly growing. In July came two significant verdicts in the courts. In Berne a Leftist weekly, *Die Nation*, won a case against a Frontist officer named Maag, a verdict which vindicated the freedom of the press. And in Zürich, Zander [1] and a number of his associates were convicted by Dr. Strebel, according to recent legislation of June 1936 and December 1938, on account of their intrigues in Germany; further, the trial had made clear that they had a mere handful of followers in Switzerland itself. Feeling against Italy was rising too, both on account of the South Tyrolese affair and because Mussolini now banned Swiss newspapers like the *Bund* and the *Neue Zürcher Zeitung*, which had sometimes shown sympathy for Italy, for instance in the days of the Abyssinian War. Meanwhile Swiss

[1] See above, p. 290.

defences, including the air force, were being substantially strengthened. A shooting festival at Lucerne
and, above all, the Zürich Exhibition, proved to be
great national rallies, the latter providing a real
counterblast to National Socialist pageantry beyond
the Rhine.

Nazi Germany had brought all her weight to bear
upon Switzerland, the pressure of a large and powerful
State upon a small one, the technique of mixing the
hope of advantage with downright fear, sugar alternating with the whip. She had condemned Switzerland, as a *Nationalitätenstaat* instead of a racially
homogeneous political unit, to dissolution, and in
doing so had raised what were elsewhere called
minority questions. She had hoped to coerce Switzerland through her own economic size and strength.
Yet up to the summer of 1939 it may be said that the
undeclared war against this essentially Western society
had failed in spite of the particular appeal made
possible by the Germans to three-quarters of the
Swiss, on grounds of the *Zusammengehörigkeit* created
by a common written language and literature. East of
the Axis Germany undoubtedly exerted a powerful
attraction through her size and efficiency and her habit
of "clearing up the place"; there were Roumanians,
for instance, who were reconciled to the German
occupation of Bucharest in 1918 on account of the
hygienic effects as compared with those of the presence
of Russian troops in the country. Again the Scandinavians were kept from political co-operation with
Poland and the Baltic States partly by the feeling that
the East was squalid and Germany clean. But the
Swiss were clean without German help, their towns

were superbly organized, their public buildings as large as any of those in the Reich. As for the attraction of belonging to a huge political society, which affected non-Nazi Austrians very forcibly before 1938, and has been felt in Slovenia, Polish Upper Silesia and perhaps Transylvania, the Swiss, with the exception of a handful of "*treue Eidgenossen nationalsozialistischer Weltanschauung*," [1] do not feel it. The descendants of the earliest rebels against the Habsburgs and the Holy Roman Empire are not merely indifferent to the imperialism to which Adolf Hitler at last confessed in 1939, but are fundamentally hostile to the historical traditions which he claims as his justification. The *élite* of Switzerland—and perhaps not only the *élite*— are intensely aware of the extraordinary potentialities of a country where life is lived on the scale of the canton yet in terms of Europe. What do they need with political imperialism? Three *Weltsprachen* open three doors for the Swiss into the very citadel of civilization, while their political training has taught them the advantages of smallness with diversity as opposed to bigness with regimentation.

The whole idea of the human quality of the individual, without which society can have none, is implicit in the attitude of the Swiss. They have organized a society which is the exact antithesis of the barbaric tribalism of Nazi Germany, for it rests upon agreement, and, through its various peoples, links the individual with humanity as a whole, instead of breaking up humanity into primitive biological groups which can know no law but force. Swiss political life is built from the bottom up to the top, from commune

[1] See above, p. 290.

to canton and from canton to confederation,[1] in exact
contradiction of the *Führerprinzip*; it aims at the
spontaneous development of the citizen's personality
and responsible feeling. As Dr. Strebel has said,
democracy, because of its virtues, is the most difficult
form of government to work,[2] but those who em-
phasize the difficulties condemn not democracy but
themselves. To watch the Zürich cantonal election
campaign in that week in March when the Germans
completed the subjection of the Czechs was a consoling
experience. There was vigorous struggle between the
parties, but not one in which any man could feel fear,
could experience the degradation of belying his
opinions in order not to lose his job, his home, health
or life. And with the struggle went a common
allegiance to the political principles which were being
trodden underfoot in Prague. The Freethinking
Party and the Social Democrats, together with the
Peasants' Party and the Catholics, were the chief
political groups, but they were all at one in their main
political assumptions. The Freethinkers and the
Socialists had an old and very bitter quarrel over
finance, and the Socialists reproached the others as
reactionary. Yet much of the Freethinking Party's
appeal to the electors might have been fully approved
by the Socialists themselves as an appeal to the world
against National Socialism. "The essence of the form
of our state requires the decision of the people through
referenda and elections in commune, canton and confederation. Therefore there can be no question of
struggling to obtain totalitarian power or to destroy
an enemy, but rather the effort to arrive at a rational

[1] See Dr. J. Strebel, *op. cit.*, p. 18.   [2] *Ibid.*, p. 20.

understanding between differing views. Honest and decent differences of opinion preserve the vigour of democracy and do it no harm. . . . We wish to defend it (our country) through fidelity to our inheritance of freedom and through respect for the free human being, for right and for law. We challenge every totalitarian doctrine on our soil." In a special appeal to the young electors were included the words:— "The most beautiful pages in the history of Swiss civilization are those which tell of readiness to help the persecuted and those who are hungry in body and soul." It was strange to read this appeal for tolerance within so few miles of the frontiers of the Third Reich.

CHAPTER VI

CONCLUSION

THE students of National Socialism are aware that its theories are those of pre-war Pan-Germanism; in other words, its aim is precisely that world-domination declared by Mr. Neville Chamberlain, in the most critical days of September 1938, to be something which it is necessary to resist. When, therefore, British politicians or leader-writers beg the Germans to keep their National Socialism to themselves they are making a meaningless request. To the Treaty of Versailles the National Socialists owe mainly gratitude for supplying them with admirable propagandistic material which their ingenuity would, no doubt, have discovered elsewhere. Pre-war Pan-Germanism was an offshoot of nineteenth-century nationalism as one knew it in other parts of Europe, but it was also consciously obscurantist in a spirit of rebellion against the West. In order to be German, Germany's nationalists rejected the rational and humane ideals of the Anglo-Saxons and the French. This enabled them to pervert the idea of freedom into meaning nothing but the independence of a group within which its members might be coerced to any extent. And external freedom in this sense will be found to mean only the ability to coerce, or resist coercion by, other groups. The other main elements in pre-war Pan-Germanism were the Prussian and Baltic cult of the Teutonic Knights and

310

the German Mission in the East, and the racialism of the Austrian or Sudeten Germans, Georg von Schönerer and Karl Hermann Wolf. It is platitudinous to point out that when Bismarck divided Austria from the rest of Germany, he transformed the Austrian Germans into a minority within the Habsburg Empire. Adolf Hitler is an Austrian and a follower of Schönerer, and his and Rosenberg's theories are the theories of aggressive minorities, of *Auslandsdeutschen*; it is natural that they should have set about their pursuit of world power by stirring up their own old minority emotions wherever they could. Thus National Socialism means the dissemination of Pan-Germanism among the masses, and depends upon borrowed Communist technique combined with post-war mechanical devices like broadcasting, which have made it possible to disturb the tranquillity of the peasants in the remotest villages of Europe. National Socialism pursues its aims through undeclared war until no more can be gained without continuing the policy in the form of open war, and the over-stimulation of Germans outside Germany has been one of the most successful methods hitherto employed. It has been seen that the collapse of pre-war Russia and Turkey, but most of all the breakdown of old Austria-Hungary, provided fertile territory for this stratagem, and for the disturbance of other racial groups at the same time; the old common-sense reasons for different kinds of people to live together could be ridiculed, and in Eastern Europe no others had had time to mature.

In the West the minority device was not directly so important, but it was a splendid way of arousing sympathy on behalf of the sufferings of Germans, and of identifying German ambition with the Wilsonian notion of self-determination which, in Western minds, was still connected with individual freedom. It did not occur to people in the West that for the Nazis, who declared that every man was nothing but the slave of his physical descent, there could be no such thing as self-determination in the Western sense. Indeed the ruthless and "total" cynicism of the minds of those who directed Nazi policy, making use of much confused idealism in the men who were their tools both at home and abroad, was enough to deceive public opinion in the democratic States at least until March 1939. The few experts who had occasion to study these things observed with apprehension that, on the one hand, German theorists condemned a "nationalities-state" like Switzerland because they declared that a State should be racially homogeneous (however impracticable this might turn out to be), while on the other, in 1936, 1937 and 1938, Konrad Henlein was demanding that Czechoslovakia, ceasing to behave like a Czech national State, should *become* a second Switzerland. Democratic opinion applauded this "constructive" demand, which then turned out to be purely destructive in aim. In the pre-Munich days those who doubted Henlein's words and pointed to pre-war Sudeten German chauvinism were ignored, because it was believed that the Henleinists could never be guilty even of the chauvinism of the Czechs since they complained of it so loudly. To-day conditions in the Sudeten German districts and in Bohemia and Moravia show a ruthless oppression of the Czechs, with which the pre-Munich lives of the Sudeten Germans compare so favourably that there is no comparison. This throws light upon Nazi technique, or at least upon two of its principles. The first of these is—"Always denounce others for things you would not hesitate to do yourself—abuse your enemy as oppressive, although you oppress ten times more grimly when you can." Why?—"Because people are deceived into believing that you could not have the effrontery to do the things you yourself have so bitterly denounced." It is the same with the abuse of the Bolsheviks for terrorism and theft. The second of these principles—a special case of the first—is "Germanize ruthlessly." The census taken on May 17th, 1939, showed how much consideration the non-German subjects of Hitler have to expect, whether in Memel-land, the Sudeten German districts or Carinthia. Germany must expand and dominate, but she must remain as far as is possible a national state, not on any account a "nationalities-state." It remains to be seen how soon the Czechs of the Protectorate will be ordered to become Germany's unqualified subjects—many of them have already been moved into the inner Reich, while Germans have been brought into Bohemia, Moravia and Slovakia as well. The reorganization of the South Tyrol is proceeding along the same lines; it destroys the whole case for self-determination and minority rights as it was formulated by the Nazis until 1939. Their propaganda, nevertheless, continues along the old lines in order to dissuade the French or the British from "dying for Danzig," although in their own words, "Danzig is neither urgent nor vital; it is purely a question of power politics." [1] If ex-

[1] Quoted, in a letter to *The Times*, by Mr. Harold Callender on July 7th, 1939.

pedient, the rights of the Germans in Bessarabia may still be championed as warmly as those of the Sudeten Germans once were; and it is worth while to remember that the Germans had already discovered an ethnical claim to Dobrogea or a section of Southern Bessarabia in 1918.[1]

New mechanical devices are thus combined by the Nazis with a mendacious audacity on an unprecedented scale. Few governments have been altogether innocent of hypocrisy and brutality, but the present rulers of Germany have made a science of unscrupulousness. For years they have abused the Bolsheviks for terrorism and theft which they have never hesitated to practise themselves. To-day it is the brutality of the British by which they are piously appalled. Since Socialism had become the issue of the day the Nazis stirred up social discontent among the poor and declared themselves more Socialist than the Socialists; at the same time, by their anti-Marxist ardour, they convinced the owners of property that they alone could provide them with protection. That their Nazi sons thus induce social disruption in order to exploit it is not realized by innocent Pan-German fathers.

Another Nazi device which has had great success is that of occasionally announcing Hitlerist Germany's real aims—to see how they are received; at the same time, so that too great alarm shall not be created, it is implied through other agencies that this is the fantasy of an eccentric or megalomaniac. When Dr. Funk, for example, revealed his economic programme, the effect was toned down by the comments of moderates about Funk "poetry." When at Königsberg, on August

[1] R. W. Seton-Watson, *A History of the Roumanians*, p. 519.

21st, 1938, he put forward the idea of German bulk purchases from Hungary, Roumania, Yugoslavia, Bulgaria and Greece, from which Germany would resell as she chose, and spoke of a unified economic area from the North Sea to the Black Sea, he was perfectly serious; at Belgrade some six weeks later he advocated long-period agreements for wholesale purchases over a period of years at "guaranteed and stable prices" (which in fact divorce those who accept them from the world market), and he has been steadily pursuing this aim ever since. Again there is no reason to feel surprise, for German economists had had large ideas of this kind both before and during the war. It has been seen that three months after the "Bread Peace" with the Ukrainians, the Germans on May 7th, 1918, made a treaty with Roumania to monopolize Roumanian agricultural produce for nine years. On March 7th, 1918, they had made a commercial treaty with Finland before they proceeded to "liberate" her, which also reminds one of the German-Roumanian Treaty twenty-one years later, for by it the Finns were compelled to agree that Germans were to be placed on an equal footing with themselves, "regarding their admission as members or directors in commercial, industrial and financial associations," and so on.[1] After the Munich Agreement it may be remembered that the Czech press was not allowed to refer to Little Red Riding Hood and the Wolf, lest the Germans should feel "provoked."

The inconsistency in German pronouncements about German economic policy is thus as great as the actual consistency of the policy itself. Any student of

[1] See J. Hampden Jackson, *The Slavonic Review*, July 1939, p. 98.

modern German history and political literature knows
that the Germans believe in the continued extension
of Prussia's *Zollverein* policy of the early nineteenth
century, because they are convinced that economic
leads to political domination; during the war they
prepared to extend their *Mitteleuropa* up to the frontiers
of their ally, Bulgaria. The pronouncements of
German economists, recently, have frankly favoured
the partition of the world into a few large economic
areas or *Versorgungsräume* in each of which one great
Power in practice rules as it will; thus they presume
that only a few large States can enjoy a real independence, while apparently taking no thought for the
conflicts that arise when the boundaries of each
Versorgungsraum have to be fixed. Among Pan-
Germans and Nazis, economic plans, whether they
speak of Germany's necessary *Lebensraum* or *Leis-
tungsraum* or what it may be, have always contradicted
the talk about independent racial States. These people
believe that they themselves should be ruled by only
one consideration, the advantage of the German
people. At the same time it has been possible for
Dr. Funk and his colleagues to travel around Europe
expounding the altruistic benevolence of Germany's
economic plans. It has been eloquently explained to
the small Powers that Germany offers them the
marvellous advantages of a new system based on
labour, not upon "artificial" wealth, a system which
by cutting out speculating middlemen, is free of the
old trade-cycle fluctuations—is in fact *krisenfest*.[1] The
Germans have splendidly advertised the "benevolence" of their credits as compared with those supplied

[1] Proof against economic crisis.

by the "usurious" West; in fact they regard the generous preferences they have offered in South-Eastern Europe as a cheap price to pay for the imperialistic power these preferences may bring. It is true that the Nazis, being revolutionaries without fear of destruction, show far greater enterprise than the Western Powers, and their willingness to take risks sometimes brings new economic life to poor areas. On the other hand, their rage when Great Britain dares to compete with them in attempting to stimulate trade or to supply the military needs of smaller powers is illustrated by the "Blood-Money" outcries. "Great Britain pays and the others are to shed their blood," the *Völkischer Beobachter* wrote on July 7th, 1939. Phrases of this kind have effectually stimulated the belief in Britain's degeneracy.

Just as the different reactions of Eastern and Western Europe to German political propaganda depend upon the difference of political structure between East and West, so the reactions to economic pressure vary according to the difference of social structure. The peasant countries of the East have found the markets supplied by Germany irresistible. They are impressed with the standard of life in Germany as compared with their own. Though they resent German *Herrenvolk* theories, they are sufficiently oriental to feel a certain fatalism towards them. The industrial countries of the West are primarily susceptible to the news that Germany has abolished unemployment. The fear of unemployment in big industrial cities, where it means starvation, is something which undermines all the humanistic theories of the West—when starvation stares men in the face, they lose their freedom of will, they mostly become the slaves of any *Führer* who offers them work. Indeed a big decrease in unemployment may be as important to the West as all its anti-aircraft guns.

In the early days of Hitler's rule one constantly heard that his anti-Semitism would undo him. On the contrary, anti-Semitism is an invaluable weapon in the undeclared war, quite apart from the proceeds of the plunder involved. In the East of Europe the lack of a mature middle class had given the Jews a monopolizing position which created a feeling of strong antagonism against them. The National Socialists have gained much popularity by posing as the champion of the peoples against Jewish exploitation—anti-Semitism was long ago recognized as the socialism of the stupid; at the same time, by causing the Jews to be expelled, they have dealt a serious blow at industries which were able to compete with their own and prevent South-Eastern Europe from becoming their "colonial space." In the West, generally, just as in Switzerland, there was no Jewish problem, because society has not been dependent upon Jews to be its business men or its intellectuals. But by casting thousands of refugee Jews out into the Western countries, the great Western problem of the urban unemployed, which is not a question of the working-man alone, is aggravated, and the seeds of anti-Semitism are sown. And everywhere, whether in the East or the West, suspicion and anxiety are intensified by Nazi Germany's attitude towards the Jews. All this is part of the war of nerves. Few people in Western Europe are able to believe what unlimited funds, often derived from complicated foreign-trade transactions, are placed at the disposal of poverty-stricken Germany's propagandists; nor do they at all comprehend the science of spreading rumours which has been evolved by them—*Flüsterpropaganda* it is appropriately called, or propaganda by whispering. In all the small countries one of the most terrible results of the undeclared war is that decent behaviour is continually stigmatized. It is not only the humiliating question a man may have to put to himself, "What if they discover that my grandfather was a Jew?" but equally "What if they discover that I have helped Jews?" In the South-Eastern countries one constantly meets men with liberal beliefs who have allowed their pupils at a University, perhaps, to hear them defend tolerance and individual freedom, men who have championed the free circulation of literature, men who are known to be Anglophil or Francophil, who, for those reasons alone, live in a state of unceasing anxiety. University teachers are State employees on the Continent, and in any case their semi-dictatorial governments can easily cause their dismissal from their posts if German pressure is brought to bear. And since the occupation of Prague, people in Poland, Hungary, Roumania and Yugoslavia are bound to think in terms of a possible German invasion and annexation, involving death, exile, or the concentration camp in retrospective punishment for their anti-Nazi views. To live in this state of anxiety is far more demoralizing than those who have not experienced it are usually able to realize. The opposite phenomenon is also observed in many small countries to-day. In other words people with no particular ability are surrounded with a carefully engineered publicity so that they are easily put forward as the candidates for vacant posts; in this way Ministries of Commerce in South-Eastern Europe have a mysterious way of acquiring a Germanophil personnel.

Whereas in the Eastern countries National Socialist propagandists can profit by the dictatorial interests of the governments, in the Western countries they can exploit the liberties of the subject in order to try to destroy the very systems which exist to preserve civic rights. Habits of legality induced by centuries of political evolution have also made the Western countries vulnerable in the undeclared war. The Swiss, the French, the British or the Dutch have for many years found it satisfactory—even profitable—to observe a system of laws, whether national or international; even their cynics have adhered to the letter of these laws. It has taken them years to be able to believe that the present rulers of Germany have no respect whatever for existing codes; on the contrary, the National Socialists are proud of tricking their opponents by momentarily undertaking conventional obligations only to ignore them later. The civilized West could not even believe that it could suit the present rulers of Germany to break their word flagrantly, for that sort of thing does not seem to pay in the West. This is why the West was able to accept the German Chancellor's word when he declared so recently as the *Sportpalast* speech on September 26th, 1938, that he wanted no Czechs under his rule.

In the West, too, the claim hurriedly emphasized from the moment he took over power in 1933 that Adolf Hitler meant peace, a curious echo of Napoleon III's "*L'Empire, c'est la paix*," was tremendously potent for six years. The Western countries had every reason to thirst for peace where the East was accustomed to turmoil. In the West men had immensely much to lose by war. Nor was it only the men of property who feared to be deprived. The humanitarian tradition, to which perhaps the *philosophes* had contributed most in their day, had been woven into the fabric of Western life and had created a genuine pacifism—it was for this reason that the men of the West found it so difficult to believe that National Socialism despised peace, and that war, open or undeclared, was a condition of its life. The West longed to protect and preserve the civilization which had descended to it directly from Greece and Rome through so many generations, and to which Christianity had contributed so much. But to the rulers of Germany to-day that civilization is alien and worthless; it costs them nothing to destroy it.

Love of peace and horror of destruction have combined with the failure of the League of Nations to undermine the meagre beginnings of international co-operation, political or economic; the Swiss have returned to greater insistence upon their neutrality, and other small nations, the Netherlanders, the Scandinavians and the Balts, increasingly aware of the fact that the Nazi criterion of force by definition destroys the independence of the weak, have hastened to take refuge behind the same principle, while the Balkan countries try to poise themselves between the Axis Powers and the West. In the East of Europe this policy is easily understood in view of an inherited dislike for Russia and the fears induced by her social system, but it is seldom realized to how great an extent the pursuit of neutrality suits Germany's plan. All genuine ideas of international co-operation are condemned by Hitler's doctrine; in *Mein Kampf* and elsewhere it is made plain that Nazi Germany must first become dominant—then he will see. . . . Neutrality tends towards acceptance of Germany's condemnation of international action, towards acceptance of Germany's encirclement cries which mean nothing but dislike of the tardy appreciation of her aggressive designs. During 1938 Germany's encirclement of Czechoslovakia was skilful and complete (the Ruthenian-Roumanian frontier excepted), yet even the Germans scarcely believed that Prague cherished aggressive intentions. The Czechs, nevertheless, were required to drop their alliances and become "neutral," or, in other words, helpless. National Socialist Germany knows very well that one cannot be neutral towards totalitarianism—it is something which, by definition, one must accept or reject. In the name of "moral" neutrality Germany claims the submission of all the small States, for any sign of resistance to her doctrines on their part she condemns as unwarrantably "provocative" action; the power she has gained by her influence on the press in the Scandinavian, Baltic and Balkan countries has been seen. Another Nazi method in the undeclared war has been to exploit Europe's thirst for peace by denouncing all ideas of international co-operation as chestnut tactics on the part of Great Britain and France. Divide to destroy. If each small country waits till its own territory is openly attacked or a prey to "spontaneous revolt" from within, each separately is helpless before Germany, and every vow to defend that territory to the "last drop of blood" is as aimless as suicidal mania.

From January 1933 to March 1936 Hitler was engaged in consolidating the power he had grasped. From March 1936 to March 1939 he launched the first offensive in the undeclared war with racialism as its avowed *motif*. This first phase was so successful that in March 1939 the rulers of Germany were ready to discard the racialist cry and admit the imperialism to which they now hoped to reconcile world opinion by historical phrases, but chiefly by appealing to the pacifism which they themselves so much despised. On March 25th the *Völkischer Beobachter* headed its foreign news page with the words *Deutschlands Friedenswerk in Osten* [1] with the injured sub-heading "Paris and London without any understanding." The German invasion of Bohemia and Moravia (though it followed logically enough from the disastrous Munich Agreement) not only initiated what may later be recorded as a revolution in British foreign policy, it also tremendously strengthened a conviction scattered among the non-German peoples that some day soon one of them would have to stand up to the Germans since Nazi Germany understands no argument but force. And if official jargon required the phrases about shedding one's last drop of blood in defence of one's territory, there were more and more men in each country who knew that they must be ready to face destruction in order, perhaps, to save Europe by their example. The traveller from the West asked himself whether it would be the Poles or the Yugoslavs, who had shown such remarkable spirit in resisting the pressure from Berlin

[1] =Germany's Work for Peace in the East.

and even from their own rulers, but who had relatively little to lose. Would it perhaps be a resurrected Panslavism, of which there were signs? Or would it be the immensely civilized Swiss with their multiple Latin and German, their humanist, inheritance, and the feeling, lurking here and there among them, that the "other Germany" needs their help?

The ordinary Swiss people are stolid and untalkative, even inarticulate. They do not appear to concern themselves with the elaboration of "ideology"—they respond most warmly to the idea of their unbreakable historical union, to the very words of the pact of 1291 "to stand by one another . . . against any and all who threaten oppression and injustice." Their feeling is perhaps very much the same as that of the ordinary Englishman, who, if Mr. Harold Nicolson's two territorials were typical,[1] do not wish to be told about the defence of democracy, but want to "get at" Hitler for breaking his word. It is simply human decency which has to be defended. National Socialism is fundamentally a dehumanizing process, it drags men down to divide them into categories according to their breed, it sets out to frighten or bribe them, as if they were performing animals. Both Lord Halifax and MM. Daladier and Paul Reynaud, like President Roosevelt or the intellectuals of Switzerland, have been formulating the notion of human dignity, that *Menschenwürde* about which Gottfried Keller felt so differently from the Germans; this is the issue in the war, open or undeclared, of to-day.

[1] See *Spectator*, July 14th, 1939.

INDEX

Abyssinia, 172

Adams, Alexander, *Report on Economic and Commercial Conditions in Roumania*, 88

Albania, 72, 128, 133, 135, 137, 138, 142, 172

Alexander I, of Russia, 218

Alexander, King of Yugoslavia, 106, 109, 110, 111, 112, 113, 114, 115, 116, 117, 124, 135, 147

Altgayer, leader of the *Kultur- und Wohlfahrtsvereinigung des deutschen Slawoniens*, 147, 148, 152

Anglo-Turkish Pact, the, 138, 172

Anti-Comintern Pact, the, and Hungary, 23

Anti-Semitism, in Hungary, 9, 10, 18, 19, 22, 25-28, 43-45; in Roumania, 54, 55, 57, 61, 71; in Yugoslavia, 127; in Poland, 178; its value in the Undeclared War, 318, 319

Arndt, Ernst Moritz, early Pan-German, 257

Ausnitt, M., and Madame Lupescu, 99

Aussiger Chemical Company, the, Roumania, 91

Austria, 4, 5, 7, 17, 18, 19, 38, 39, 40, 42, 91, 103, 113, 122, 123, 128, 140, 141, 155, 159, 164, 172, 175, 239, 247, 283, 301, 311

Austria-Hungary, different races in, 4, 5, 104, 114, 131, 179, 196

Austro-Prussian War, the, 1866, 48

Awender, and the Regeneration Movement, 147

Axis policy, Italy's rôle, 172, 173, 177

Bacinsky, M., 216

Bánffy, Count Nicholas, leader of Hungarian Minority in Roumania, 85

Barth, Professor Karl, 293

Barthou, M., 180

Basch, Dr. Franz, 35, 36, 37, 38

Beck, Colonel, 178, 182, 188, 191, 234, 235, 236, 245, 246

Bela Kun, 8, 15

Belgium and Nazi Germany, 256, 257, 258

Belgrade, contrasted with Bucharest, 48, 105, 106; corruption in, 110; visit by Dr. Beneš, 121; visit by Dr. Maček, 121, 122, 124, 125, 127, 131, 134, 136, 140, 166; retail prices in, Oct. 1938, 169

Beliţa incident, clash between Roumanians and Bulgars, 72

Beneš, Dr., and Hungary, 20, 21; visit to Belgrade, 1937, 121, 123, 181, 249

Bernstorff, Count, 219

Bessarabia, 87, 94, 95, 314

Bethlen, Count, of Hungary, 14, 25, 28, 73, 85

Beuve-Méry, M., 215

Bismarck, 197, 218

Bleyer, Professor, leader of German Minority in Hungary, 32, 33

Blum, M., 56, 292, 297

Bohemia, 6, 36, 42, 80, 91, 95, 128, 137, 153, 158, 161, 164, 171, 215, 241, 246, 270, 279, 300, 312, 313, 323

Boris, King, 135, 136

Bornemisza, M., 20

Bosnia, 6, 103, 113, 118, 124, 125, 131, 132, 138

Böszörményi, M., and the Scythe Cross party in Hungary, 15

Brest-Litovsk, by J. W. Wheeler-Bennett, 198

Brest-Litovsk, the Treaty of, 198, 204, 219, 220

British Documents on the Origins of the War, by G. P. Gooch and H. W. V. Temperley, 89, 257

Brody, M., 214, 216

Buć, M., on racial theories, 127, 128

Bucharest, contrasted with Sofia and Belgrade, 48

Bucharest, poverty in, 98, 99; cost of living, 99; tension between Sofia and Bucharest, 138

Budak, M., 127

Buell, R. L., author of *Poland—Key to Europe*, 186

Bulgaria, 72, 120, 129, 134, 135, 136, 137, 153, 162, 171, 317
Bulgars, the, and self-determination, 6, 105, 108, 109, 115, 133, 134, 135, 137, 138, 241
Bülow, von, 219
Bunsen, Count, 197
Bürckel, Herr, 149
Burckhardt, Jakob, *bâlois* scholar, 281

Callender, Harold, letter on Danzig in *The Times*, 313
Calvin, 259
Calinescu, M., Prime Minister of Roumania, 63
Cantacuzino, General, and the Roumanian All for the Fatherland Movement, 57
Carinthia, Slovenes in, 139; and Germany, 171
Carlsbad, 5, 33, 152
Carol, King, 59, 60, 61, 62, 63, 64, 84, 99
Carpatho-Ukraine, and Germany, 23
Catherine the Great and Cossack autonomy, 194, 229
Catholic Nazis in Hungary, 16
Cetnici, armed bands of terrorists in Croatia, 111, 117
Chamberlain, Houston Stewart, 218, 219
Chamberlain, Neville, 249, 310
Charles of Hohenzollern, and Napoleon III, 48, 49
Chevchenko, Russian Ukrainian poet, 195, 217
Choulguine, M., editor of *Revue de Prométhée*, 218
Chust, Ruthenia, 21, 71, 224, 227, 231, 233, 234, 239
Ciano, Count, 176, 177, 236
Cisleithania, 4, 5
Codreanu, Zelea, leader of the Roumanian Iron Guard, 55, 56, 57, 58, 62, 63, 64, 70, 71
Conscience de la Suisse, by M. Gonzague de Reynold, 268, 269, 298
Croatia-Slavonia, 103, 145, 146
Croat leaders, murder of, in the Skupština, 109
Croat Peasant Party, the, 108, 112, 117, 119, 130, 133
Croats, the, 103, 104, 105, 106, 107, 108, 109, 110, 111, 112, 113, 114, 115, 116, 117, 118, 119, 120, 121, 124, 125, 126, 127, 128, 129, 130, 131, 132, 135, 137, 138, 139, 140, 141, 142, 146, 147, 148, 150, 151, 155, 160, 174
Croat village life, 107, 108
Csáky, Count, 38
Cuza, Professor, and the Christian Defence League, in Roumania, 54, 61
Cvetković, M., 128, 129, 131, 132, 161
Cvijić, Dr., Serb academic theorist and racial beliefs, 114
Czechoslovakia, 7, 13, 14, 20, 21, 37, 38, 39, 40, 41, 55, 56, 58, 63, 64, 69, 79, 80, 81, 84, 89, 90, 95, 112, 123, 149, 152, 155, 162, 176, 181, 182, 183, 191, 192, 211, 212, 213, 214, 217, 223, 234, 235, 243, 249, 276, 295, 312, 322
Czech Chauvinists, 6
Czechs and Germans, by Elizabeth Wiskemann, 270
Czechs, the, sympathy with Allies, 49; capital invested in Yugoslavia, 157; relations with the Poles, 180, 181; with the Ruthenes, 211-214, 249

Daladier, M., 324
Dalmatia, 103, 108, 111, 118, 123, 148, 173, 174
Danubian Destiny, by Graham Hutton, 43
Danzig, 178, 184, 186, 188, 209, 236, 238, 239, 245, 247, 248, 249, 313
Declaration of Corfu, the, 105, 106
Democratic Peasants Party, in Poland, 178, 182
Denmark and Germany, 254, 255, 256
Der Grüne Heinrich, novel by Gottfried Keller, 279
Die Nation, Leftist weekly, of Berne, wins case against Frontist officer Maag, 305
Die Revolution des Nihilismus, by H. Rauschning, 6
Dollfuss, Chancellor, murder of, 113
Dragomir, Silviu, Minister for Minority Interests in Roumania, 83, 84, 86
Duttweiler, Herr, Swiss pro-German, 301

East Prussia, 189, 249
Eckhardt, M., leader of Hungarian Small Farmers' Party, 27, 35, 37, 38

Erasmus' Basle, and the humanistic heritage, 281
Esthonia, 178, 185, 188, 243, 249
Eugene, Prince, 18
Eye-witness in Czecho-Slovakia, by Alexander Henderson, 225

Fabritius, Herr Fritz, 77, 79
Fencik, M., 214, 216
Ferdinand, King, of Roumania, 52
Festetics, Count Alexander, 17, 28
Finland, 178, 185, 220, 242, 249, 257, 315
Fisher, Professor Allan G. B., on Bulgarian Currency System under German control, 162
Foreign investments (capital and credit) in Yugoslavia, 156, 157, 158
France, v
Francis Ferdinand, Archduke, 196
Francis Joseph, the Emperor, 49
Franco-Russian Pact of 1935, 13
Frank, Dr., and the Frankists, 112, 128, 130
Frankel, Professor Jonas, of Berne University, 278, 279, 280
Frankfurter, assassin of Gustloff, 289, 290
Frederick William IV, King, 197
French Revolution, the, 3
Fueter, Dr. E., 298
Funk, Dr., 41, 94, 161, 162, 163, 198, 314, 315

Gafencu, M., 63
Gdynia, the port of, 184
Germany and Italy in the Axis, 172, 173, 177
German capital in Yugoslavia, 153-171
German capital in Roumania, before the Great War, 88, 89 ; after the war, 87-101, 168
German Minority in Poland, 188-191, 192
German Minority in Roumania, 56, 70, 72, 73, 74, 75, 76, 77, 78, 79, 80, 83, 149, 152, 247
German Minority in the South Tyrol, 175, 176
German Minority in Yugoslavia, 143-153, 158-161, 247
German policy and Greece, 171-173
German-Polish Agreement, 1934, 178, 179, 180, 183, 190

German-Roumanian Commercial Treaty, the, signed, 23, 44, 92, 93, 94, 95, 96, 97, 98, 161, 198, 237
German-Yugoslav Agreement, Oct. 23rd, 1938, 163, 164
Goebbels, Dr., 217, 248
Goering, General, 120, 243
Goethe, 278, 280
Goga, M., 61, 90, 91
Gömbös, General, 14, 15, 19, 27
Gooch, G. P., and H. W. V. Temperley, *British Documents on the Origins of the War*, 89, 257
Graczynski, the Voivod of Upper Silesia, 191, 246
Grassl, Herr, German senator in Yugoslavia, 160, 161
Gratz, Dr. Gustav, 38
Grdjić, Dr., *Affaires Danubiennes*, 164, 167, 168
Greece, 120, 134 ; and Germany, 171, 172
Gustloff, leader of Germans in Switzerland, 289, 290, 291

Habsburgs, the, 7, 17, 49, 74, 105, 113, 120, 145, 155, 197, 258, 259, 307
Halifax, Lord, 324
Hamm, Herr, pro-Nazi in Yugoslavia, 153
Hausammann, Captain, of St. Gallen, 290
Haushofer, Paul, author of *Raum ohne Volk*, 256
Helikon, review published in Transylvania by Hungarian Intellectuals, 85, 86
Henderson, Alexander, author of *Eye-witness in Czecho-Slovakia*, 225, 226, 227
Henlein, Herr Konrad, 32, 38, 79, 144, 152, 216, 232, 276, 312
Henry of Pless, Prince, 189
Hess, Rudolf, 286
Hindemith, and the Zürich Music Festival, 300
History of the Russian Revolution, by Leon Trotzky, 187
Hitler, and anti-Semitism, 10, 11, 12 ; and Hungarian independence, 46
Hitler and Germans in the South Tyrol, 175, 176
Hitler, Herr, 15, 18, 19, 23, 24, 32, 35, 46, 62, 63, 77, 92, 122, 128, 142, 150, 175, 176, 179, 182, 183,

Hitler, Herr (*contd.*)
185, 187, 189, 190, 208, 209, 220, 221, 224, 228, 236, 237, 239, 240, 242, 245, 246, 247, 255, 284, 286, 290, 291, 292, 297, 307, 311, 318, 320, 321, 322, 323, 324
Hitler, Herr, anti-Communist talk, 8
Hitler's racialism, 8, 10, 11, 12
Hofer, Andreas, leader of Tyrolese peasants in 1809, 175, 176
Hoferlied, song by Mosen in celebration of Andreas Hofer, 175
Hofmann, Ernst, of Zürich, the National Front, 290, 291
Holland and Germany, 256, 257
Holland and Nazi Germany, 256, 257
Homan, M., Hungarian pro-Nazi, 24
Horthy, Admiral, 16, 19, 20, 22, 24, 28
Hruchevsky, Ukrainian historian, 204
Hubay, M., 17, 24, 25, 26, 27
Huber, Professor Max, 298
Hungary, 4, 5, 7, 8, 9, 10, 11, 12, 13, 14, 15, 16, 17, 18, 19, 20, 21, 22, 23, 24-46, 49, 50, 51, 52, 63, 64, 65, 74, 75, 80, 81, 92, 100, 101, 103, 104, 112, 113, 120, 129, 135, 137, 153, 168, 173, 183, 186, 187, 212, 213, 238, 246, 247, 276, 319
Hungary and Her Successors, by C. A. Macartney, 29, 82
Hungarian Minority in Roumania, 73, 81, 82, 83, 84, 85, 86, 87, 97 ; in Yugoslavia, 146, 153, 213
Hungarians, the, and self-determination, 6, 83-87, 146
Hutton, Graham, author of *Danubian Destiny*, 43

Imrédy, M., 20, 22, 23, 27, 28, 34, 35, 43, 46, 125
Imrédy Cabinet in Hungary, 20
Inculet, M., Roumanian Minister of the Interior, and the Iron Guard, 58
Iron Guard, the, of Roumania, 54, 55, 56, 57, 58, 60, 62, 63, 68, 70, 71, 83, 211
Italo-Hungarian Treaty, the, of 1927, 8
Italy, 7, 39, 72, 102, 112, 113, 119, 120, 121, 126, 128, 133, 135, 137, 138, 139, 142, 154, 172, 173, 174, 175, 176, 177, 270, 273, 275, 305
Italy and the Axis, relations between Germany and Italy, the latter's rôle, 172, 173, 177

Italy and Yugoslavia, offer of credits, 173, 174

Jackson, J. Hampden, article in *The Slavonic Review*, July 1939, 315
Jaggi, Herr Arnold, 298
Jaros, M., Hungarian pro-Nazi, 24
Jevtić, M., Serb Radical leader, 116, 124
Jews, the, 8 ; Jewish intellectuals, 9 ; anti-Semitism in Hungary, 9, 10, 11, 18, 19
Jorga, Professor, 63
Jovanović, Professor Dragoljub, 115, 123

Kaganovich, of the Soviet Union, 201
Kaiss, Hans, author of article "The New Face of Europe," in the *Siebenbürgisch-deutsches Tageblatt*, 95
Kánya, M. de, 43
Katowice, 189
Keller, Gottfried, Swiss poet, 278, 279, 280, 281, 283, 324
Klein, Herr Anton, supporter of M. Eckhardt, 37
Klöti, Dr., Swiss Social Democrat, 264, 266, 296
Koc, Colonel, 178
Komarinskyi, Dr., 226
Konovalec, Ukrainian terrorist leader, 208, 209, 225
Konradi, Arthur, of the German Bucharest Legation, 78
Korfanty, Polish Catholic Democrat, 190, 191, 249
Korošec, Father, Slovene leader, 105, 116, 117, 125, 140
Koscialkowski, M., Polish Prime Minister, 210, 211
Kunder, M., 44, 45

Lachenal, M., Radical, of Geneva, 292
Lajos affair, the, in Hungary, 46
Latvia, 178, 185, 188, 243, 249
Leitha, the, river, 4, 18, 104
Lemberg, 194
Lessing's plea for toleration, *Nathan der Weise*, 299
Lithuania, 178, 185, 199, 241, 242
Little Entente, the, 12, 13, 64, 89, 114, 120, 124, 126, 136, 137, 155
Litvinoff, M., 180
Liubchenko, President of the Council of Commissars in the Ukraine, 204

Lódż, 189
Ludendorff, von, 220, 238
Lupescu, Madame, 58, 99
Lupu, Dr., 57, 69
Luther contrasted with Zwingli, 259, 260
Luxembourg and Nazi Germany, 256, 257

Maag, Frontist officer in Switzerland, loses case against Leftist weekly Die Nation, 305
Macartney, C. A., author of Hungary and Her Successors, 29, 82, 105, 215
Macedonia, 103, 106, 133, 134, 137, 138
Macedonian Revolutionary terrorist Organization, 112
Macedonians, the, 110, 112, 133, 134, 135, 147
Maček, Dr., Croat leader, 107, 113, 117, 119, 121, 122, 124, 125, 127, 128, 129, 130, 131, 132, 137, 150, 170, 296
Madgearu, V., La Politique Économique Extérieure de la Roumanie, 90, 100
Magyars, the, 4, 5, 8, 9, 11, 12, 18, 19, 21, 24, 26, 29, 30, 31, 33, 40, 43, 48, 50, 51, 64, 69, 70, 73, 74, 75, 76, 80, 82, 85, 107, 113, 146, 147, 212, 236, 247
Malaxa, M., of the Roumanian Malaxa Locomotive Works, 99
Malnasi, Edmund, Hungarian historian, 16
Maniu, M., 51, 52, 54, 59, 60, 69, 82
Manolescu-Strunga, M., 98
Max of Baden, Prince, 220
Mayer, M., Swiss Minister of Finance, 264
Mécser, M., Hungarian pro-Nazi, 22, 27
Mediterranean in Politics, The, by Elizabeth Monroe, 171
Mein Kampf, by Herr Hitler, 94, 187, 228, 322
Memel, 184, 185, 186, 188, 237, 241, 242, 313
Metaxas, General, 171
Metternich on the limits of the Dual Monarchy, 104; and Ukrainian nationality, 195
Mihailoff, Macedonian revolutionary leader, 135, 138

Mihalache, M., 51, 59, 69
Miklič, M., 144
Mixed Race problem in Switzerland, the, 271-300
Moldavia, 47
Montenegro, 102, 103
Mosen, author of Hoferlied, song in celebration of Andreas Hofer, 175
Monroe, Elizabeth, author of The Mediterranean in Politics, 171
Motta, M., Swiss Foreign Minister, 263, 264, 265, 294, 296
Mudrij, M., 209, 211
Müller, Lugwig, Bishop, 148
Munich Agreement, the, 7, 34, 64, 77, 91, 123, 124, 129, 137, 152, 153, 162, 177, 183, 240, 244, 246, 256, 293, 300, 301, 315, 323
Mussolini, 40, 120, 142, 172, 173, 176
Mylnik, Colonel, 225, 227

Napoleon and the Ukraine, 218; and the Swiss, 261, 270, 281
Napoleon III, 48, 281, 321
Nathan der Weise, by Lessing, 299
National Peasant Party, the, of Roumania, 51, 52, 54, 57, 59, 60, 63, 64
Nazi ideology in Hungary, 11, 26, 27
Nazi propaganda, failure of the West to comprehend Nazis' technique, 318, 319, 320, 321.
Nazi propaganda, in Hungary, 15, 25; in Yugoslavia, 141-153
Nazis and Belgium, 257, 258; and Holland, 256, 257; and Luxembourg, 256; and Munich Agreement, 7; and the Poles, 233, 234, 235, 236, 237, 241, 242, 243, 244-249; and Scandinavia, 2′4-257; and Switzerland, 257-309; and the Ukrainians, the, 217-234
Nazis, in elections or plebiscites, 6
Nazis, the, nihilism of, 6
Nauhausen, Herr Franz, 123, 150, 158, 160
Neutrality of small States suits Germany's plan, 321, 322
Nezavismost, newspaper edited by M. Bué, 127
Nicholas I, 191
Nicole, M., Socialist Mayor of Geneva, 292, 297
Nicolson, Harold, 324
Niš, the Bishop of, 125
Nordic Man, the, 8
Norway and Germany, 254

Obrecht, Dr., 303
Oehler, Herren, of the National Front, Switzerland, 290
Oil Fields, the, of Roumania, 52, 53

Palnski, Polish Ukrainian, 240
Paneyko, B., 200
Pan-Germanism, the *Verein*, 32, 76 ; and Hitler, 89, 149, 220, 246, 247, 257, 281, 310, 311
Pan-Serbism, 105, 130
Pan-Slavism, 13, 14, 137, 138, 187, 197, 323
Papen, Herr von, 20
Pašić, M., the Serbian Premier, 106
Paul, Prince of Yugoslavia, 116, 125, 126, 127, 129, 130, 132, 161, 170
Pavelić, Dr., 112
Peace Treaties, the, after the Great War, 3, 5, 6, 7, 8, 11, 49, 50
Peter, King, of Yugoslavia, 116
Petljura, 200, 209
Petrusziewicz, Dr., 199
Philip, Duke of Hesse, brings Zwingli and Luther together at Marburg, 1529, 260
Picot, M., Radical, of Geneva, 292
Pieracki, M., 208
Pilsudski, Marshal, 178, 181, 185, 199, 201, 208, 209, 218
Poland, 6, 7, 66, 102, 177 ; Jewish population, 178 ; Polish-German Agreement, 1934, 178 ; democratic Peasants' Party, 178 ; anti-Russian feeling in, 179, 180 ; pro-German policy, 180, 181 ; relations with the Czechs, 180, 181, 182, 183, 184-189 ; German minority in, 188-191 ; Polish minority in Germany, 191, 192, 193, 194, 195-200 ; Ukrainian post-war situation in, 204-211, 223, 232-236, 237-249, 323
Poland—Key to Europe, by R. L. Buell, 186
Polish Chauvinists, 6
Polish Corridor, the, 184, 185, 209, 245
Polish Minority in Germany, 191, 192
Polish Peasant Party, the, 210
Polish Western Society, the, 191
Pomorze, 189, 209
Popp, Dr., Protestant Bishop of Yugoslavia, 148
Potocki, Count Andrew, 204

Poznania, 189, 209
Pribičević, M. Svetozar, leader of the Prečani, 106, 115, 116
Prokop, Adam, landowner, of Raćinovci, 160
Propaganda, failure of the West to comprehend Nazis' technique, 318, 319, 320, 321

Radić, Antun, 107, 108
Radić Family, the, famous Croats, 107, 108, 109
Radić, Stepan, 107, 108, 109, 115, 130, 134, 135
Rainis, Dr., and the Hungarian National Front, 16
Rappard, Professor, 298
Rassay, Dr., leader of Hungarian Liberal Group, 28, 38
Raum ohne Volk, by Paul Haushofer, 256
Rauschning, H., *Die Revolution des Nihilismus*, 6, 178, 299
Revay, M., 216
Reynaud, Paul, 324
Reynold, M. Gonzague de, author of *Conscience de la Suisse*, 268, 269, 283, 298
Rhodes, Italian activity at, after seizure of Albania, 172
Ribbentrop, Herr von, 235, 236
Riga, 188
Rohrbach, Paul, German publicist, 197, 198, 219, 223, 224, 237, 238
Romanoffs, the, 197, 198
Rome-Berlin Axis, the, 141, 172, 173, 177
Romier, M. Lucien, 239
Roosevelt, President, 324
Rosenberg, Alfred, 83, 220, 221, 222, 223, 237, 238, 254, 311
Roumania, 4, 5, 7, 23, 29, 30, 40, 44, 47-101, 120, 129, 137, 138, 148, 152, 153, 173, 186, 198, 211, 237, 247, 315, 319
Roumania, British guarantee to, 66
Roumania, German Minority in, 56, 70-83, 149, 152
Russia, Roumanian distrust of, 53, 55, 56, 57, 58, 59, 71, 122, 137, 170, 187, 188, 193-197, 198, 199, 200, 201, 202, 203, 204, 205, 206, 207, 208, 209, 210, 222, 223, 230, 231, 232, 234, 237, 238, 239, 243, 311, 321
Russo-Turkish War, the, 1877-78, 53

Ruthenia, Chust, the new capital, 21, 23, 41, 64, 65, 75, 84, 173, 183, 195, 212, 213, 214, 215, 216, 217, 224, 233, 239, 240, 241
Ruthenes, the, in Hungary, 28, 29; in Roumania, 71, 195, 196, 197, 205, 211, 212, 213

Saar Plebiscite, the, 1935, utilized by the Banat Germans, 77
Sarajevo, the murder of the Archduke, 105
Scandinavia and Nazi Germany, 254-257
Schacht, Dr., 39, 41, 156, 161
Schaffner, Jakob, Pan-German Swiss writer, 301, 302
Schiller, 278
Schindler, Professor, Swiss legal expert, 299
Schönerer, Georg von, 311
Schuschnigg, Herr von, 20, 122, 123
Self-determination, 3, 6
Serbia, 102, 104, 105, 113, 114, 115, 118, 125, 128, 140
Serb Chauvinists, 6
Serbs, the, 103, 104, 105, 106, 108, 109, 110; police methods with Croats, 111, 112, 113, 114, 115, 117, 119, 120, 121, 122, 123, 124, 126, 128, 129, 130, 133, 134, 135, 137, 138, 139, 140, 141, 142, 146, 160, 241
Seton-Watson, R. W., author of A History of the Roumanians, 47, 75, 314
Sidobre, André, 201, 202, 238, 239
Silesia, 189
Skoda factories, the, 65, 92
Skoropadski, Hetman of Russian Ukraine, 198, 199, 207, 208
Skrypnik, Minister of Education in the Ukraine, 202, 203
Slavonia, anti-Croat campaign, 150; Slavonian Brod, 150, 151, 159, 160
Slovaks, the, v, 4, 12, 13, 21, 23, 29, 36, 41-44, 87, 95, 112, 131, 136, 181, 183, 212, 216, 241, 245, 246, 249, 313
Slovene Clerical Party, the, 140
Slovenes, the, 5, 103, 105, 106, 107, 110, 113, 114, 120, 121, 123, 133, 137, 139, 140, 141, 142, 143, 144, 145
Slovenia, 103, 105, 118, 138, 139, 141, 142, 143, 144, 145, 148, 155, 158, 159, 160, 173, 307

Smigly-Rydż, Marshal, 178, 199, 209
Sobieski, John, 194
Sofia, contrasted with Bucharest, 48, 134, 136, 138
Sorel, Albert, 4
South Tyrol, the, removal of German population, 175, 176, 305, 313
Soya bean production in Roumania by Germans, 90
Spaho, M., leader of Bosnian Moslems, 116, 117, 125
Stalin, 239
Stambulisky, M., and Stepan Radić, 108, 134, 135, 136
Stojadinović, Dr., Premier of Yugoslavia, 116, 117, 118, 119, 120, 121, 123, 124, 125, 126, 128, 136, 139, 140, 149, 150, 160, 161, 169, 170
Strebel, Dr., 299, 305, 308
Strumberger, Protestant Pastor at Slavonian Brod, 148
Styria, 103, 142, 145, 160
Sudeten Germans, 31, 34, 35, 84, 155, 190, 215, 239, 274, 311, 312, 313
Sufflay, Croat writer on racial theories, 126
Sweden and Germany, 254, 255, 256
Swiss Constitution and democracy, 262, 263, 264-270
Swiss exports to Great Britain, Holland, and U.S.A., increase of, 304
Swiss Nationality, a series of sonnets by Gottfried Keller, 279, 280
Swiss opinion during the World War, 281, 282
Switzerland, different races in, 4, 5
Switzerland and Germany, 257-309, 324
Switzerland and its mixed races, 271-300
Switzerland and the Jews, 293, 294
Szálasi, Major Ferenc, in Hungary, 15, 16, 17, 18, 19, 20, 22, 24, 25, 27, 55
Széchenyi, Count Louis, 22, 28
Székelys, the, of Transylvania, 73, 74, 80, 84, 85
Szeptycki, Mgr., Uniate Primate of Lwów, 225
Sztrányávszky, M., 20

Teleki, Count Paul, 20, 22, 24, 25, 28, 37, 38, 45, 85
Tell, William, 258, 278, 299

Thierry, M., French Minister in Buckarest, 56

Thirty Years' War, the, and the Swiss, 260

Titulescu, M., 58, 59, 71

Tobler, of the National Front, Switzerland, 290

Transleithania, 4

Transylvania, 6, 14, 23, 24, 48, 49, 51, 65, 66, 73, 74, 75, 80, 81, 84, 85, 86, 87, 90, 94, 95, 102, 109, 268, 307

Treaty of Berlin, the, and Bismarck and the Roumanians, 50, 53

Treaty of Bucharest, the, May 1918, 89, 93

Treaty of Neuilly, the, 1919, and Bulgaria, 72

Treaty of Trianon, the, 13, 30, 73

Treaty of Versailles, 255, 310

Treaty of Westphalia, the, 257

Trianon-Hungary, 7, 14

Trieste, diversion of Austrian exports, 172, 173, 174

Trotzky, Leon, author of *History of the Russian Revolution*, 187

Trumbić, Dr., Croat, and the Declaration of Corfu, 105, 106

Tsankoff, Professor, 136

Turkey, 53, 69, 72, 73, 102, 104, 120, 122, 134, 146, 172, 311

Ukraine and its People, The, by Hugh P. Vowles, 203

Ukrainians, the, 28, 171, 192, 193, 194, 195-242; scattered here and there, 200, 201; Communists in, 201-203; situation in post-war Poland, 204-211; in Roumania, 211; in Ruthenia, 214, 215; the Nazis and the Ukrainians, 217-234, 237, 238, 239, 240, 241, 249, 315

Union of Socialist Soviet Republics, 170, 200, 207, 209, 210, 223, 234

Upper Silesia, 188, 189, 190, 191

Vienna, 5; Nazi conquest of, and Roumania, 77, 155

Vilna, 184, 185, 242

Vistula, the, 184

Voevod, Dr. Vaida, and anti-Semitism, 54, 59, 60

Voivodina, 103, 118, 133, 138, 145, 146, 147, 150, 159, 160

Vološin, Father, 215, 216, 225

von der Goltz, General, 220, 242

von der Vogelweide, Walther, troubadour, 175

Voron, M., 226, 227

Vowles, Hugh P., author of *The Ukraine and its People,* 203

Wallachia, 47, 75

Warsaw, 189, 190

Weimar Germany, 8, 207, 235, 281, 282

Westen, Herr, owner of heavy industry of Slovenia, 158

Wetter, Dr. Ernst, 264, 266

Wheeler-Bennett, J. W., author of *Brest-Litovsk,* 198

Wille, Colonel, 286, 302

William II, of Germany, 218, 219

Wilson, Sir Arnold, 248

Wilsonianism in Eastern Europe, 6, 312

Wiskemann, Elizabeth, author of *Czechs and Germans,* 270

Witos, M., 182, 210, 249

Wohltat, Dr., in Roumania, 66

Wolf, Karl Hermann, 311

World Depression, the, and Switzerland, 288, 289

Yugoslavia, 7, 30, 40, 42, 64, 77, 89, 90, 101, 102-171; activities of Germans in, 102; elements of population in, 103, 104, 109, 110, 111, 112, 118, 119, 120, 123, 126, 127, 128, 129, 133, 137, 138, 139, 140, 141, 142-176, 247, 319, 323

Yugoslavia and Italian policy, offer of Italian credits, 173, 174

Yugoslavia, foreign investments in, 156-158; German capital in, 156-171

Yugoslavia, German minority in, 143-153, 158, 159, 160, 161

Yugoslav National Party, the, 124

Zander, Herren, of the National Front, Switzerland, 290, 305

Zivković, General, joins with M. Jevtić, 124

Zwingli, Ulrich, Swiss reformer, 259; contrasted with Luther, 259, 260